THOSE WHO WEEP SHALL LAUGH

THOSE WHO WEEP SHALL LAUGH

Reversal of Weeping in the Gospel of Luke

Sung Min Hong

☙PICKWICK *Publications* • Eugene, Oregon

THOSE WHO WEEP SHALL LAUGH
Reversal of Weeping in the Gospel of Luke

Copyright © 2018 by Sung Min Hong. All rights reserved. Except for brief quotations in critical publications or reviews, no part of this book may be reproduced in any manner without prior written permission from the publisher. Write: Permissions, Wipf and Stock Publishers, 199 W. 8th Ave., Suite 3, Eugene, OR 97401.

All rights reserved unless otherwise indicated, all Scripture quotations are from ESV® Bible (The Holy Bible, English Standard Version®), copyright © 2001 by Crossway, a publishing ministry of Good News Publishers. Used by permission. All quotations are from 2011 text edition of the ESV

Pickwick Publications
An Imprint of Wipf and Stock Publications
199 W. 8th Ave., Suite 3
Eugene, OR 97401

www.wipfandstock.com

PAPERBACK ISBN: 978-1-5326-3544-1
HARDCOVER ISBN: 978-1-5326-3546-5
EBOOK ISBN: 978-1-5326-3545-8

Cataloging-in-Publication data:

Names: Hong, Sung Min

Title: Those who weep shall laugh : reversal of weeping in the Gospel of Luke / by Sung Min Hong

Description: Eugene, OR : Pickwick Publications, 2018 | Includes bibliographical references.

Identifiers: ISBN 978-1-5326-3544-1 (paperback) | ISBN 978-1-5326-3546-5 (hardcover) | ISBN 978-1-5326-3545-8 (ebook)

Subjects: LCSH: Bible. Luke—Criticism, interpretation, etc. | Crying—Religious aspects.

Classification: LCC BS2595.52 H6 2018 (print) | LCC BS2595.52 (ebook)

Manufactured in the U.S.A.   08/20/18

To my wife
Jin Hee Hong
for her tears, long sacrifice, sincere prayer, and love
in weeping turning to laughter

You have turned for me my mourning into dancing;
> you have loosed my sackcloth
> and clothed me with gladness,
that my glory may sing your praise and not be silent.
O LORD my God, I will give thanks to you forever!

Ps 30:11–12

CONTENTS

ACKNOWLEDGMENTS | ix
ABBREVIATIONS | x
INTRODUCTION | xiii

CHAPTER ONE: HISTORY OF RESEARCH AND METHODOLOGY | 1
  History of Research | 1
  Methodology | 16
  Conclusion | 23

CHAPTER TWO: REVERSAL OF WEEPING IN THE OLD TESTAMENT AND SECOND TEMPLE LITERATURE | 24
  The Use of κλαίω | 25
  The Reversal of Weeping in the Old Testament | 27
  Reversal of Weeping in Second Temple Literature | 42
  Conclusion | 57

CHAPTER THREE: THE REVERSAL OF WEEPING TO JOY | 60
  Luke 6:21b as the Programmatic Statement of the Reversal of Weeping | 61
  The Weeping Widowed Mother of Nain (Luke 7:11–17) | 68
  The Weeping Woman (Luke 7:36–50) | 80
  The Weeping Father (Luke 8:40–56) | 90
  The Weeping Disciple (Luke 22:54–62) | 102
  Conclusion | 108

CHAPTER FOUR: THE REVERSAL OF JOY TO WEEPING | 109
  Luke 6:25b as the Programmatic Statement of the Reversal of Weeping | 109
  The Weeping Generation (Luke 7:31–35) | 111
  The Weeping Savior (Luke 19:41–44) | 119
  The Weeping Women (Luke 23:27–31) | 127
  Conclusion | 136

CHAPTER FIVE: THE NARRATIVE INTENTION AND IMPLICATION OF THE REVERSAL OF WEEPING | 137
   Luke's Purpose in Telling of the Reversal of Weeping | 138
   Theological Implication: Phenomenon of the Kingdom of God | 144
   Conclusion | 147

CHAPTER SIX: CONCLUSION | 148

BIBLIOGRAPHY | 151

ACKNOWLEDGMENTS

It is indescribable to express my feeling of gratitude to those who have supported to finish this book, the revision of my doctoral dissertation. There are too many people to mention but I would like to say a few words of appreciation for several people here.

I am grateful particularly to Chris Spinks. As my main editor, he read my manuscript and made it better by giving valuable advice. I also want to thank my PhD advisor, Brandon D. Crowe, for his consistent encouragement and valuable comments throughout the writing and publication. He provided me a lot of helpful and insightful advice from recent scholarship and shared his experience as a scholar. Vern S. Poythress, who was my second reader, should be mentioned. By giving valuable comments and demonstrating his love for God's word, he was an example to me of what a scholar should be. My indebtedness goes to my former teachers, Dan G. McCartney, Stephen S. Taylor, Douglas J. Green, Michael B. Kelly, and Peter E. Enns. They all have helped me to grow up in God's word.

My good friends Rev. Taehoo Lee, Rev. Eunjae Joo, and Sungheum Lee gave me great insights through joyful fellowship. Not only by academic discussion but also by causal conversation, they reminded me the importance of everyday life that God has given to us.

I would like to express words of thanksgiving to my family. My son and daughter, Josh and Irene, have always been my great joy. Josh understood my hard situation during writing and consistently prayed for me. Irene also gave great words of love. I thank God for allowing me to have these great blessings.

Finally, I would like to thank my wife, Jin Hee Hong, for her endurance, love, and faithfulness. Her prayer and encouragement have always been great inspirations for my writing. She is the most deserved one to have my thankfulness. This book is dedicated to her. I pray that God may use this study to comfort those who weep now in this present world.

Soli Deo Gloria!

ABBREVIATIONS

AB	Anchor Bible
ABRL	Anchor Bible Reference Library
AJT	*American Journal of Theology*
ATLA	American Theological Library Association
BBB	Bonner Biblische Beiträge
BECNT	Baker Exegetical Commentary on the New Testament
BT	*Bible Translator*
BZNW	Beihefte zur Zeitschrift für die neutestamentliche Wissenschaft
CBQ	*Catholic Biblical Quarterly*
ETL	*Ephemerides theologicae lovanienses*
EVQ	*Evangelical Quarterly*
ICC	International Critical Commentary
JBL	*Journal of Biblical Literature*
JETS	*Journal of the Evangelical Society*
JSNT	*Journal for the Study of the New Testament*
JSNTSup	Journal for the Study of the New Testament Supplements
JSOT	*Journal for the Study of the Old Testament*
JSOTSup	Journal for the Study of the Old Testament Supplements
JTI	*Journal of Theological Interpretation*
JSS	*Journal of Semantic Studies*
KEK	Kritisch-exegetischer Kommentar über das Neue Testament (Meyer-Kommentar)

NAC	New American Commentary
NIGTC	New International Greek Testament Commentary
NICNT	New International Commentary on the New Testament
NICOT	New International Commentary on the Old Testament
NovTSup	*Supplements to Novum Testamentum*
NTS	*New Testament Studies*
OTP	*Old Testament Pseudepigrapha.* Edited by J. H. Charlesworth. 2 vols. New York, 1983
RTR	*Reformed Theological Review*
SANT	Studien zum Alten und Neuen Testaments
SBAB	Stuttgarter biblische Aufsatzbände
SBLDS	Society of Biblical Literature Dissertation Series
SE	*Studia evangelica I, II, III (= TU 73 [1959], 87 [1964], 88 [1964]. etc.)*
TR	*Theological Review*
TynBul	*Tyndale Bulletin*
VT	*Vetus Testamentum*
WBC	Word Biblical Commentary
WMANT	Wissenschaftliche Monographien zum Alten und Neuen Testament
WUNT	Wissenschaftliche Untersuchungen zum Neuen Testament
ZNW	*Zeitschrift für die neutestamentliche Wissenschaft und die Kunde der älteren Kirche*
ZECNT	Zondervan Exegetical Commentary on the New Testament

INTRODUCTION

The Gospel of Luke is full of reversal stories.[1] The Song of Mary, which is also called the Magnificat (Luke 1:46–55), opens the Gospel of Luke with a reversal of status: The mighty becomes dethroned, while those of humble estate are exalted; the hungry will be filled by God with good things, whereas the rich will be sent away empty (Luke 1:52–53). The parable of the Rich Man and Lazarus also illustrates the reversal of status eloquently. The rich man in this world experiences a tragic destiny in his afterlife, while the miserable man, Lazarus, enjoys a happy life after his death (Luke 16:19–31). In fact, the theme of reversal can be found in many passages in the Gospel of Luke.[2] Among these passages, the Beatitudes and Woes (Luke 6:20–26) is perhaps the most concise and direct statement.[3] The Beatitudes and Woes displays diverse aspects of reversal: the poor are blessed because they will

---

1. In this study, I will use the term "reversal" as "bi-polar reversal," which John York defined in his work. See York, *The Last Shall be First*. Simply speaking, "bi-polar reversal" is that the fortune of A becomes that of B and vice versa. "Bi-polar refers to oppositions whose 'poles' are reversed—for example *good* becomes *bad* and *bad* becomes *good*" (ibid., 42). York discusses bi-polar reversal with the help of Burke's concept of "the role of antithesis" and Tannehill's demonstration of the importance of repetitive patterns. See ibid., 39–43; Burke, *Language as Symbolic Action*; Tannehill, *The Sword of His Mouth*, 39–57. In this dissertation, "reversal story (stories)" or "reversal theme" refers to the story (stories) or theme that shows the bi-polar reversal explicitly or implicitly.

2. According to Drake, the theme of reversal can be found elsewhere in the Gospel of Luke. He lists many passages in Luke that could possibly be construed as dealing with reversal. See Drake, "The Reversal Theme in Luke's Gospel." York has also studied reversal in the Gospel of Luke extensively. York places reversal into two categories, explicit bi-polar and implicit bi-polar. The former are the Magnificat, the Beatitudes and Woes, the Rich Man and Lazarus, the Pharisee and the Publican, 14:11//18:14; 9:24//17:33; and 13:30: the latter are 2:34; 3:4–6; 7:36–50; 10:25–37; 14:7–24; 15:11–32; and 18:18–30. York, *The Last Shall be First*.

3. "One of the striking expressions of presenting the theme of eschatological reversal is shown in the beatitudes in both Matthew and Luke" (Dunn, *Jesus Remembered*, 412).

have the kingdom of God, those who are hungry will be filled, those who are weeping will laugh, those who are persecuted will receive their reward in heaven, and vice versa. Thus, Luke's Beatitudes and Woes provide the frame on which subsequent appearances of the theme of the reversal are hung. In this sense, it is not an exaggeration to say that the Lukan Beatitudes and Woes is a microcosm of the reversal theme.[4]

It is the presupposition of this study that many reversal stories in the Gospel of Luke illustrate the aspects of reversal found in his Beatitudes and Woes (6:20–26). Unfortunately, most commentators have treated many aspects of reversal as derived only from the reversal of poor and rich,[5] and as a result, not much attention has been paid to other aspects of reversal, especially those found in the Beatitudes and Woes.[6]

---

4. A dominant theme in the Gospel of Luke is that of "reversal," also called "eschatological reversal." Dan McCartney rightly says that this eschatological reversal "represents that intrusion of God's retroactive justice as then ending of the old age and the inauguration of the promised new age. This reversal is especially prominent in Luke" (McCartney, foreword *At the Heart of Luke: Wisdom and Reversal of Fortune* by Martin Emmrich, xi). This kind of approach to finding a theme in narrative has become a popular trend in the study of Luke–Acts, especially since the appearance of narrative criticism. Narrative criticism is a complex process that requires attention to numerous literary dynamics. Powell, "Narrative Criticism," 169–72. As narrative criticism has developed, attempts have been made to find topics or themes in Luke–Acts and to understand how they function in the narrative structure. From larger and more prominent themes such as the temple or the Holy Spirit, to such specific themes as repentance, physiognomy, response to praise, and feasting, many works have dealt with various themes and motifs within a literary/narrative perspective. One of the fine studies among them is Rowe, *Early Narrative Christology*. Some more recent works include Hur, *A Dynamic Reading of the Holy Spirit in Luke–Acts*; Anderson, *"But God Raised Him From the Dead"*; Voorwinde, *Jesus' Emotions in the Gospels*; Holmås, *Prayer and Vindication in Luke–Acts*; Parsons, *Body and Character in Luke and Acts*. Works in German include Hotze, *Jesus als Gast: Studien zu einem Christologischen Leitmotiv im*. Also see Inselmann, *Die Freude im Lukasevangelium*. "The use of 'reversal' as a technical term for a literary pattern or theme is a recent development. The impetus for such usage has come primarily from literary and structural studies of the parables and sayings of Jesus" (York, *The Last Shall be First*, 9).

5. This will be discussed in the following section, including the works that focus on the poor and rich.

6. One of the main reasons for focusing on the poor and rich in the study of reversal is that Luke demonstrates heavy interest in such marginalized groups as the poor, widows, and sinners. Most studies have focused on the poor, or on other groups somehow included in the category of the poor. Interestingly, the trajectory of studies of reversal in the Gospel of Luke matches that of studies of marginalized groups in that Gospel. For Lukan interest in marginalized groups, see Beavis, "'Expecting Nothing in Return': Luke's Picture of the Marginalized," 357–68. Beavis places marginalized people into two categories: the poor in contrast with the rich, and women in contrast with men. Blomberg affirms that Jesus' humanity shines through his compassion and concern for the outcast of society See Blomberg, *Jesus and the Gospels: An Introduction and Survey*,

INTRODUCTION

The purpose of this study is to show that the reversal of weeping is a theme in Luke that is distinctive from the reversal of poor and rich, and it is therefore deserving of attention on its own. There are many examples of the theme. For instance, in Luke 7:11–17, the widow of Nain who lost her son was weeping at the time of her son's funeral. However, after Jesus raises him up, her weeping turns to laughter and joy. She finally rejoices because her son has been resurrected from death. Luke 8:40–56 shows the same pattern: weeping turns to joy through Jesus' raising up the daughter of Jairus. The weeping woman who anointed Jesus was forgiven her sin (Luke 7:36–50).[7] Through the forgiveness of sin, the woman is honored, and this results in joy and laughter. Luke also illustrates the "reversal" of this reversal through the weeping of Jesus in Luke 19:41–44 and the judgment oracle in 23:38. The end result for those who laugh will be weeping—not blessing, but woe.

Luke's display of the reversal of weeping as a distinctively Lukan interest is intensified by his use of κλαίω, "weep." In all seven accounts of the reversal of weeping (Luke 7:11–17: 7:31–35; 7:36–50; 8:40–56; 19:41–44; 22:54–62; 23:27–31), Luke uses κλαίω rather than other words that convey the same meaning, such as πενθέω. This suggests that Luke purposefully uses the technique of repetition to illustrate his point.[8] In so doing, Luke not only presents the reversal of weeping as a theme distinctive to his narrative, but he also demonstrates what the theological implications of the reversal of weeping are.

Firstly, Luke shows his concern and sympathy toward marginalized people through these accounts. These people include a widow, a Gentile, a sinner, and the disciple Peter, who cursed his beloved teacher as a criminal. Luke wants to show how these marginalized people will be restored from their suffering and will enjoy a reversal of fortune. This corresponds to one of the unique aspects of Lukan theology, the interest in marginalized groups and people.[9]

Secondly, Luke does not only demonstrate his interest to sympathetic concern for marginalized people. Rather, the purpose of his various descriptions of the reversal of weeping is to teach his readers the nature and the phenomenon of the kingdom of God as well. This kingdom has a character different from what people anticipate. As Crossan says, "Reversal is the

---

163–65.

7. The debate over whether this woman had already been forgiven before she came to Jesus or she was forgiven after she anointed Jesus will be discussed in chapter 3.

8. This technique of repetition, which is called *Leitwort*, will be discussed in the following section.

9. For the interest in marginalized groups in Luke 4:21, Strauss, *The Davidic Messiah in Luke-Acts*, 196–260.

challenge the Kingdom brings to the complacent normalcy of one's accepted world."[10] In this case, Luke wants to describe a new kingdom inaugurated with the coming of Jesus; Jesus' mission shown in Luke 4:18-20 would be fulfilled in an unexpected way.[11] By reversing the fortune of the marginalized people, such as the poor, the prisoners, the blind, and the oppressed, Jesus proclaims that he is the one who bring God's reign to this world: ἤρξατο δὲ λέγειν πρὸς αὐτοὺς ὅτι σήμερον πεπλήρωται ἡ γραφὴ αὕτη ἐν τοῖς ὠσὶν ὑμῶν (Luke 4:21).[12]

Finally, Luke portrays Jesus not only as the bringer of the kingdom and the anticipated Messiah, but also as the longed-for prophet whom God had promised in the OT that he would send (Luke 7:16, 39). This study will show how Luke uses the reversal of weeping to promote these theological implications.

The work is divided into six chapters. Chapter 1 will explore previous studies of reversal in Luke. This will be limited to the reversal of poor and rich due to the scarcity of materials dealing with the reversal of weeping. I will also suggest that the compositional approach to Luke helps readers see that Luke arranges his material with specific intent, which is to highlight his theme of reversal of weeping. In addition, by utilizing narrative criticism, we will see that repetitive words form a literary pattern, leading the reader to focus on specific reversals, e.g., weeping to laughing and vice versa.

Chapter 2 pursues the historical background of the reversal of weeping in the context of the Old Testament and Second Temple literature. This background survey reveals how Luke uses traditions familiar to him and how he develops and distinguishes his treatment of the reversal of weeping from the way this theme is treated in the OT and Second Temple literature. Some insights and principles of the reversal of weeping from the OT and Second Temple literature will be provided.

Chapter 3 will deal with the positive direction of reversal of weeping, how weeping turns to laughter. First, I will delve into Luke 6:21 as the foundational text on the reversal of weeping. By considering four passages that illustrate the reversal of weeping (Luke 7:13; 7:36-50; 8:40-56; 22:54-62), I will argue that the reversal of weeping occurs in the present world, not only

10. Crossan, *In Parables*, 75.

11. This unexpectedness is shown in Luke 7:18-23, which retells that the disciples of John the Baptist ask Jesus whether he is the one who was to come or not. See an excellent discussion of Hays, "Reading the Bible with Eyes of Faith: The Practice of Theological Exegesis," 5-21. See his related essay, Hays, "Reading the Bible with Eyes of Faith: Theological Exegesis from the Perspective of Biblical Studies," 82-102.

12. Dunn, *Jesus Remembered*, 439. Also see Arnold, "The Kingdom, Miracles, Satan, and Demons," especially 157-58; McCartney, "ECCE HOMO," 1-21.

in the eschatological[13] lives of those who weep, and their fortune is reversed by the prophet Jesus, who is the bringer of the kingdom of God. The exegesis of these passages will support this argument.

Chapter 4 takes an approach similar to that in chapter 3 except that it focuses on the "Negative Reversal of Weeping." In other words, the reversal is shown in the way that laughter turns to weeping. The foundation for this theme will be laid with a discussion of Luke 6:25. After that, three passages (Luke 7:31–35; 19:41–44; 23:27–31) will be examined to show the Luke is also interested in this direction of reversal. Those who laugh will be turned into people who weep.

Chapters 5 and 6 respectively synthesize and conclude the present study.

---

13. Lukan eschatology is a widely debated and discussed area. In particular, it was the view of H. Conzelmann that Luke wrote against a background of concern because Jesus had not yet returned. Luke supposedly met this alleged "delay of the parousia" by reworking Jesus' teachings that the church is to continue. See his *The Theology of St. Luke*. However, Tuckett refutes Conzelmann position by saying that Luke already recognizes that Jesus coming is not imminent, as people expect. "In this sense, Conzelmann is right: Luke is concerned about the delay of the parousia. But Luke may *not* have yet given up the hope and expectation of the End for his own day. Thus, Conzelmann may be wrong to suggest that Luke has postponed the parousia into the indefinite future. Rather, Luke may still want to reaffirm the eschatological hope in his own time and hence preserves some of the elements in his tradition which warn of a sudden End that may arrive at any moment. Thus, for Luke, Jesus predicts delay, and Luke tones down some of the predictions of the parousia that Jesus makes; but this is not because Luke himself surrendered all such hope completely. Rather it may be precisely in order to reaffirm such hope in his own day that Luke rewrites his sources in this way. . . Moreover, rather than postponing the *eschaton* into the indefinite future, *Luke* still has a firm hope for an imminent eschatological event, while at the same time affirming a belief in the present as in a very real sense a realization of some of these eschatological events" (Tuckett, "Luke," 280–81, 84). In this study, I will use "eschatology" of Luke with this sense of Tuckett, understanding that not solely future but also realization of some eschatological events in this present world, now. For more bibliography on Luke's eschatology, see Wolter, "Eschatology in the Gospel according to Luke," 106–8.

CHAPTER ONE

HISTORY OF RESEARCH AND METHODOLOGY

This chapter is a survey of previous materials that discuss reversal in the Gospel of Luke. Because of the paucity of studies concerning the reversal of weeping,[1] this survey will focus on the context of the poor and rich, which is the most frequently treated category in the study of reversal. This chapter also discusses two main methods of criticism, composition and narrative criticism, which I will employ throughout the study. In addition, Luke's purpose for using repetition, frequently noted by narrative critics, is his way of intensifying the theme of the reversal of weeping.

History of Research

Studies of reversal in Luke have focused on the reversal of rich and poor because, as John Nolland says, "Hunger and weeping are not being considered as separate conditions from poverty but as characteristic manifestations of poverty."[2] David Garland agrees: "The hungry and those beset by grief are subgroups of the poor."[3] Amanda C. Miller explains that the reversal is not separable from the schema of poor and rich: "Closely related to the ethics of wealth, poverty, and possessions in the Gospel of Luke is the theme of status reversal, the idea that the current power structure and values of this

---

1. There has been no single volume that discusses solely the reversal of *weeping* in Luke. York has only passing comments on the issue. See York, *Last Shall be First*, 61–62.
2. Nolland, *Luke*, 1:283. "The theme of 'good news to the poor' belongs at the heart and center of the Lukan story" (Pilgrim, *Good News to the Poor*, 64).
3. Garland, *Luke*, 276.

world will be turned upside down by the reign of God."[4] As a result, scholars have tended to subsume all other reversals under the category of poverty and wealth.

With this tendency, the previous attention to reversal has taken the following four focuses: (1) passing comments about the significance of reversal without consistent attention on reversal itself; (2) discussion of the reversal theme in relation to literary concerns; (3) treatment of reversal as a distinctive Lukan theme; and (4) discussion of reversal in the context of an apocalyptic motif.

Observations about Reversal

In most of the passing comments about reversal in the Gospel of Luke, the emphasis falls on three significant passages in which the reversal theme is explicitly shown: the Magnificat, the parable of the Rich Man and Lazarus, and the Beatitudes and Woes.[5]

First to be considered here is the Magnificat.[6] The reversal theme is clearly found in 1:52-53, which read, καθεῖλεν δυνάστας ἀπὸ θρόνων καὶ ὕψωσεν ταπεινούς, πεινῶντας ἐνέπλησεν ἀγαθῶν καὶ πλουτοῦντας ἐξαπέστειλεν κενούς. A sharp contrast is shown between δυνάστας and ταπεινούς in v. 52. It is God who exalts those who are in humble status (ταπεινούς), while He puts down the mighty (δυνάστας). Also πεινῶντας and πλουτοῦντας in v. 53 shows another contrast by reversal of fortune: Those who are hungry are full, whereas the rich are sent away empty.[7] Many have recognized that the

---

4. Miller, "Bridge Work and Seating Charts," 417.

5. See Introduction

6. See Bailey, "The Song of Mary," 29-35; Brown, *The Birth of the Messiah*; Brown, "The Annunciation to Mary," 249-59; Minear, "Luke's Use of the Birth Stories,"; Luccio, "La Megillá de Ester," 39-55; Thaidigsmann, "Gottes Schöpferisches Sehen," 19-38.

7. Because of the contrast between πεινῶντας and πλουτοῦντας, hunger has been thought as a characteristic of the poor. Thus, Bovon comments that "one reads about both God's transcendence over rich and poor, and his active decision in favor of the little ones" (Bovon, *Luke*, 1:62). This contrast is intensified by Nolland's chiastic structure. The parallelism is clearly shown in v. 52 and v. 53. See Nolland, *Luke*, 1:61.

51 He has shown might with his arm:
He has scattered those who are proud in the thought of their hearts;
52 He has brought down potentates from their thrones,
and exalted the lowly;
53 He has filled the hungry with good things,
and sent away empty those who have become rich;
54 He has taken the part of Israel his servant,
In remembrance of his mercy—
55 just as he spoke to our fathers—

reversal is a significant component, especially in these two verses.[8] Robert Tannehill says, "In its dynamic unity this text holds together the small and great, the birth of a baby to an unimportant woman and the fulfillment of Israel's promise through the overturn of human society. By means of the text what would otherwise appear ordinary and insignificant becomes great with significance."[9] John Drury agrees, pointing out that it is one of Luke's peculiar traits to illustrate "God's classical action of raising the low and bringing down the lofty."[10] Tannehill's interest is in the repetitive pattern (or contrast) within the Magnificat that contributes to the dynamic unity of the whole narrative of Luke, while Drury treats the theme of reversal in the context of Luke's use of the Old Testament, not in the context of the poor and rich. Although neither scholar focuses explicitly on reversal *per se*, both notice that reversal is an important component in the Magnificat.

Richard Hays views reversal in the Magnificat as part of the fulfillment of Deuteronomistic command and the ethics of God's renewed people. "Luke . . . proclaims God's liberating power on behalf of the poor and hungry (Luke 1:52-53, 4:18-19) and highlights the vision for a new community of believers who share all possessions in common so that there are no poor among them, in fulfillment of the Deuteronomistic command."[11] Hays includes vv. 52-53 in the category of eschatological reversal and argues that the liberating power of God can make a new community for his renewed people. The renewed community of God's people is marked by the sharing of their possessions with the poor.

Anke Inselmann understands the reversal as being on more a social and political level. "Bei aufmerksamer Lektüre wird dem impliziten Leser das Bild eines erhofften Messias mit politischen beziehungsweise eschatologischen Ansprüchen vermittelt. Wie in der Prophetie oder der weisheitlichen Psalmentradition zeigt sich die heilsgeschichtliche Wirkweise Gottes an politischen und sozialen irdischen Konsequenzen."[12] She rightly connects the verses to the tradition of the Psalms and points out that this OT tradition of God's salvation results in political and social reversal. Both

---

to Abraham and his descendants forever."

8. Bock, *Luke 1:1–9:50*, 1:156; Bovon, *Luke*, 1:62–63 Fitzmyer, *The Gospel according to Luke I-IX*, 360–61; Green, *The Gospel of Luke*, 98–104; Seccombe, *Possessions*, 77–81.

9. Tannehill, "Magnificat as Poem," 275. For the genre of the Magnificat, see Simons, "The Magnificat," 25–46. Also see, Bemile, *The Magnificat*, 63–73.

10. Drury, *Tradition and Design*, 50.

11. Hays, *Moral Vision*, 464. In exegesis of Luke 1:52–53, Hays puts more emphasis on the role reversal of the women in the Gospel of Luke. See, ibid., 132–33.

12. Inselmann, *Die Freude im Lukasevangelium*, 181. Bock also thinks that the ruler in v. 52 refer to the Romans and those like them. Bock, *Luke*, 1:156.

Hays' and Inselmann's analyses show that the reversal is not confined to the spiritual realm, but also happens in this present world. Thus, the Magnificat demonstrates that reversal brings a change of people's social status as well as salvation for God's people.

Christopher Hays closely examines the reversal of the fortune of the poor and rich in the Magnificat. He admits that the soteriological reflection on the poor and rich should not be overlooked here, but, at the same time, "since any number of images might have been adopted to express Mary's jubilation, we ought to appreciate that Luke is emphatically (though not exclusively) concerned about the material aspects of the Messiah's redemption."[13] In saying this, Hays contends that Luke's one of the main emphasis in the Magnificat is the reversal of the poor and rich. Moreover, he recognizes that the reversal theme is expanded as Luke's narratives goes on. The most interesting thing is that "the envisioned reversal is nationalistic, but Luke will later clarify that many *within* Israel will be counted among the rich against whom God bares his arm (e.g. 6.20–26)."[14] Here Hays rightly understands that the details of the reversal theme are brought out in the Beatitudes and Woes, with only reversal in general being foreshadowed in the Magnificat. Specifically, the beneficiaries of reversal are not clearly described in the Magnificat. Rather, as Luke's narrative goes on, the identity of those beneficiaries becomes clear. Hays thinks that the Beatitudes and Woes is one of the clearest place to show their identity: poor, hungry, weeping, persecuted.[15]

Hays' works is about Luke's wealth ethics that "all the possessions of the follower of Jesus ought to be committed to the propagation of his message about the Kingdom of God"[16] but his discussion of status reversal of the poor and rich is insightful in that the status reversal is developed throughout the narrative of Luke.

Second, a number of Jesus' parables present the reversal theme (Luke 14:7–24; 15:11–32), but the parable most often studied is that of the Rich Man and Lazarus (Luke 16:19–31).[17] Here the fortunes of the rich man and the poor man, Lazarus, are reversed after their deaths. The rich man, who enjoyed his wealth and comfortable life in this world, encounters suffering,

---

13. Hays, *Luke's Wealth Ethics*, 102.

14. Ibid.

15. Hays also lists Luke 7:22 (blind, lame, lepers, deaf, dead, and poor); 14:13, 21 (poor, crippled, lama, and blind), and 16:20, 22 (poor, hungry, ulcerated). Ibid., 104.

16. Ibid., 270.

17. The parable is also called "the parable of Dives and Lazarus," for "Dives" is Latin for "rich man" in *Vulgate* (homo quidam erat *dives* et induebatur purpura et bysso et epulabatur cotidie splendide) (Luke 16:19).

while Lazarus, who has experienced harsh suffering for a long time in this life, is comforted after death. This parable is a popular subject not only for narrative approaches, but also for apocalyptic approaches, which will be discussed in detail below.[18]

Finally, it is in the Beatitudes and Woes that Luke makes his most direct statements about the reversal of fortune or destiny. Here marginalized people in society will experience the reversal of fortune or status. This becomes clearer when the Lukan Beatitudes and Woes are compared to Matthew's. One notable difference between Luke and Matthew is Luke's de-spiritualization of the characteristics of the poor.[19] Luke leaves out the τῷ πνεύματι[20] found in Matt 5:3 so that he may focus on the poor in this world.[21] Whether the poor in the Beatitudes can be identified as objects of God's salvific action or not, their fortune shall be reversed in this present world.[22] The focus is "this present world." Not only in the promised blessings in the Beatitudes but also in the future woes, Luke creates a sharp focus on the reversal of fortunes (6:24–26). Drake rightly explains that since the woes present the results of failure to receive God's gift, Luke employs them

18. See, Bauckham, "The Rich Man and Lazarus," 225–46; Bishop, "A Yawning Chasm," 3–5; Boyd, "Apocalyptic and Life after Death," 39–56; Cadbury, "The Name of Dives," 73; Himmelfarb, *Tours of Hell*; Hintzen, *Verkündigung und Wahrnehmung* Omanson, "Lazarus and Simon," 416–19; Vogels, "Having or Longing," 27–46. For more bibliographies, see Kissinger, *The Parables of Jesus*, 371–76.

19. Davies and Allison admit this fact in his commentary: "The addition does, admittedly, shift the emphasis from the economic to the religious sphere" (Davies and Allison, *A Critical Commentary on the Gospel according to Saint Matthew*, 1:443).

20. Note some mss, such as À2, Q, Q and others, have τῷ πνεύματι. However, it seems a harmonization with Matthew (Fitzmyer, *The Gospel according to Luke I–IX*, 632).

21. Bock summarizes five major differences between Matthean and Lukan beatitudes: Luke has four while Matthew has eight; the order of the common beatitudes is different; the addresses are different. While Luke uses second person whereas Matthew does the third; the character of those addressed differs. One example is Matthew puts "in spirit" in the character of the poor; and, Luke alone has the woes. Bock, *Luke*, 1:549–50. I will discuss later Luke's emphasis on this present age by using νῦν. Also see Betz and Yarbro, *The Sermon on the Mount*.

22. The identification of the poor in Matthew and Luke is another big issue, which is not the major concern for this study. However, see Hoyt, "The Poor/Rich Theme in the Beatitudes," 31–41. Many commentaries on Matthew and Luke deal with the issue. Specifically see Betz, *The Sermon on the Mount*; Davies and Allison, *Gospel according to Saint Matthew*; Meadors, "The 'Poor' in the Beatitudes of Matthew [5:3] and Luke," 305–14. Also Seccombe identifies the poor as a characterization of Israel in her need of salvation. Thus, "'The hungry' was seen to be open to a similar interpretation and it can easily be demonstrated that the picture of weepers being comforted and having their mourning turned to joy is also part of the traditional imagery of national salvation." See Seccombe, *Possession and the Poor in Luke–Acts*, 88.

"to point out a vivid and total reversal of conditions."[23] Garland agrees: "The beatitudes combined with woes emphasize a reversal of circumstances that will occur in God's future."[24]

Most discussions of the Lukan Beatitudes and Woes have been done from the perspective of literary concerns or apocalyptic motifs, which I will discuss below. However, Verhey discusses the great reversal in the Lukan Beatitudes and Woes apart from any apocalyptic motif. He thinks that Luke revises the material content of apocalyptic expectation and emphasizes the reign of God in the present age: "The nationalistic hope for Israel's lordship over and revenge against the nations is strikingly absent."[25] He summarizes the significance of this great reversal: "The 'great reversal' of the kingdom brings a transformation of values. The present order, including its conventional rules of prestige and protocol, pomp and privilege, is called into question by Jesus' announcement of the coming kingdom."[26] Verhey attempts to show how NT messages provide the proper ethics for Christians. Thus, by portraying the Lukan reversal of values as occurring in this present age, he shows how Scripture bridges the moral level of the people of God with what God wants his people to do.

From the above, we can see that passing comments on reversal come from interest in such varied topics as the distinction between rich and poor, the distinction between the powerful and the powerless, and New Testament ethics. These comments provide insights helpful to the understanding of reversal in the Gospel of Luke: reversal is not necessarily confined to one specific scheme.

Literary Concerns

Other scholars have focused on reversal from literary concerns. In discussing the Beatitudes in Luke 6, Dodd tries to find the reversal theme only in the context of the poor and rich, arguing that the reversal—eschatological reversal—was a common device in the plots of Greek tragedies. Dodd thinks that Luke adopted the concept of περιπέτεια, first noted by Aristotle, which means "a sudden change over of what is being done to the opposite in the way we have said, and—as we have also just said—according to likelihood or necessity,"[27] and spiritualized it: "If the parable of Dives and Lazarus

---

23. Drake, "The Reversal Theme in Luke's Gospel," 154.
24. Garland, *Luke*, 277.
25. Verhey, *The Great Reversal*, 15.
26. Ibid.
27. Aristotle, *Aristotle's Poetics*, 87.

is allowed as an illustration, the 'etherealized' character of the reversal of conditions is emphasized."[28] Dodd's contribution is that the motif of reversal in the Gospel of Luke is a plot commonly found in the contemporary literature, so Luke might have adopted περιπέτεια and utilized it not only in the parable of the Rich Man and Lazarus but also in the Beatitudes and Woes. However, there are not many places where περιπέτεια is clearly seen and used throughout the Gospel of Luke. In other words, only these two texts clearly show περιπέτεια.

Luke Timothy Johnson identifies a literary pattern concerning the poor and the rich in Luke. He suggests that "acceptance and rejection" is a unique literary pattern of Luke's narrative (1:52–53; 6:20–26; 14:12–15; 16:19–31). The most intriguing thing is that the pattern of acceptance and rejection appears explicitly in reversal.[29] This pattern is applied to Jesus and his apostles in Luke-Acts by Luke's portrayal of Jesus as a rejected prophet.[30] More to the point, Johnson's argument is that "the preaching of the Gospel to the poor and the proclamation of woes to the rich signify that by God's visitation in the Prophet Jesus, these conditions are reversed, that the outcast are called to salvation and the men who enjoy present acceptance are to be rejected."[31] Accordingly, Luke presents the poor as those who accept the message of the rejected prophet and are finally vindicated by God. They are the truly accepted people. In contrast, those who are rich—sometimes described as the leaders—who reject the prophet and his message will be outcasts when God's judgment falls (Luke 14:12–15).[32] In other words, the acceptance and rejection that brings the reversal of fortunes is the acceptance or rejection of Jesus' message.[33]

Johnson shows that this pattern occurs not only in the Magnificat but also in the Beatitudes and Woes.[34] He acknowledges a pattern of reversal here, but he does not discuss it in detail. Rather, he identifies the poor

---

28. Dodd, *More New Testament Studies*, 6.

29. Drake and York well summarize the content of Johnson's work. Drake, "The Reversal Theme in Luke's Gospel," 15–17. Also see, York, *The Last Shall Be First*, 20–23.

30. Jesus and his disciples are described as the prophetic model of Moses. Johnson, *The Literary Function of Possessions*, 77–78.

31. Ibid., 140.

32. Ibid., 124.

33. Johnson lists a number of passages to show this pattern other than the Magnificat and the Beatitudes and Woes, such as 4:18; ch. 7; 14:1, 12, 1 3, and 15. These passages show that "the poor take a prominent place among others to whom the Good News." However, his focus is, as seen the below, the Beatitudes and Woes of Luke. Ibid., 132–33.

34. Johnson, *The Literary Function of Possessions*, 135–37.

as the rejected, and "this rejection is associated with the rejection of the prophets."[35] Johnson focuses on the fourth beatitude (6:22) and woe (6:26), which clearly show an acceptance and rejection pattern. The series of verbs denoting persecution (μισήσωσιν, ἀφορίσωσιν, ὀνειδίσωσιν, and ἐκβάλωσιν) in v. 22 well illustrate the outcast character of the poor.[36] For this reason, he understands that not only weeping and hunger but also persecution are specific characteristics of the poor.[37] Johnson develops his argument by analyzing the parable of the Rich Man and Lazarus. He thinks that this parable sheds light on the pattern of acceptance and rejection in the Gospel of Luke as well.

Johnson successfully argues that the reversal affects the poor and the rich because they respectively accept and reject the message of Jesus; in addition, the reversal of fortune is not a moralistic one but is "simply the Divine reversal."[38] Thus, it is directed to the Pharisees, who reject the prophet Jesus. "As the rich man had scorned the demands of the Law and the Prophets to give alms, so the Pharisees reject the teaching of the living Prophet Jesus on almsgiving."[39]

Johnson's main concern is to find a literary pattern with identifying reversal as a theme. He utilizes the reversal theme to find the literary pattern of acceptance and rejection.[40] He therefore fails to notice the variety of reversals, such as weeping turning to laughter, the hungry being filled, and those who are persecuted being comforted. Rather, he puts all these into one category, the poor and the rich, in order to show his literary pattern of acceptance and rejection.

---

35. Ibid., 134–35.

36. μακάριοί ἐστε ὅταν μισήσωσιν ὑμᾶς οἱ ἄνθρωποι καὶ ὅταν ἀφορίσωσιν ὑμᾶς καὶ ὀνειδίσωσιν καὶ ἐκβάλωσιν τὸ ὄνομα ὑμῶν ὡς πονηρὸν ἕνεκα τοῦ υἱοῦ τοῦ ἀνθρώπου· (Luke 6:22). See the contrast which is shwon in v. 26. οὐαὶ ὅταν ὑμᾶς καλῶς εἴπωσιν πάντες οἱ ἄνθρωποι· κατὰ τὰ αὐτὰ γὰρ ἐποίουν τοῖς ψευδοπροφήταις οἱ πατέρες αὐτῶν (Luke 6:26). The fortune of the rich people who are already accepted and enjoying their reputation will be reversed. They will be outcasts. Ibid., 135.

37. Ibid.

38. Ibid., 142. For Johnson, "Divine reversal" refers: "The present situation of the poor and rejected will be reversed by God" (ibid., 135).

39. Ibid., 143.

40. See Drake, "The Reversal Theme in Luke's Gospel," 16. Also See York, *The Last Shall Be First*, 21–22. For the critique of Johnson's work, see Karris, "The Literary Function of Possessions," 653–54. Also see Tiede, "The Literary Function of Possessions," 445–46. Tiede raises the question of modernity of Johnson's method, such as using "literary device." So, "Could it not also be argued that the content of the 'literary device' would have affected its peculiar force in the text as a document of its times?" (ibid., 446).

York's discussion of reversal in the Gospel of Luke is one of the most explicit studies of reversal so far. The purpose of his study is to "understand better Luke's use of double or 'bi-polar' reversal,[41] the impact of these passages on our overall perspective of Lukan eschatology, and the message a first-century audience would have 'heard' in the combined reading of these reversals."[42]

York divides Lukan reversal into two types, explicit bi-polar and implicit bi-polar. The former are: the Magnificat (1:53–55); the Beatitudes and Woes (6:20–26); the Rich Man and Lazarus (16:19–31); the Pharisees and the Publican (18:9–14); Exalted/Humbled–Humbled/Exalted (1:11//18:14); Losing by Saving–Saving by Losing (9:24//17:33); Last/First–First/Last (13:30). The explicit bi-polar reversal shows repetitive patterns with similar structure and terminology, while the implicit one is not as explicit, but the reader can draw the conclusion that they are stories of reversal. One of the most interesting parts of York's work is that he recognizes the repetition of the terms found in the Beatitudes and Woes and shows how the pattern works throughout the narrative. He relates the Lukan Beatitudes to the Magnificat within this framework: "The repetitive patterns first seen in the Magnificat are amplified in the beatitudes and woes, and this amplification links the two texts together."[43] For instance, the terms, such as πτωχός, and πλούσιος, which are used in the Beatitudes, are rooted in the Magnificat.[44] Through this repetitive pattern, "the theme of bi-polar reversal emerges as part of the value-system of the narrative."[45]

However, the most important feature that York identifies related to the reversal of weeping is those who experience the reversal: "It is in the reversal experienced by each group that the use of repetitive words decisively links the beatitudes and woes together and exhibits the bi-polar structure. This is emphasized in the second and third members of each group where νῦν is also repeated."[46] Touching on the reversal of weeping in conjunction with the hunger/full reversal, York states,

> Jesus responds to the tears of those who are weeping (κλαίω), first by raising a dead child back to life, then offering forgiveness of sins and salvation to a "sinful woman." In ch. 9, Jesus feeds the 5,000 and they are "satisfied." Following the exaltation of Jesus,

---

41. For definition of bi-polar reversal, see Introduction note 1.
42. York, *The Last Shall Be First*, 38.
43. Ibid., 58.
44. Ibid., 59.
45. Ibid., 60.
46. Ibid., 58.

Luke depicts the church as a community in which there are no poor, hungry, or weeping people because the community's lifestyle overcomes such needs.[47]

However, York does not extend his discussion to the reversal of weeping, but only includes the reversal of weeping in the category of the repetitive use of specific words or terms. Although he rightly recognizes that this pattern is a feature of the Lukan narrative, he deals with the reversal of weeping within the broad framework of reversal, not as a distinctive theme or subject.[48] In addition, York's discussions are based more on the Greco-Roman than on the Jewish concept of honor and shame.[49] Nevertheless, York's idea is timely in that he recognizes that the pattern of reversal in the Gospel of Luke is emphasized by repetition and the use of similar terminologies in the narrative.[50]

Reversal as a Distinctive Lukan Theme

Not many works treat reversal as a distinctive Lukan theme. However, some scholars, such as Nils Dhal, Howard Marshall, John York, and Larry Drake, understand reversal as a theme that is distinctive in the Gospel of Luke.

Nils Dahl views reversal as the overarching message of Luke and Acts, insisting that it is found in the context of proof-from-prophecy.[51] He focuses on Acts rather than on the Gospel of Luke to prove that the fulfillment of the Old Testament prophecy is shown in Acts, especially in Acts 2–5, 10, and 13. In Acts, as the gospel spreads, the pattern of reversal is more clearly demonstrated as the suffering apostles are miraculously delivered or saved.[52] However, his interest does not lie in reversal specifically, nor does

---

47. Ibid., 61–62.

48. York only mentions the reversal of weeping in a bit more detailed fashion, not exhaustively, in his footnote by using the word, "weeping/laughter reversal." Moreover, he includes only three passages into weeping reversal (7:13, 38, and 8:52). See, ibid., 62.

49. York heavily relies on Bruce Malina's sociological analysis, which focuses on Greco-Roman context of honor and shame. For Malina's work, see Malina, *The New Testament World*. Also see Malina, *Social Science Commentary on the Synoptic Gospels*.

50. The conclusion of York is somewhat perplexing in that the effect of repetition has a bi-polar effect: "Repetition would naturally have lessened the 'surprise' or shock typically attributed to the bi-polar texts. However, the repetitive pattern also would have served to solidify the value system inherent in the divine principle" (York, *The Last Shall Be First*, 183).

51. Also see Johnson, *The Literary Function of Possessions*. See the discussion of Johnson above.

52. Dahl, "The Purpose of Luke–Acts," 91.

he discuss instances of reversal in detail. Rather, he wants to show that the reversal is brought about as a fulfillment of prophecy.

Howard Marshall also views reversal as a distinctive theme in Luke. Although he does not explicitly deal with the theme, he devotes a chapter in *Luke, Historian and Theologian*, "The Rich and the Poor," to reversal.[53] He says that the Lukan beatitudes and woes seem to teach that there will be a reversal of status in the Kingdom of God. This is confirmed by several similar passages such as the Magnificat, the parable of the rich fool (12:13–21, in contrast to God's care for disciples in 12:22–34), the parable of the wedding feast (14:7–11), and the parable of the Rich Man and Lazarus. He concludes, "Luke teaches a simple reversal of conditions. Wealth is a bad thing; it leads to loss in the next world, and therefore it is better to renounce it now in the hope of spiritual reward."[54]

Although Marshall extends the scope of reversal to persecution and comfort in 6:22, he still considers the weeping and the hungry as the poor. However, his argument is helpful in that it shows that the reversal of fortune is the result of a change in attitude toward God as well as what Johnson calls "divine reversal": "Luke does not present poverty as an ideal in itself, nor wealth as intrinsically evil. When his teaching on wealth and poverty is seen in the context of the Gospel as a whole, the underlying attitude to God is what really matters."[55] Furthermore, the more significant point that Marshall makes is that this reversal occurs in the Kingdom of God. He understands that the reversal in the Kingdom takes place only in the future, so there is a tension between the present world and the coming future. However, the reversal of status is not solely future. Rather, Jesus shows by his earthly ministry that the reversal of fortune can happen in this world as well.[56]

Drake's work identifies all passages that contain reversal in the Gospel of Luke. He wants to show that reversal is not confined to a single passage or specific parable, such as the Rich Man and Lazarus, but it is a theme that can be found throughout the Gospel of Luke.[57] To show that reversal is a distinctive Lukan theme, Drake argues that Luke's reversals do not have the same literary pattern as those in Greco-Roman literature, although there are some similar patterns found in Greek comedy and tragedy.[58] Drake thinks

---

53. Marshall, *Luke, Historian and Theologian*, esp., 141–44.

54. Ibid., 142.

55. Ibid., 143.

56. It will be discussed in my chapter 3 and 4.

57. Drake, "The Reversal Theme in Luke's Gospel," 1, 265.

58. Ibid., 44–74. However, his discussion of Greco-Roman literature is mostly focused on περιπέτεια.

that Lukan reversal is a continuation of that found in the OT and Jewish literature. After surveying the related literature, Drake places all the passages of reversal in the Gospel of Luke into five categories:

> (1) specific statements by authors who use the phrase "reversal theme" or some synonymous expression; (2) a pattern of acceptance and rejection of Jesus by groups within and beyond Judaism; (3) reversal of the plight of the oppressed and those who are oppressing (generally in the context of wealth/poverty in Luke–Acts); (4) apocalyptic or eschatological reversal; and (5) reversal in parables, aphorisms/proverbs and stories.[59]

Each of these five categories contains both explicit and implicit reversals. However, Drake's argument needs to be refined if it is to be useful: his categories are not always clearly defined. For example, his first category is too general. Authors who use the phrase "reversal theme" (or synonymous expressions) have their own criteria for analyzing reversal themes. Drake uses the works of Dahl and Marshall as examples of the first category, but they combine acceptance and rejection of Jesus in the same category as oppressed poor and wealthy, where Drake makes them, respectively, his second and third categories.[60] In other words, "Drake's dissertation demonstrates the difficulties inherent in any attempt to collect other scholars' references to reversal in Luke or Luke–Acts."[61] In addition, categories three and four are not always separable because apocalyptic or eschatological reversal usually occurs with the poor and rich. In other words, the reversal of the oppressed is one of the distinctive features of the apocalyptic literature in the following section. Thus, though Drake properly understands the theme of reversal as distinctive to the Gospel of Luke, he does not present a convincing list of categories for the theme of reversal.

Reversal Within the Apocalyptic Motif

The reversal of the fortune of the rich and the poor is a typical characteristic of apocalyptic literature.[62] For this reason, reversal has been studied by many scholars within the context of apocalyptic motifs.

---

59. Ibid., 9–36.

60. Ibid., 10–14. See Dahl, "The Purpose of Luke–Acts." Also see Marshall, *Luke, Historian and Theologian*.

61. York, *The Last Shall Be First*, 38.

62. Frederick Murphy lists elements of an apocalyptic worldview. They are somewhat lengthy but worth to mention: an unseen world affects or even determines this one; the unseen world is accessible only through revelation; after death, humans are

In discussing Jesus' parable within an apocalyptic context, Boomershine argues that "instead of envisioning from the present to a new age in the future which will reverse present order in a manner that provides comfort and certainty in the present, these parables present the turn of the ages by reflecting back from the future into the present in a manner that creates discomfort and confusion about the present."[63] He extensively analyzes the parable of the Rich Fool (Luke 12:16–21) and argues that this parable is one of the greatest examples of apocalyptic reversal, since the turn of the ages is a radical reversal of expectations.[64] He finds apocalyptic reversal in many passages in the Gospel of Luke, but he does not recognize the reversal of weeping as a distinct element of the parables of Jesus. Rather, he only thinks that reversal is an important element because an apocalyptic worldview is depicted therein. For Boomershine, reversal is a "reversal of expectation" with the turn of the ages.

---

judged and rewarded or punished; there is often a future world that entails a renewal of the present one or its replacement with a better one; God's sovereignty is at issue. Humans and/or angels have rebelled against God's rule, but divine rule will soon be reasserted. Resistance to the coming of God's rule is common. God sometimes accomplishes the reestablishment of divine rule alone, sometimes with angelic aid and sometimes with human aid. God's sovereignty is contrary to earth's empires, especially those that oppress Israel or Christians; Dualism pervades apocalypses—humanity is divided into the righteous and the unrighteous; time is divided into the present world and the one to come; cosmic power are seen to be either for or against God; There is dissatisfaction with the present world; The coming of the eschaton is often accompanied by cosmic disturbances, as well as by social upheaval; the coming of a messiah is not present in every apocalypse but is not uncommon; the apocalyptic worldview is deterministic. At least on the macro level, things happen according to God's plans, regardless of human action. Individuals and groups can affect their own fate by aligning with or against God; the apocalyptic worldview has a developed angelology and demonology, and; Apocalyptic language is used to communicate the apocalyptic worldview. Murphy, *Apocalypticism in the Bible and Its World*, 8–14. For more details of apocalyptic worldview, see chapter 2.

63. Marcus and Soards, "Epistemology at the Turn of the Ages," 159.

64. Ibid., 157–58. The parables that Boomershine thinks to show apocalyptic reversal are: the parable of vineyards (Luke 20:9–18); the budding fig tree (Luke 21:29–31); the unmerciful servant (Matt 18:23–35); the good employer (Matt 20:1–16); the great supper and the guest without a wedding garment (Luke 14:16–24); the servant entrusted with supervision (Luke 12:42–46); the ten virgins (Matt 25:1–13); the talents (Luke 19:12–27); the last judgment (Matt 25:31–46); the prodigal son (Luke 15:11–32); and the rich man and Lazarus (Luke 16:19–31). Boomershine aptly explains apocalyptic characteristics of Jesus parable. He does not specifically how parables of Jesus relates the poor/rich context. However, he relevantly shows that eschatological reversal is one part of apocalyptic characters and how it is shown in Jesus' parables including the reversal of the rich and poor.

Nickelsburg also finds similarities between *1 Enoch*[65] and Luke; he especially focuses on the reversal of the fortunes of the poor and the rich. His work is more detailed than that of Boomershine in that he compares *1 Enoch* to the Gospel of Luke comprehensively, focusing on the poor and rich. Nickelsburg examines the work of Sverre Aalen, who had dealt with the same topic previously.[66] Aalen compares the verbal similarities (i.e., vocabulary and expression) of the Gospel of Luke and the last chapter of *1 Enoch* (*1 Enoch* 102:10/Luke 10:29, 16:15; *1 Enoch* 104:8/Luke 12:5; *1 Enoch* 99:9/Luke 14:18; *1 Enoch* 100:5/Luke 16:9; *1 Enoch* 98:7, 99:10, 100:4; 101:1/ Luke 1:32, 35, 76, 6:35) and draws conceptual parallels between two, such as woes against the rich (*1 Enoch* 97:8–10 and the parable of the rich fool in Luke 12:15–21; *1 Enoch* 98:9, 97:9, 104:5, 103:3, 5 and the Rich Man and Lazarus in Luke 16:19–31),[67] concluding that Luke depends on *1 Enoch*. In spite of many obvious parallels between Luke and *1 Enoch*, Nickelsburg concludes that Aalen's proposal is not persuasive since verbal similarities do not prove and guarantee literary dependence.[68] Nickelsburg rather bases his argument that the Gospel of Luke depends on *1 Enoch* on the evidence that both authors presume an apocalyptic worldview in the reversal of the fortune of the poor and rich after death. Both works attempt to "adjudicate the present unjust prosperity of the rich and the suffering of the poor whom they oppress or disregard,"[69] although there is an important difference in that Luke gives the rich the greater chance for repentance.[70] Nickelsburg's work is valuable because it illuminates the reversal of the poor and rich in the context of an apocalyptic worldview.[71]

---

65. More detailed information on *1 Enoch* will be discussed in §2.2.3.

66. Aalen, "St Luke's Gospel and the Last Chapters of I Enoch," 1–13. Aalen has more detailed work on this topic, although he does not relate the Gospel of Luke extensively. See Aalen, *Heilsverlangen und Heilsverwirklichung*.

67. The date of *1 Enoch* is much debated. However, Charlesworth's conclusion is the most persuasive: it is dated as late as the end of the first century. See Charlesworth, *Old Testament*, 1:4–8.

68. Neusner and Avery-Peck, *George W. E. Nickelsburg in Perspective*, 522. Especially, see 522–23.

69. Ibid., 570.

70. For example, the call for repentance by John the Baptist (3:7–9); the sinful woman (7:36–50); and ten lepers (17:15–19), while *1 Enoch* has only 104:9 according to Nickelsburg. Although Nickelsburg admits that some verbal parallels are common between *1 Enoch* and Luke, he thinks the common theological pattern such as the reversal of the status of the rich and poor is more comprehensively shown. Ibid., 530–32.

71. Nickelsburg emphasizes the characteristic of apocalyptic worldview on dualism. Thus he affirms that the great reversal of the rich and poor is "set within the framework of a special and temporal dualism: this world/heaven and Sheol and Hades; the present life or time/its end through a judgment that ushers in a new life or time" (ibid., 570).

Richard Batey also links the poor and rich motif to eschatological reversal within an apocalyptic context. He treats the problem of the poor in the Gospels as part of his discussion of "Theology of Reversal." Eschatological reversal occurs when the current social order is reversed. In other words, economic structure is reformed by God's power.[72] He selects several passages in the Synoptic Gospels to support his point. However, Batey's core interest lies in the Beatitudes of Luke. He "finds Luke 6:20–24 as a clear example of economic reversal or revolution."[73] Batey's view is simple but clear, for he presents the important character of reversal by using the phrase "turning tables." However, he limits the scope of reversal to the category of economics, not expanding to other categories such as weeping, filling, and persecution.

Walter Pilgrim, from research on the poor in the Old Testament and Judaism, puts reversal in an apocalyptic category as well. In particular, he argues that the portrayal of God, especially from the OT, as the defender of the poor and needy is one of the most significant element in apocalyptic.[74] This portrait becomes normative in early Judaism, while mixing with "apocalyptic hopes for a coming reversal and with a growing rabbinic separation for the poor."[75] Pilgrim connects "the poor" to the pious poor (עֲנִיִּים), and he tries to show that this class of poor is represented by Jesus, whose reign brings a reversal effected by God. Pilgrim discusses important passages that show an eschatological reversal, including the Magnificat, the Beatitudes of Matthew and Luke, the parable of the Rich Man and Lazarus, and many other passage in the Gospel of Luke and Acts.[76] Regarding the Lukan Beatitudes specifically, he says,

> He (Jesus) can offer the kingdom to the poor. But that is not all. The blessings upon the poor as recipients of the kingdom are made concrete in what follows; their present hunger will be satisfied, and their present afflictions will turn to laughter. . . . Now they are poor, hungry, weeping, yet as inheritors of the kingdom they will then be satisfied and full of joy. A total reversal of social status is envisioned, a point made even more vivid by the contrasting woes upon the rich in Luke's Gospel[77]

---

72. Batey, *Jesus and the Poor*, 18.
73. Drake, "The Reversal Theme in Luke's Gospel," 18.
74. Pilgrim, *Good News to the Poor*, 38.
75. Ibid.
76. He surveys almost all passages from Luke and Acts.
77. Pilgrim, *Good News to the Poor*, 58.

Pilgrim relates these passages of Luke (and Acts) to the theme of reversal, but he does not expand the reversal to dimensions other than the material. So, the reversal of weeping is not discussed here or in other scholars' discussions of reversal.

Based on the research, then, the theme of reversal has most often been explored under three main categories: literary concerns, distinctive as a Lukan theme, and apocalyptic context. In dealing with these categories, scholars have focused almost solely on the dyad of rich and poor. For this reason, it is necessary to look at other aspects of reversal in a more detailed fashion. The study of the reversal of weeping is a good place to begin because it is an important Lukan theme.

Methodology

No single methodology is used in this dissertation. The primary method is composition criticism in light of redaction criticism. Composition criticism will be used to demonstrate how and why Luke arranges his materials (or sources) in his unique way. Narrative criticism is also used in order to articulate the unity of Luke's arrangement of his materials. These methods are employed throughout this work.

Composition Criticism

Composition criticism, which treats the arrangement or rearrangement of the material according to the author/redactor's concerns, is subsumed under redaction criticism. The broad aim of redaction criticism is to discover something about the author's own concerns and ideas.[78] For this reason, composition criticism is considered within the framework of redaction criticism. However, Norman Perrin thinks that redaction criticism and composition criticism are interchangeable terms:

> It is concerned with studying the theological motivation of an author as this is revealed in the collection, arrangement, editing, and modification of traditional material, and in the composition of new material or the creation of new forms within the traditions of early Christianity. Although the discipline is called redaction criticism, it could equally be called "composition criticism" because it is concerned with the composition of new material and the arrangements of redacted or freshly created

---

78. Tuckett, "Luke," 266.

material into new units and patterns, as well as with the redaction of existing material.[79]

Here Perrin acknowledges the difference between redaction and composition, but he does not discuss any specific distinction between them, even while expressing the view that composition criticism will be separated from redaction criticism in the future. "It may well be that one day the discipline will have developed to the point where composition criticism has to be distinguished from redaction criticism as redaction criticism now has to be distinguished from form criticism."[80] Thus, Perrin uses the term "redaction criticism" as an umbrella term, embracing composition criticism and excluding form criticism. While Perrin's broad definition provides us a useful overall framework, acknowledging the differences between redaction and composition criticism highlights the latter's usefulness for understanding the reversal of weeping in the Gospel of Luke. The difference in perspective between the two can be clearly recognized in Smalley's explanation of composition criticism: "One (redaction criticism) is the study of the observable changes introduced by the Gospel writers into the traditional material they received and used. The other (composition criticism) examines the *arrangement* of this material, an arrangement which is motived by the theological understanding and intention of the evangelists."[81] In this regard, the main motivation behind composition criticism is that the evangelists deal the meaning of the whole. Thus, Grant Osborne asserts, "At both the micro and macro levels the rearrangement of the inherited tradition is significant."[82] Even though Osborne's explanation of composition criticism is much closer to a definition of redaction criticism, especially in the use of the phrase "rearrangement of inherited tradition," the focus in composition criticism is on the whole text rather than on specific sources or tradition.

Randall Tan argues that composition criticism is a more text-centered approach than redaction criticism. In other words, composition criticism is

79. Perrin, *What Is Redaction Criticism?*, 1. "It is becoming evident that one problem connected with redaction criticism is and will increasingly become the problem of the relationship between redaction and composition" (ibid., 65). Ernst Haenchen first coined the term composition criticism. See Haenchen, *Der Weg Jesu*, especially 24.

80. Perrin, *What Is Redaction Criticism?*, 66–67. Perrin develops his methodology from redaction criticism to literary criticism later. For more detail, see Mercer, *Norman Perrin's Interpretation of the New Testament*.

81. Smalley, "Redaction Criticism," 181. Also note Soulen's definition to distinguish composition criticism from redaction criticism. "It refers to an analysis of the total effect of a redacted text, treating the composition as a whole rather than concentrating only on the specific redactional elements within a text" (Soulen, *Handbook of Biblical Criticism*, 38).

82. Osborne, "Redaction Criticism," 662–69.

a synchronic approach in that its focus is on the final text rather than prehistory, while redaction criticism is a diachronic method that focuses on the differentiation of redaction from tradition and interpreting the redaction as separate from the tradition.[83] In this regard, what characterizes composition criticism is its focus on "the Gospels as wholes and [its] search for patterns and emphases without discrimination, which presupposes a Gospel that has been so thoroughly reshaped by the evangelist that the final product reflects the literary and theological accomplishment of an individual."[84]

Thus, composition criticism can overcome the weaknesses of redaction criticism, which focuses on sources or traditions that the evangelist wants to redact.[85] By considering the text as a whole and final product, composition criticism leads us to see the whole theology of the evangelist. Furthermore, it sheds lights on the pattern or the way in which the evangelist arranges the material. Chapters 3 and 4 will show how composition criticism helps to deal with Luke's reversal of weeping.

Narrative Criticism

As seen above, various forms of literary criticism can be employed in composition criticism; these include narrative criticism, structuralism, reader response criticism, rhetorical criticism, and so on.[86] This work adopts narrative criticism more than these other methods. Resseguie gives an adequate description of narrative criticism:

> Narrative criticism focuses on how biblical literature works as *literature*. The "what" of a text (its content) and the "how" of a text (its rhetoric and structure) are analyzed as a complete

---

83. Tan, "Recent Developments in Redaction Criticism," 600, 611.

84. Telford, "Pre-Markan Tradition," 2:707.

85. For critique of redaction criticism, see Carson, "Redaction Criticism," 123–28. Carson lists twenty weaknesses of redaction criticism from the perspectives of evangelical and general scholarship. However, it is not our purpose to survey every aspect of redaction criticism. Accordingly, the focus should be the points that are relevant to composition criticism for the purpose of the study.

86. "Literary criticism" is a very broad term that has been used at least three different ways: (1) It originally referred to a particular approach to the historical study of Scripture that appeared in systematic form in the nineteenth century; this is now more familiarly known and practiced as source criticism. (2) In the early and mid twentieth century, it began to be used to refer to attempts to explicate a biblical author's intention and achievements through a detailed analysis of the text's rhetorical elements and literary structure. (3) In contemporary usage, it often refers quite broadly to any attempt to understand biblical literature in a manner that parallels the interests and theories of modern literary critics and theorists. Soulen, *Handbook of Biblical Criticism*, 105.

tapestry, an organic whole. Narrative critics are primarily concerned with the literariness of biblical narratives—that is, the qualities that make them literature. Form and content are generally regarded as an indissoluble whole. Narrative criticism is a shift away from traditional historical-critical methods to the way a text communicates meaning as a self-contained unit, a literary artifact, an undivided whole.[87]

Indeed, narrative criticism appeared on the scene with Robert Alter's famous 1981 work *The Art of Biblical Narrative*. After Alter's work, narrative criticism began to be considered a critical method independent of literary criticism. Based on Resseguie's definition, narrative critics see the biblical narrative as a story (or literature). Because Scripture is viewed as a complete tapestry, the interest of narrative criticism is the final form, not a specific fragment of the story. Accordingly, key items of interest include plot, characterization, structure, implied reader, and intended reader.[88]

However, the methodology of narrative criticism is not unified, but complex. One of narrative criticism's useful tools is the close reading employed by the New Critics,[89] the so-called *explication de texte*, which is the "painstaking analysis of the nuances, ambiguities of words, images, metaphors, and small units of a text."[90] The close reading pays attention to the words on the page rather than to the contexts that produced them,[91] and it recognizes the significance of repetitions and patterns that are found in the biblical narrative.[92] However, close reading is not limited to small units of the text; it extends to each gospel as a whole and to the other books of the New Testament as well. For this reason, Mark Powell analyzes the apparent

---

87. Resseguie, *Narrative Criticism of the New Testament*, 18–19, italics in original.

88. Resseguie explains all these concepts in his *Narrative Criticism of the New Testament*. For narrative criticism of Luke, see Kurz, *Reading Luke–Acts*; Powell, "Toward a Narrative-Critical Understanding of Luke," 341–46. For general information about narrative criticism, see Powell, *What Is Narrative Criticism?*

89. The term New Criticism comes after the publication of Ransom, *The New Criticism*. New Critics focus on the text solely and argue that "the background information about an author such as his or her designs and intentions for a work are irrelevant to the understanding of a text. New Critics also did not take into account factors of race, gender, politics, and sexuality in their readings." See Resseguie, *Narrative Criticism of the New Testament*, 22. For New Critical work, see Richards, *Principles of Literary Criticism*. Also see Midgley, *Science and Poetry*. For an overview of New Criticism, see Abrams, *A Glossary of Literary Terms*.

90. Resseguie, *Narrative Criticism of the New Testament*, 23–24.

91. Ibid., 24.

92. The importance of repetition is articulated in Alter, *The Art of Biblical Narrative*.

distinction between how the Gospel of Luke is analyzed under narrative criticism and how it is analyzed under historical criticism:

> Narrative critics prefer to analyze Luke's Gospel with reference to story and discourse. Whereas *story* refers to the content of the narrative—what is about, *discourse* refers to its rhetoric—how the story is told. Narrative critics try to identify the basic storylines of the narrative and consider such questions as how the narrator guides the reader, how characters are constructed in the experience of reading, how literary motifs and patterns are developed and how the logic of the story is maintained.[93]

Using narrative criticism, we will see especially how the literary motif of the reversal of weeping is patterned and developed in the narrative of Luke's gospel. Although the concern of narrative criticism is not historical investigation and historical reliability but the text itself, it is useful for analyzing the final text as a literary whole without necessarily denying its historical reliability. This work will employ a narrative-critical approach integrated with compositional analysis. In doing so, it will make a detailed study of Luke's use of *Leitwort*, one technique of repetition that is discussed in the following section.

Leitwort, a Technique of Repetition

In *The Narrative Unity of Luke–Acts*, Tannehill pays much attention to internal connections among different parts of the narrative. "Themes will be developed, dropped, then presented again. Characters and actions may echo characters and actions in another part of the story, as well as characters and actions of the scriptural story which preceded in Luke–Acts."[94] Certainly, these internal connections are important elements in the creation of the narrative as a work of inherent unity. Tannehill recognizes that telling a story involves narrative rhetoric, which the narrator constructs a world where readers are invited to imagine according to certain values and beliefs. These values and beliefs are purposed to be appealing and convincing.[95] In order to convince the readers, some particular literary techniques are used.

> We may speak of narrative rhetoric both because the story is construed to influence its readers and because there are particular literary techniques used for this purpose.... Readers are

---

93. Powell, "Toward a Narrative–Critical Understanding of Luke," 344.
94. Tannehill, *The Narrative Unity of Luke–Acts*, 1:3.
95. Ibid., 8.

led to believe or to reaffirm their belief in the central character, Jesus, and are thereby influenced in complex ways—in their attitudes, controlling images, patterns of actions, feelings, etc.[96]

Tannehill understands the power of narrative. The Gospel of Luke invites readers to its narrative world and influences them through various literary techniques, among which repetition is important because Luke uses κλαίω in describing the reversal of weeping throughout his narrative. There are also many techniques of repetition, such as verbal repetition (including *Leitwort*), motif, theme, sequence of actions, and types of scenes.[97] The simple purpose of all these techniques of repetition in a narrative is to make a point, but more specifically, repetition helps "identify the norms, values, beliefs, and point of view that the narrator considers important."[98]

Among many literary techniques of repetition, the center of our interest is *Leitwort*, a German term coined by Martin Buber:

> By *Leitwort* I understand a word or word root that is meaningfully repeated within a text or sequence of texts or complex of texts; those who attend to these repetitions will find a meaning of the text revealed or clarified, or at any rate made more emphatic. As noted, what is repeated need not be a single word but can be a word root.[99]

The importance lies in "a word or word root that is meaningfully repeated." However, *Leitwort* is not mere repetition within the narrative; rather, it is repetition that provides a dynamic to the narrative. Thus, "I say 'dynamic' because what takes place between the verbal configurations thus related is in a way a *movement*; readers to whom the whole is present feel the waves beating back and forth.... Such measured repetition, corresponding to the inner rhythm of the text—or rather issuing from it—is probably the strongest of all techniques for making a meaning available without

---

96. Ibid.

97. There are many books that deal with the literary techniques, including the technique of repetition. Resseguie, *Narrative Criticism of the New Testament*, esp. pp. 42–54, provides basic understanding of the literary techniques and narrative criticism. Another fine book that focuses on repetition is Kawin, *Telling It Again and Again*. Alter, *The Art of Biblical Narrative*, esp. 88–113, is the foundational work on literary criticism of the biblical narrative, dealing extensively with the techniques of repetition described above. For a more extensive study on literary techniques in the Bible, see Sternberg, *The Poetics of Biblical Narrative*, esp. 365–440. For specific reference material on repetition for biblical study, see Anderson, *Matthew's Narrative Web*.

98. Resseguie, *Narrative Criticism of the New Testament*, 42.

99. Buber, "Leitwort Style in Pentateuch Narrative," 114. For his German work, see "Leitwortstil in der Erzählung des Pentateuchs," 1131–49.

articulating it explicitly."[100] Although Buber seems to overemphasize the impact of *Leitwort*, it is apparent that *Leitwort* intensifies the meaning by repetition. It is a technique that the narrator employs deliberately. Although Alter thinks that Buber goes to extremes in order to explain and preserve all instances of *Leitwort*, he agrees with Buber about the significance of *Leitwort*,[101] providing his own definition: "Through abundant repetition, the semantic range of the word-root is explored, different forms of the root are deployed, branching off at times into phonetic relatives (that is, word-play), synonymity, and antonymity; by virtue of its verbal status, the *Leitwort* refers immediately to meaning and thus to theme as well."[102] Thus the repetition of the word (or word-root) highlights not only the meaning but also the theme. This is how Luke uses κλαίω in reversal.

A fine example of the *Leitwort* is Kavin Rowe's work, *Early Narrative Christology*. He describes *Leitwort* as "a regular recurrence of similar features variously put to use in the service of a coherent meaning."[103] Rowe demonstrates that Jesus and God share the identity of κύριος ("the LORD"), so that Luke provides the high Christology as Paul and John by Luke's repetitive use of κύριος. Although he does not explicitly say that he uses the technique of *Leitwort*, he thinks that *Leitwort* provides a coherent meaning in Luke's Gospel to see Jesus as the LORD.[104] Indeed, by employing the technique of repetition, especially *Leitwort*, Luke aims to reach his narrative goals, which will be discussed in the following chapters.

Conclusion

In this chapter, it has been proposed that the reversal of weeping is a distinctive Lukan theme. The reversal of weeping is deserving of attention on its own in contrast to the previous studies of the reversal theme, which have focused mainly on the distinction between poor and rich.

By understanding Luke's third beatitude (6:21b), "those who weep now shall laugh," and third woe (6:25b), "those who laugh now shall weep," as two pegs on which the theme of the reversal of weeping is hung, the reversal of weeping is a distinctive theme in Luke.

100. Ibid.
101. Alter, *The Art of Biblical Narrative*, 93.
102. Ibid., 95.
103. Rowe, *Early Narrative Christology*, 199.
104. Ibid. Rowe insists that his methodology is mainly narrative–critical. See ibid. 9–16.

It has also been proposed that Luke uses the technique of repetition, *Leitwort*, to illustrate the seven stories of reversal of weeping in his narrative. By using κλαίω in each story, Luke highlights the reversal of weeping. This *Leitwort* has been discussed under narrative criticism. In addition, composition criticism has suggested that Luke arranges the stories according to his specific purpose, which is to demonstrate the theme of the reversal of weeping.

In the following chapters, we will examine the reversal of weeping in the context of the Old Testament and Second Temple literature, as well as in the Gospel of Luke. The theological implications and Luke's narrative intention will be discussed after examination of those texts.

CHAPTER TWO

REVERSAL OF WEEPING IN THE OLD TESTAMENT AND SECOND TEMPLE LITERATURE

The purpose of this chapter is to describe the historical background of the reversal of weeping in the context of the Old Testament and Second Temple literature. By analyzing some passages from OT and Second Temple literature as test cases, we can see how Luke uses traditions familiar to him and how he not only develops but also distinguishes his treatment of the reversal of weeping from the way this theme is treated in the OT and Second Temple literature. Special attention will be paid to the passages that utilize the word κλαίω in relation to reversal.

The first task is to examine the use of κλαίω in the LXX and NT. Although it is not the purpose of this work to consider every usage of κλαίω, looking at a representative sample will enable us to see its semantic range and to determine its nuanced meaning within the context, especially in the context of reversal.

The next task is to delve into several OT and Second Temple literature passages that contain κλαίω as test cases. Obviously, the passages that illustrate the reversal of weeping are not necessarily limited to those containing κλαίω.[1] If, however, Luke utilizes the tradition and highlights the reversal of weeping by repetitive use of κλαίω, it is reasonable to focus on the passages with κλαίω. The outcome will be an understanding of the dynamics of the reversal of weeping in the Gospel of Luke. In other words, the reversal of

---

1. The passage from the Qumran document, 4Q179 is the case. Although 4Q179 is not written in Greek, it will give some insights for how the reversal of weeping is used in one of the important Second Temple document, which is the Qumran.

weeping in the OT and Second Temple literature provides some important precedents and principles for the Lukan reversal of weeping.

The Use of κλαίω

The lexical meaning of κλαίω is "to weep, cry" or "to weep (for), bewail."[2] It is used forty times in the New Testament.[3] Other Greek words denote "weep" or "mourn": πενθέω, which is used in Matt 5:4, denotes "to mourn" as well.[4] κλαίω is used in the NT more generally and frequently than πενθέω.[5] The most frequent Hebrew verb corresponding to κλαίω is הָכָב, which denotes "to weep by reason of joy or sorrow, the latter including lament, complaint, remorse or repentance."[6] The LXX translates הָכָב as κλαίω 117 times, and as πενθέω 49 times.

Because of this common use of κλαίω, some scholars think that πενθέω is used in a way specifically related to sin, while κλαίω is not.[7] For example, Paul rebukes the Corinthian church for their sins in 1 Cor 5:2: καὶ ὑμεῖς

---

2. "κλαίω," BDAG, 545. The distinction between a word and its concept has been pointed out by many scholars. James Barr criticizes the failure of modern scholarship to distinguish linguistic concepts and structures from theological ones. For this reason, he criticizes Kittel's *TDNT* vehemently: "The work of the dictionary is to be in the realm of 'concept history'; but the dictionary itself is a dictionary of Greek *words*. The construction of the work thus brings right to the fore the difficult problem of the relation of word and concept." For more balanced discussion on the issue, see Silva, *Biblical Words and Their Meaning*. Silva admits and even recommends word study: "We need to recall the distinction between the word, or linguistic symbol on the one hand, and the extralinguistic referent (the concept of theological idea) on the other." D. A. Carson also points out the danger of word study. Carson, *Exegetical Fallacies*, 27–64. See also Poythress, "Kinds of Biblical Theology," 129–42. I view Luke's use of κλαίω through my own understanding of the word/concept distinction as the technique of repetition the so-called Leitwort, as seen in chapter 1.

3. Luke uses κλαίω the most (eleven times), followed by the Gospel of John (eight time) and Revelation (six times).

4. According to BDAG, πενθέω denotes "to experience sadness as the result of some condition or circumstance, *be sad, grieve, mourn*" and "to engage in mourning for one who is dead, ordinarily with traditional rites, *mourn over*" (κλαίω, BDAG, 795). Besides πενθέω there are words that also denote "to mourn; to weep; to tear": θρηνεῖν (John 16:20), ταλαιπωρεῖν (Jas 4:9), ὀλολύζειν (Jas 5:1), κόπτεσθαι (Rev 18:9), and λυπεῖσθαι (John 16:20). However, they do not appear as frequently as κλαίω and πενθέω.

5. Bovon, *Luke*, 1:226. It is only used ten times in the New Testament (Matt 5:4; 9:15; 16:10; Luke 6:25; 1 Cor 5:2; 2 Cor 12:21; Jas 4:9; Rev 18:11, 15, 19), four times less than κλαίω.

6. "הָכָב," BDB, 113.1. Harris, Archer, and Waltke, *Theological Wordbook of the Old Testament*, 107.

7. Betz, *The Sermon on the Mount*, 577.

πεφυσιωμένοι ἐστὲ καὶ οὐχὶ μᾶλλον ἐπενθήσατε, ἵνα ἀρθῇ ἐκ μέσου ὑμῶν ὁ τὸ ἔργον τοῦτο πράξας. Rosner argues strongly that the use of πενθέω is related to mourn over sin (of brothers).[8] However, not only πενθέω but also κλαίω is used to indicate sorrow for sin. In Luke 7:38, the sinful women weeps (κλαίουσα) for her sin.[9] In addition, Ezra 10:1 (LXX) has three instances of κλαίω to show Israel's repentance over their sin (κλαίων, ἔκλαυσεν, and κλαίων).[10] In this regard, Plummer's distinction of κλαίω from πενθέω is insightful; he points out that the latter has to do with the mental and emotional aspects of mourning,[11] while the former implies outward manifestation of grief in loud weeping.[12] In this sense, κλαίω is more expressive than πενθέω.

Κλαίω is associated with death or loss in most cases in the LXX and NT. A clear example occurs in John 20, which uses κλαίω extensively.[13] After Jesus' death, a disappointed Mary stood weeping (v. 11, κλαίουσα) outside of the tomb, and as she wept (v. 11, ἔκλαιεν), two angels came to ask her the reason for her weeping (v. 13, κλαίεις). Mary recognized that it was Jesus who was standing behind her only after he called her name. Mary thought he was a gardener when Jesus asked her, "Why are you weeping (κλαίεις)?" (v. 15). Here all four usages are associated with death, specifically Jesus' death.

On the topic of weeping related to death, Sirach 22:11 is more explicit than John 20. It reads, ἐπὶ νεκρῷ κλαῦσον ἐξέλιπεν γὰρ φῶς καὶ ἐπὶ μωρῷ κλαῦσον ἐξέλιπεν γὰρ σύνεσιν ἥδιον κλαῦσον ἐπὶ νεκρῷ ὅτι ἀνεπαύσατο τοῦ δὲ μωροῦ ὑπὲρ θάνατον ἡ ζωὴ πονηρά "Weep for the dead, for he has left the light behind; and weep for the fool, for he has left intelligence behind. Weep less bitterly for the dead, for he is at rest; but the life of the fool is worse than death" (NRSV).[14] Here κλαίω is directly connected to the dead and the fool

---

8. Rosner, *Paul, Scripture and Ethics*, 71–73. Rosner examines the usages from the LXX with reference to sin and relates them to Paul's use of πενθέω. BDAG also shows that πενθέω has to do with sorrow for sins (κλαίω, BDAG, 795).

9. Whether the weeping of the sinful woman is that of repentance or sorrow for her sin, or that of gratitude for her forgiveness, is a controversial and difficult issue that I will discuss in more detail in chapter 3.

10. "While Ezra prayed and made confession, weeping and casting himself down before the house of God, a very great assembly of men, women, and children, gathered to him out of Israel, for the people wept bitterly" (ESV).

11. Friberg indicates that κλαίω expresses strong inner emotion. *Analytical Lexicon of the Greek New Testament*, 230–31.

12. Plummer, *A Critical and Exegetical Commentary on the Gospel according to St. Luke*, 180.

13. It is used in vv. 11 (twice), 13, and 15.

14. Here all four instances of "weep" translate κλαῦσον.

as well as death; Sirach emphasizes the importance of wisdom.[15] However, the point is that κλαίω is associated with the dead in this context.[16]

The use of κλαίω is not limited to death or loss. It is also used in other contexts that depict strong emotions of grief before great distress, unexpected sadness, or shock. When the Chaldeans took Jerusalem and burned it with fire, the people wept (καὶ ἔκλαιον καὶ ἐνήστευον καὶ ηὔχοντο ἐναντίον κυρίου [*Baruch* 1:5]). In Luke 19:41, Jesus wept and lamented over the imminent destruction of Jerusalem (Καὶ ὡς ἤγγισεν ἰδὼν τὴν πόλιν ἔκλαυσεν ἐπ' αὐτήν).[17] When Job's friends saw Job's suffering, they wept aloud (וַיִּבְכּוּ, ἔκλαυσαν, Job 2:12; also 30:25).

Weeping is not always associated with loss or distress; it can also be associated with joy. Esau met Jacob with joy and he wept (ἔκλαυσαν; also see 45:15). Here κλαίω is used to express joy and happiness. While the primary usage of κλαίω is to weep due to death and loss, the context determines the meaning and nuance of the word. On this basis, we will examine the passages from the OT and Second Temple literature, which show the reversal of weeping with κλαίω.

The Reversal of Weeping in the Old Testament

One area that provides a number of illustrations of reversal is the Old Testament. According to Larry Drake, reversal can be found in all sections of the OT: the Pentateuch, Deuteronomistic History, Prophetic literature, and Wisdom literature. Hence, "It is incorrect to argue, as some do, that any one area of the OT provides 'the' background to such Lukan interests as his interest in the poor, his beatitudes, or his aphoristic sayings."[18] Although

---

15. Di Lella, and Skehan, *The Wisdom of Ben Sira*, 311. For more information of Sirach, see Coggins, *Sirach*; Snaith, *Ecclesiasticus or The Wisdom of Jesus Son of Sirach*; Witte, "Theologien im Buch Jesus Sirach," 91–128.

16. Also see Gen 21:16; 37:35; Lev 10:6; Num 20:29; Judg 11:37.

17. See Isa 16:9; Jer 13:17; 22:10; and Lam 1:6. Luke 19:41 will be fully discussed in chapter 4.

18. Drake, "The Reversal Theme in Luke's Gospel," 108. Although his discussion is lengthy, Drake's categories of reversal in the OT are worth mentioning. In the Pentateuch, he lists six aspects of reversal: (1) reversal of chaotic situations (Gen 1:28; 3:7–8; 18:10–15; Exod 1–2;); (2) equity of justice (poetic justice—Exod 22:33–34; Num 33:55–56); (3) reversal of primogeniture (Gen 25:19–25; 27); (4) those who are lowly are raised, those who are last are first, and the elevation or deliverance of those who are downtrodden, those who are unjustly oppressed (Gen 29:31–35); (5) reversal of expectation (Gen 38; 50:20). In Deuteronomistic History, he has seven categories: (1) rebellion, punishment, and forgiveness (Deut 29:22–24; 30:3; 1 Kgs 8); (2) land, land loss, and restoration to the land (Judg 2:6; 2 Kgs 24:14–15; Deut 7:1–5); (3) barrenness

Drake identifies the prevalence of the reversal theme in the OT, he does not find the reversal of weeping as an independent and distinctive theme of Luke. The task that remains to be done, then, should be to examine reversal in association with weeping, especially focusing on κλαίω.

There are two places in the OT where reversal is related to weeping more explicit than in other sections: Psalms and the Prophets. Bosworth discusses different uses of weeping in the Psalms, specifically in Ps 6; 42:4; 80:6; 102:30; 56.[19]

First, weeping is a petition to God and a way to get him to respond, as in Ps 6: "Weeping is a plea for pity and help, and the speaker of Psalm 6 verbalizes his weeping to motivate God to heed his petition, then identifies his weeping as the key to God's favorable response."[20] Although Bosworth thinks that Ps 6 is different from Ps 56 in that the latter shows confidence in God more clearly than does Ps 6, the two psalms are similar in that they use weeping as a demonstration of their plea to God and expect his response. He also categorizes Pss 126 and 137 as communal petitions that are different from individual petition like Ps 6 and 56. In these Psalms, the reasons for weeping are enemies (sometimes unidentified, Pss 6 and 56), danger (69), and exile (126 and 137). Psalm 126 in particular is closely related to the reversal of weeping, as will be discussed later.[21] Second, weeping is used as

---

is made into abundance with Yahweh's presence (Sarah and Hannah story) (4) kings are raised up from lowly positions (1 Sam 9:15–21); (5) the humble are exalted and the exalted humbled; (6) ironic reversals and reversed expectations (Deut 7:6–16; 1 Kgs 12:7; 2 Kgs 19:21–28); (7) poetic justice (1 Kgs 21:19; 1 Kgs 22:37–38). In Prophetic Literature, which Drake views the place where the most material on reversal occurs in the OT, he lists five aspects: (1) those who abuse privileged positions will be put to shame [the humble are exalted and the arrogant are humbled] (Amos 2:14–16; Isa 3:4; 5, 12; 10:24—34; 13:11, 1925:11–12; 37:26–29; Jer 50:33–34; Ezek 29:7); (2) image reversals where deliverance/salvation from exile is frequently pictured as moving from darkness to light, and resurrection, movement from death to life, becomes an image to describe the new kingdom (Isa 58; 61:4,–7; 65; Amos 5:18–20; Jer 11:17); (3) the ideal king cares for the oppressed and downtrodden and he works to reverse their plight (Isa 8:21–9:2; Jer 22–23); (4) in a restored kingdom the lame, blind, and afflicted are the select subjects of the kingdom and their station in life is reversed. Drake focuses on exile in this category (Isa 35; 42:5–9; Ezek 36:13b–15); (5) poetic justice (Jer 14:15, 19; 34:16; Obad 15). Finally, Drake gives five forms of reversal in the Wisdom and didactic material: (1) the humble are exalted and those who exalt themselves will be humbled (Ps 18:27; 22:24a, 26a); (2) Yahweh and the king reverse the plight of the downtrodden (Pss 3; 5:4–6; 6:3, 10; 7:12–16; 9:11–18; 10; 11; the story of Job); (3) reversal in story plots (Esth 6:1; 7:10; Ruth's life); (4) the tragic reversal of the exile (Lam 2:1; 14–16); (5) reversal of societal expectations. Drake, "The Reversal Theme in Luke's Gospel," 75–117.

19. Bosworth, "Weeping in the Psalms," 36–46.

20. Ibid., 40–44. Also see Kuckhoff, *Psalm 6*; Loretz, "Psalm 6," 75–102.

21. "Psalm 126 places the motif in the context of a desired future in which present

an image to indicate tears as food and drink (Ps 42:4; 80:6; 102:30).²² Finally, there are several psalms that equate weeping with joy and happiness (Pss 30 and 130). Using Bosworth's analysis, we can find major reasons for weeping in the Psalms such as enemies, danger, exile, and joy.²³ However, all psalms listed by Bosworth do not relate to the reversal.

In his analysis of the Prophetic literature and Wisdom literature, Drake finds that weeping comes because of such things as arrogance, affliction, exile, darkness, and death.²⁴ He takes Jeremiah 13:15–27 as an example of self-exaltation reversed to abasement: those who are proud (v. 15) will weep bitterly, and tears will run down (v. 17). Jeremiah 13:15–27 shows a reversal of laughter too: there the cause of weeping is arrogance in not giving glory to God (v. 16).²⁵

Many scholars have discussed the OT background of the reversal of weeping as found in the Gospel of Luke. As noted in chapter 1, since the fundamental Lukan statement of the reversal of weeping is in the Beatitudes and Woes (6:21b, 25b) the OT background for the reversal of weeping is discussed mostly with these passages.

While many scholars agree that the OT background of Matthew's second beatitude, μακάριοι οἱ πενθοῦντες, ὅτι αὐτοὶ παρακληθήσονται, is Isa 61:1–3,²⁶ Luke 6:20 is not confined to a single passage. This is because Matthew and Luke use different terms. Matthew clearly echoes the LXX of Isa 61:2, which says that the Spirit-anointed one has come παρακαλέσαι πάντας τοὺς πενθοῦντας. The same words (παρακαλέω, πενθέω) are used in both passages as well as the same content, "to comfort those who mourn." While the OT uses both πενθέω and κλαίω to denote weeping, Luke contains no similarly clear parallel with the OT as Matthew.

For this reason, many Lukan scholars find the OT background for the Lukan reversals of weeping in different texts from Isa 61.²⁷ Bovon re-

---

weeping contrasts with future joy, whereas the thanksgiving psalms contrast past weeping with present joy" (ibid., 45).

22. Ibid.

23. Ibid., 46.

24. Drake, "The Reversal Theme in Luke's Gospel," 90–100. See note 18 above [x-ref].

25. Although Drake thinks that Jer 13:15–27 demonstrates the reversal from self-exaltation to self-abasement, the fundamental cause for the weeping is the having been taken captive, which is exile.

26. Betz, *Sermon on the Mount*, 119–24, esp. 121. See also Davies and Allison, *Gospel according to Saint Matthew*, 1:447–48; Gundry, *Matthew*, 68–69; Hagner, *Matthew 1–13*, 92; Luz, *Matthew 1–7*, 193–94; France, *The Gospel of Matthew*, 165–66; Turner, *Matthew*, 150–51.

27. Fitzmyer connects "weeping" in Luke 6:21 (par. Matt 5:2) to Isa 61:2, as do the

lates the reversal of weeping in Luke 6:21b to God's comfort in the OT: "The quintessential experience of mourning was the exile in Babylon (Ps 137[LXX 136]:1), just as the return became the symbol of greatest joy (Jer 31:7–14)."[28] Bovon argues that the essential comfort of God is return from exile, as encapsulated in Isaiah 66:10: "Rejoice with Jerusalem, and be glad for her, all you who love her; rejoice with her in joy, all you who mourn over her (πάντες ὅσοι πενθεῖτε ἐπ' αὐτῆς)."[29] Bovon rightly sees that the exile is the primary reason for the weeping or mourning of the Israelites and coming home from exile is their ultimate hope and God-given comfort.[30]

Howard Marshall also points out that the reversal of weeping in Luke has its foundation in the OT.[31] He lists some important passages that show the reversal of weeping in the OT, such as Isa 35:10; 60:20; 61:3; 65:16–19; 66:10; Jer 31:13; Bar 4:23; 5:1; Ps 126:2, 5f, although he does not provide specific exegesis.[32] He insists that the passages of the OT and NT are connected by the theme of God's promise. For example, the promise of God in Isa 65:16–19 is the eschatological promise of God's restoration and reversal of his people's fortune, which not only occurred in Luke 6: 21b (and 25b) but will also be fulfilled on the final day (Rev 7:17 and 21:4).[33] Marshall explains that the one who can reverse the fortune of those who weep is God. He also understands the reversal as a part of an "already and not yet" scheme in which promises of God will be fulfilled eschatologically.[34]

In agreement with other scholars that weeping is a condition of the poor, Darrell Bock gives a broader scope to the OT background of the reversal of weeping in Luke 6:21b. He thinks that the reason for weeping and mourning comes from the suffering or injustice of this world, but this is only one cause among others: "The OT background for weeping pictures a person in mourning for a variety of reasons, but primarily for the suffering

---

Matthean scholars above. He thinks that weeping in Luke 6:21b to some degree reflects God's comfort for those who mourn, longing for God's vengeance in His day. In this sense, the reversal of weeping is eschatological. It will be accomplished in the Day of the LORD's vengeance. However, Fitzmyer stops short of elaborating on this point, saying, "In the Lucan context, the 'weeping' would seem to refer to oppression of some sort" (Fitzmyer, *The Gospel according to Luke I–IX*, 634).

28. Bovon, *Luke*, 1:226.

29. Ibid.

30. The understanding of exile will be discussed throughout the following section.

31. Marshall, *The Gospel of Luke*, 251.

32. Ibid. Marshall does not distinguish πενθέω from κλαίω. Rather he has a thematic approach to the reversal of weeping.

33. Ibid.

34. Marshall thinks that "human need will be met by the fullness of divine salvation," which means eschatological fulfillment of God's promise. Ibid., 249.

of painful injustice in a world where God's people are pressured, persecuted, and exiled, just as the prophets were (Ps 126:5–6; 137:1; Isa 40:1–2)."[35] Bock sees this reversal as eschatological: "Fortunately, that pain is reversed into eschatological joy. Old Testament images for joy are laughter, the removal of grief, and the time of everlasting day (Ps 126:1–3; Isa 60:20; 61:3; 65:19; 66:10; Jer 31:13)."[36]

William Hendriksen understands the reversal of weeping from a somewhat different perspective from that of the scholars just mentioned. He thinks that the people of God mourn the despoilment of the glory of God; they weep because God's name is being dishonored.[37] This weeping is spiritual one: "Their weeping is God-centered. They sigh and cry not only over their own sins, nor only over these plus the power of the wicked to oppress the righteous (Hab 1:4; II Tim 3:12), but over 'all the abominations that are done in the midst of Jerusalem' (Ezek 9:4). It grieves them that God, *their own* God whom they love, is being dishonored."[38] Hendriksen considers Ps 119:136 a good example of this grief: "My eyes shed streams of tears, because people do not keep your law" (ESV). Hendriksen's argument is relevant to the context of the Lukan reversal of weeping in that the concept of weeping is sometimes used in contrast to laughter, which is also a positive contrast to the negative concept of gloating.[39] In other words, weeping over God's honor is righteous crying. However, Hendriksen overlooks that those who weep suffer because of their present life. He puts too much emphasis on the spiritual dimension. Luke's concern in 6:21, 25 is not only spiritual but also earthly, concerned with the present realm. Luke's use of νῦν clearly shows his concern for this present world, in which the reversal occurs.[40]

All this shows that the theme of reversal of weeping is rooted in and derived from the OT. In the following section, three passages from the OT that deal with the reversal of weeping using the word κλαίω will be discussed. The selected OT passages are not explicitly examined by the commentators above, although they recognize that these passages show the reversal of weeping in the Gospel of Luke, especially in 6:21b and 25b.

---

35. Bock, *Luke*, 1:577.
36. Ibid.
37. Hendriksen, *Exposition of the Gospel according to Luke*, 342.
38. Ibid.
39. Bovon, *Luke*, 1:226.
40. Note Luke's concept of eschatology, which is explained in note 13 of Introduction.

Jeremiah 31:15–17

Although Lukan scholars have not categorized it as such, Jeremiah 31, well known for its description of the new covenant (vv. 31–37),[41] is one of the most significant examples of the reversal of weeping.[42] The context of the new covenant that God will write on his people's heart is when he turns mourning to joy by causing his people return from exile, from, as declared in vv. 1–9. Specifically, v. 9a says, "with weeping (κλαυθμῷ, יְכָבְ), they will come, and with supplications I will lead them back."[43] The type of weeping in this verse has been the subject of two main interpretive streams.[44]

On the one hand, some see the people's weeping is that of repentance: the people of God will come with the weeping of repentance over their sin, which caused their exile.[45] In this case, "streams of water" in v. 9b is a reference to "a providential protection which enables [the Israelites] to negotiate [the] dangerous route" they must travel to arrive home.[46] In addition, this interpretation makes good sense in connection with 31:18–19, which describes Israel's repentance, especially in view of the words "after I had turned back, I repented יִתְמֹחַן . . ." (v. 19).

Jack Lundbom takes וּאֹבִי as "they went out" rather than "they will come." The Israelites were exiled with the weeping of repentance, but they will return by God's consolation. Lundbom's interpretation, which renders the weeping in v. 9 as that of repentance as well,[47] can be matched with the reversal of weeping in Luke 6:21 in that the fortune of "those who weep" (in Jeremiah those who "went out with weeping") shall be reversed through God's restoration. However, the problem of taking weeping as that of repentance is that there is no other instance in the OT of "streams of water" referring to a dangerous path. Rather, the image is of peace and security, as in Ps 23:2 and Deut 8:7.

In the other interpretive schema, the weeping in v. 9 is not that of repentance but of joy in parallel with "consolation" (παρακλήσει/ וְנִחַת),

---

41. Jeremiah 31 of MT is different from the LXX, which is chapter 38. Here I follow the MT.

42. See Marshall, *The Gospel of Luke*, 251; Bovon, *Luke*, 1:226; and Hendricksen, *Exposition of the Gospel according to Luke*, 342 above. They include Jer 31 to illustrate Luke 6:21 and 25, but they do not explicitly exegete or analyze the passage and make any specific relationship between Jer 31 and Lukan passages.

43. From here on, all translations are mine otherwise noted.

44. Longman, *Jeremiah, Lamentations*, 272.

45. Ibid.

46. McKane, *A Critical and Exegetical Commentary on Jeremiah*, 2:791.

47. Lundbom, *Jeremiah*, 424–45. See also the New Living Translation.

which indicates restoration from hardship.[48] In this case, God's people will come with joy from their restoration, and the "streams of water" in v. 9 can be rendered as God's "beneficent ordering of their journey."[49] However, this option is not clearly connected to vv. 18–20, which describes the repentance of Israel as God's people. Neither interpretive option is clearly aligned with the reversal of weeping in the Gospel of Luke.

The reversal of weeping in Jeremiah 31:15–17 is nearly the same as the reversal of weeping in the Gospel of Luke. In 31:15, there is a voice of lamentation and bitter weeping (κλαυθμοῦ) in Ramah. This is the weeping of Rachel who refuses to be comforted for her children. It surely "portrays the intensity of human emotions aroused by Israel's misfortune."[50] But from what does the Israelites' misfortune come? In other words, how does Rachel's weeping relate to Israel's misfortune? From the context of Jeremiah, this misfortune is no doubt the exile, especially in light of vv. 1–14. In Rachel Jeremiah provides a figurative description of Israel's sorrow:

> Rachel was the mother of Joseph and Benjamin and the grandmother of Ephraim and Manasseh. Her connection with both northern and southern tribes suggests that although her weeping may have been primarily for the Assyrian exiles (Isa 10:29), we should associate it with the Babylonian exile as well.[51]

Jeremiah demonstrates the grief of Israel's exile by using the figurative expression that Rachel is weeping for her descendants. She is weeping not only for her birth-children but also for her future descendants. This weeping reaches to Ramah, where her grave is located.[52] However, the point in 31:15–17 is not the weeping of Rachel in itself in v. 15 but God's salvific action in vv. 16–7, for God declares, "Keep your voice from weeping, and your eyes from tears, for there is a reward for your work . . . and they shall come back from the land of the enemy . . . and your children shall come back to their own country" (ESV). God's restoration will come upon the Israelites, and they shall return from exile. They will experience the reversal of fortune from exile to return. Their misfortune, represented by Rachel's weeping, shall be stopped. God will provide them the reversal of weeping. God will turn Rachel's sorrowful weeping and tears into repentance or joy (31:9).

---

48. Weiser, *Das Buch Des Propheten Jeremia*, 285–86.
49. McKane, *Jeremiah*, 2:791.
50. Clements, *Jeremiah*, 187.
51. Longman, *Jeremiah, Lamentations*, 274.
52. For detailed discussion, see Holladay, *Jeremiah 2*, 187.

From the reversal of weeping in Jer 31:15–17, it is clear that one of the main causes of weeping in the OT is exile.[53] But the God of Israel reverses the fortune of his people, and they return to their own land. Those who had wept then laughed.

Psalm 126

From the beginning, Psalm 126 straightforwardly reveals a change in the fortunes of Zion: "When YHWH restored the fortunes of Zion . . ." (v. 1). Verse 4 also tells of the hope for reversal of the fortune of God's people. There has been a major exegetical difficulty in interpreting this psalm, summarized by Hossfeld:

> There is controversy over whether vv. 1–3 offer a look back to the past or a look forward or anticipation of the future. The decision depends primarily on whether the suffix conjugations in vv. 1c and 3 are taken as information about the past or as present, as a kind of *perfectum propheticum*. Consequently, the statement in v. 2 introduced by the temporal particle אז, "at that time, then," and formulated in the prefix conjugation are interpreted as contemporary with v. 1 and likewise as statements about the past or the future.[54]

Most scholars have thought that vv. 1–3 describe the past event of YHWH's restoration, especially indicating Israel's exile.[55] In this case, vv. 4–6 that follow indicate a prophetic expectation of a great restoration in the future, which is usually thought of as an eschatological hope.[56] So, "in the composition of the psalm, this retrospective functions as a historical-theological foundation for the petition directed to YHWH in v. 4, or vv. 4–6."[57] Merling Alomia also comments that "the psalmist used a historical experience to express his hope, but in doing so, he does not speak simply

---

53. If the exile is the main cause of weeping in Jeremiah's time, and the people of God are seriously grieving for their misfortune, then the Israelites who lived in the time of Jesus, or in the Second Temple period, still experienced exile under the control of the Roman Empire. They lived in their own land but did not enjoy sovereignty. See Wright, *The New Testament and the People of God*. I will discuss this in more detail in later chapters.

54. Hossfeld, *Psalms 3*, 370.

55. See Goldingay, *Psalms*, 26–27; Hossfeld. *Psalms*, 375; Mayes, *Psalms*, 399. LXX and Targum take as return from vv. 1–3 as return from exile, or captivity. LXX uses αἰχμαλωσίαν and Targum uses גלותּ.

56. Kraus, *Psalms*, 449–51.

57. Hossfeld, *Psalms 3*, 372.

talking of a past fact but affirms in a confident way what YHWH surely will do for his people as the LORD of the eternal covenant."[58] This position is strongly supported by the fact that it regards the series of perfect tense verbs in vv. 1-3 (לְשׁוּב, לִידְגַּה, and וּנִיָּה) as past, which is common usage. Based on this rendering, the supplication to restore the fortune of God's people in v. 4 refers to the past.

On the other hand, other scholars understand the first three verses of Psalm 126 to be solely telling of the future restoration of Israel by YHWH. In other words, vv. 1-3 do not describe an event of the past, but vv. 4-6 are "a petition to YHWH to begin, at last, to fulfill this prophetic 'vision.'"[59] The scholars who support this position render the perfect tense verbs in vv. 1-3 as present.[60] However, this argument has been refuted by many.[61] As Allen points out, this interpretation is very awkward, for there are perfect tense verbs in v. 2 and 3, לִידְגַּה and וּנִיָּה.[62] Moreover, the imperfect verb used in v. 2, אָלְמִי, which may indicate a future event, cannot explain the use of the perfect verb וּנִיָּה in v. 1b properly.[63]

In addition, both the perfect tense of the verb וּנִיָּה indicating dreams and the Ancient Near Eastern background of the dream point to the past experience of Israelites.[64] Even though it is common to render סָלַח as "dream," there are other interpretations of סָלַח in v. 1c.[65] For instance, *Targum Psalms* reads v. 1c as "like the sick who were healed" (וְהֵיעָרְמַם וְאִסְתָּאַד אִיעָרְמ). This reading takes the meaning of סָלַח as "recovery from illness or sickness" rather than dream.[66] 11QPs[a] also has the same meaning as *Targum Psalms*. Similar to *Targum Psalms* but with a slightly different nuance, LXX takes סָלַח as παρακεκλημένοι (comforted), which is a paraphrase for "healthy"

---

58. Alomia, "The Psalm of the 'Blessed Hope,'" 48.

59. Hossfeld, *Psalms 3*, 371. Gunkel takes the verbs in vv. 1, 3 as a "prophetic" perfect. See Allen, *Psalms 101-150*, 228; Dahood, *Psalms*, 218-19.

60. Berlin, *Wirs sind wie Träumend*, especially 11-50. Also see GKC §106.

61. See Allen, *Psalms 101-150*, 228-33. Also see, Hossfeld, *Psalms*, 370-78, esp. 370. Crow has a different interpretation: vv. 1-3 refer not to exile or captivity but to the prosperity of the land. However, he agrees with all others who see it as a past experience. Crow, *The Songs of Ascents*, 58-66.

62. Allen, *Psalms 101-150*, 228.

63. Harmon insists that the imperfect may need to be translated by an English past tense in the context of Ps 126. "There is clear evidence that Hebrew has a combination of *yqtl* forms, one denoting the imperfect while the other, corresponding to the Accadian preterite *iqtul* is virtually the equivalent of the *qtl* forms" ("The Setting and Interpretation of Psalm 126," 77-78).

64. See also the perfect tense of the verb in v. 3b, וּנִיָּה.

65. Isa 38:16 is an exception.

66. "סָלַח," *BDB*, 321.

or "cured."⁶⁷ However, according to Allen, rendering סָלַח as "dream" rather than "healthy" or "wellness" makes sense in light of the overall context of this psalm.⁶⁸

Most important in v. 1c is not just the dream itself but the symbolic meaning or function of the dream in the ancient world. Hossfeld explains two critical implications. First, the dream can be considered a medium of divine revelation of a future event, so that those who dream were sure that their dreams are fulfilled.⁶⁹ The second point is more significant. "It is important that dreams cannot be made; they arrive suddenly and surprisingly and for that very reason are seen as divinely caused."⁷⁰ Thus, "the event itself (the return of those liberated to Zion and the restoration of Zion as YHWH's dwelling place) was reality, but it was as unexpected and God-sent as a dream whose full achievement, though in progress, was still in the future."⁷¹ Therefore, the psalmist is reflecting on the fortune that YHWH had restored for his people. Indeed, the reversal was sudden, surprising, and unexpected, even while earnestly desired.

Verses 2 and 3 tell the result of the past dream-like restoration by YHWH that brought great joy, laughter, and gladness. Because of this change in Zion's fortune, the people of YHWH proclaimed to the nations what he had done for them. Kraus captures the essence of vv. 2–3: "Also the resumption in v. 3 of the statement in v. 2 serves to produce special emphasis. Amazement, laughter, joy—that was at the time of reaction of the people of God to Yahweh's intervention."⁷²

There are two important points in vv. 1–3 concerning the reversal of their fortune. One is that YHWH is the bringer of restoration; in other words, the restoration is initiated by and executed by YHWH, not by the power of his people. The use of causitiveבְּשׁוּב supports this point. The other is that the restoration comes unexpectedly, as a sudden, surprising, and amazing event. As mentioned above, the description of the dreamlike experience of YHWH's people reflects this fact.

On this basis, the psalmist makes the supplication in vv. 4–6. Verse 4 begins with the same verb בוש, used in v. 1. But in v. 4, it is an imperative, הָבוּשׁ, rather than the participle. The petition is for YHWH to repeat the past restoration of his people. Thus, as Hossfeld rightly points out, "verse

---

67. Goldingay, *Psalms*, 491–92.
68. Allen, *Psalms 101–150*, 228. Also see Kraus, *Psalms*, 449.
69. Hossfeld, *Psalms 3*, 376.
70. Ibid.
71. Ibid.
72. Kraus, *Psalms*, 450.

4 pleads for YHWH's returning, 'surprising as the return of water into a dried-up riverbed; what is important in the comparison is that it emphasizes the unpredictability!'"[73] As we will see, this unpredictability is one of the important features of the reversal of weeping in Luke.

In v. 1c, the unexpected intervention of YHWH that results in the change of fortune is described as a dream. In v. 4 it is depicted as streams in the Negeb. While v. 1c is focused on the suddenness of YHWH's restoration, v. 4b foregrounds the actualization of the dreamlike reality. The streams in the Negeb are dried up in the summer, but winter rains transform them so that they can overflow.[74] The psalmist imagines this transformation and wishes his dream would come true.[75] Therefore, v. 4 anticipates YHWH's returning and intervention for his people in parallel with v. 1.

Verses 5 and 6, which mention weeping and laughing, provide an important background for the reversal of weeping. Particularly, the verse 6 in the LXX use κλαίω. The image of sorrowful sowing with weeping and joyful reaping is obviously agricultural. Bellinger thinks that the imagery in vv. 5–6 refers to the "harvest as a part of the fertility ensured in the New Year festival," which is suited to the entire psalm and "its reference to a change of fortunes, fertility and prosperity."[76] He concludes that this psalm should be understood in the context of the New Year festival in terms of the background.[77]

Bellinger's view is partially right, but too limited. The imagery in vv. 5–6 is not necessarily confined to the New Year festival. Rather, it represents everyday agricultural life because the image of sowing, reaping, and sheaving is that of farming.[78] In other words, the imagery should be understood as a metaphor for the *Sitz im Leben* of YHWH's people. In this sense, the metaphor not only describes the actual difficulties of agricultural life but also illustrates the hardship experienced individually and communally by YHWH's people. As a farmer sows the seeds with anxiety and fear that the harvest might fail—that is, he sows the seeds in weeping—the people of YHWH struggle with fear and anxiety. In this regard, those who go out weeping (ἔκλαιον) are the people who are experiencing the hardship or difficulty in their *Sitz im Leben*. Their weeping indicates this point. However,

73. Hossfeld, *Psalms 3*, 377.

74. Glueck, *Rivers in the Desert*, 92–94.

75. Goldingay sees this imagination as the actual untransformed state of the people. See Goldingay, *Psalms*, 494.

76. Bellinger, *Psalmody and Prophecy*, 65.

77. However, Bellinger's determination of the background of Psalm 126 does not "preclude a possible reference to a specific prior deliverance of Israel" (ibid.).

78. Hossfeld, *Psalms 3*, 377; Crow, *The Songs of Ascents*, 64–65.

all situations will be reversed. People who sow with weeping will reap with resounding joy and laughter.

This imagery is elaborated on in v. 6. The sower goes out crying and carrying the bag of seeds, but he will indeed return laughing and carrying his sheaves. The farmer's effort to sow the seeds can be burdensome. Hope that the seeds will grow up well and perseverance in working to make it so are required for a bountiful harvest. The farmer weeps, for the result is not clear at the time of sowing. Relying on YHWH's past deed of restoration, the psalmist pleads to him once again, for he is sure that the weeping of agony will be turned to jubilation. Here again, the reversal of weeping to laughing is dependent upon YHWH's intervention. If YHWH answers the prayer and begins to act, the people's fortune will be changed. Even though the future is unclear, bringing much fear and anxiety for now, the psalmist knows that the fortune of YHWH's people will certainly be reversed on the basis of his past restoration. It will be like a dream for the people, as shown in v. 1c.

Therefore, Psalm 126 provides an illuminating instance of the reversal of weeping. First, YHWH repeatedly restores his people's fortune by intervening in their lives. Second, it is implied that the bringer of restoration is YHWH. Third, the reversal and change of fortune comes about in a sudden way.[79] Luke has also these insights and tries to demonstrate them in presenting the reversal of weeping. For instance, the fortune of those who weep reversed by Jesus' intervention and it repeatedly occurs in the life of miserable people.[80] In addition, the reversal comes in a sudden and unexpected way. The death is raised (Luke 7:11–17, 8:40–56) and those who are satisfied with their life will weep (Luke 7:31–35, 23:27–31).

Isaiah 30:18–20

The last passage that we will look at, which forms the background of the reversal of weeping from the Old Testament, is Isa 30:18–20. Although this passage and Ps 126 have many similarities, their contexts are different. The setting of the passage is well illustrated by Motyer, who sees a chiastic structure in chapter 30:

A[1] Contemporary events: Egypt no help (1–7)

    B[1] Coming human events: the refusal of the word, the way of death (8–17)

---

79. This is why most commentators relate this psalm to Acts 12:9, which describes Peter's release from prison through the prayer of the church.

80. This will be shown in chapter 3.

B² Coming divine events: the waiting God, the sure glory (18–26)

A² Contemporary events: Assyria no threat (27–33)[81]

Motyer explains, "A¹ and B¹ together describe human faithlessness and B² and A² the faithfulness of God."[82] Thus, the outcome of each party's action is very different.

As Motyer points out, A¹ is about YHWH's woe decreed on Judah, who is making plans for an alliance with Egypt. Judah has set out for Egypt without asking for YHWH's direction (v. 2). She also takes refuge in the protection of Pharaoh rather than in YHWH (v. 3). Although the people of Judah had heard that their security is YHWH alone, they pursued other options. Their dependence on Egypt shall cause them to be humiliated. After all, "Egypt's help is worthless and empty; therefore I have called her 'Rahab who sits still'" (v. 7). In sum, Egypt cannot be Judah's help.

This woe will actually be realized by YHWH, which means a reversal of fortune. Judah's breaking will be "like that of a potter's vessel that is smashed so ruthlessly that among its fragments not a shard is found with which to take fire from the hearth, or to dip up water out of the cistern" (v. 14). The judgment for fleeing from YHWH and relying on other countries is consistent, inevitable, and destructive. Judgment comes not only from alliance to Egypt but also from Judah's sinful deeds, which are described in vv. 15–17. They were unwilling to return to the Holy One of Israel. They were not quiet, nor did they trust the LORD. As Motyer rightly says, "His people were in a military situation but the prophet did not recommend armaments, only the armament of faith."[83] The people of Judah relied on their horses, saying, "No. We will flee upon horses" (v. 15). However, because of this, YHWH declares that they shall flee away (v. 16).

It is in v. 18 that YHWH turns the tables on his people's fortunes. As seen in Ps 126, only YHWH can effect a change in the fortunes of his people. Willem Beuken's point is relevant: "Partly due to the term 'he will rise up' in v. 18aᵉ¢ᵉ¢, emphasis is placed on the salvific initiative of the one who stands above all earthly powers."[84] This is clearly shown in the logical sequence in vv. 18–19, as Beuken adds, "It is striking that the logical sequence of 'hearing' and display of mercy is reversed (v. 18a and v. 19b)."[85] Indeed, YHWH's mercy upon his people precedes even his hearing their cries. In a fascinating paradox, it is not the people who wait for YHWH but YHWH who waits to

81. Motyer, *The Prophecy of Isaiah*, 244.
82. Ibid.
83. Ibid., 249.
84. Beuken, *Isaiah II*, 170.
85. Ibid.

provide help. Motyer's summary is penetrating: "His grace is his sovereign determination to bless the under-serving; his compassion is the overflowing of his passionate love for his people."[86]

Weeping is found in v. 19. The people living in Jerusalem shall weep (ἔκλαυσεν) no more because YHWH will restore them in response to hearing their crying. Along with v. 18, which shows God's mercy, grace, justice, and blessing to those who wait for him, this verse demonstrates the love, grace, and mercy of YHWH toward his people: "He will surely be gracious to you" (9c). From this, we can understand that YHWH's initiative to intervene and restore the fortune of his people comes from his mercy, because his mercy precedes everything else. In other words, what reverses the peoples' fortune, so that YHWH may begin to reverse the situation of his people, is none other than his goodness and grace. He hears, answers, and intervenes because he is YHWH, who is gracious and merciful, slow to anger and abounding in steadfast love (Ps 145:8). In this regard, another principle of reversal can be found here: the reversal is due to YHWH's goodness and compassion toward his people. It moves him to take initiative to intervene in his people's *Sitz im Leben*. For this reason, their weeping will be no more. Rather, as v. 20 shows, although they are given the bread of adversity and the water of affliction, they will see their Teacher, who will not hide himself anymore.

There is a disagreement about the reference to the Teacher in v. 20b, which is ambiguous because the subject, הֹרֶ֔יךָ (teacher), is plural, but the verb יִכָּנֵ֤ף is singular. Some commentators have understood the referent to be the LORD God by taking the subject as singular, matching the verb, while others have insisted that the referent is the prophets or unidentified figures. For example, the Targum identifies the referent as God: "He will no more take away His Shekinah from the house of the sanctuary, and thine eyes shall behold my Shekinah in the house of sanctuary."[87] However, YHWH is never identified directly as a הֹרֶ֔ה (teacher) anywhere else.[88] According to Motyer, "the translation *teacher* is permissible, but the context requires the singular, which the form also allows, i.e. 'your Teacher', referring to the LORD as the law/instruction giver."[89] In addition, the hiphil form for teacher (וְהוֹרָ֑נוּ, Isa 28:26) is used of "God teaching his people."[90]

---

86. Motyer, *The Prophecy of Isaiah*, 250.
87. Blenkinsopp, *Isaiah*, 421.
88. Wildberger, *Isaiah* 174.
89. Motyer, *The Prophecy of Isaiah*, 250.
90. Watts, *Isaiah 1–33*, 400.

The importance lies in the fact that Israel will pay attention to God's instruction with eyes to see and ears to hear.[91] They will have direct contact with God. Since his concealment was deliberate,[92] his people will see his instruction and presence without any barrier. Therefore, while the reversal of his people's fortune is stimulated by the compassion of God, he reveals himself to his people in changing their fortunes. His people will know who God is in the midst of reversal.

General observations based on the three representative passages discussed above provide some insights into the reversal of weeping. First, one of the most important causes of the reversal of weeping, found more often in the Prophets than elsewhere, is exile. To be sure, the exile has various implications and meanings for Israel.[93] However, in three different contexts in the OT, the return from exile is significant because that exile has made God's people struggle with their identity as God's chosen people. Their descriptions of weeping caused by exile in Jer 31, Ps 126, and Isa 30 well illustrate the point. If this is true, the Israel's return from exile would be to restore their fortunes in God once again. Second, YHWH initiates the reversal. He is the only one who can make changes in the fortune of his people, who are the recipients of his actions. Third, the reversal is stimulated by YHWH's compassion and goodness. His mercy, goodness, and grace are one of the primary reasons and motivation for his turning the tables in his people's favor. Fourth, in reversing the fortunes of his people, he reveals himself to them. Although God's revelation has always been clear in the midst of his people's agony, they will know who God is when they experience the reversal of their fortunes. Fifth, the reversal is not just a one-time action of YHWH; rather, it recurs: YHWH repeatedly changes the peoples' affliction to joy. This is found especially in Psalm 126, which demonstrates confidence in reversal by reflecting on past experience of restoration. Without doubt, these repetitive actions are eschatologically oriented. Finally, the reversal of weeping comes suddenly as in Psalm 126, so that even God's people have a hard time, such as exile, recognizing it. They do not know when it will be, how it will come, or what its result will be. The reversal is all in the hands of God.

---

91. Brueggemann, *Isaiah 1–39*, 274.
92. See Exod 19:21 and Isa 6:5. Whoever sees the LORD cannot survive.
93. I will discuss this topic in the next section.

Reversal of Weeping in Second Temple Literature

The portrayal of the reversal of weeping in the Second Temple period is similar to that of the Old Testament. Since weeping is often mentioned in the literature of the Second Temple period, a wide range of contexts is associated with the reversal of weeping. However, the main context is more eschatologically embedded and oriented since one of the unique features in the Second Temple period is its apocalyptic worldview.[94]

The word "apocalyptic," which is from the Greek ἀποκάλυψις (meaning "revelation"), refers to a historical movement, a type of literature, or to the cluster of theological themes associated with them. More to the point, the term *apocalyptic* is used at least three different ways. First, it refers to a type of literature, apocalypse. Second, it refers to a kind of eschatology, so-called apocalyptic eschatology, which will be discussed in next section. Third, it refers to a historical movement, apocalypticism. The New Testament contains several apocalypses, such as Revelation, Matt 24, Mark 13, Luke 21, which contain many elements shared in common with Jewish apocalyptic eschatology, and many scholars would consider early Christianity itself an apocalyptic movement, or place it within the broader current of Jewish apocalypticism.[95] An apocalyptic worldview that is shaped by apocalyptic eschatology is dominated by an eschatological dualism, a perspective that views the present age as under the power of evil until the Day of the LORD, when God will save the elect, judge the wicked, and inaugurate the future age of righteousness.[96]

However, the apocalyptic worldview is not limited to Judaism. Rather, apocalyptic writings come from many different sources, including other religions in the Ancient Near East and the Mediterranean.[97] Thus, in order to understand reversal in this period, it is necessary to grasp apocalyptic eschatology in more detail.

---

94. See §1.1.4, especially Murphy's discussion, for details.

95. Collins, *The Apocalyptic Imagination*; Hanson, *The Dawn of Apocalyptic*; McNamara, *Palestinian Judaism and the New Testament*; Stone, *Jewish Writings of the Second Temple Period*; VanderKam and Adler, *The Jewish Apocalyptic Heritage in Early Christianity*.

96. There is much material written about apocalyptic worldview, features, and literature. For some fine works, see the above note.

97. Wright, *The New Testament and the People of God*, 281–82.

Apocalyptic Eschatology

The term *apocalyptic eschatology* designates the eschatological teachings distinctive of, or common to, the Jewish apocalypse. Paul Hanson defines it more precisely as "the mode assumed by the prophetic tradition once it had been transferred to a new and radically altered setting in the post-exilic community."[98] He argues that eschatological prophecies are mixed with semi-mythological conceptions in Isa 24–27. Ezekiel 40–48, which shows the vision of a new or ideal Jerusalem, reveals YHWH as the eschatological tabernacle.[99] In Zech 1–8, such visions are clarified by an angelic interpreter. Thus he maintains that Isa 24–27, Ezek 40–48, and Zech 1–8 show prophetic eschatology beginning to grow into apocalyptic eschatology.[100]

However, as N. T. Wright points out, "Apocalyptic language uses complex and highly coloured metaphors in order to describe one event in terms of another, thus bringing out the perceived 'meaning' of the first."[101] In other words, this language should be read carefully, understanding what the symbols or metaphors stand for in their historical context.[102] For this reason,

---

98. Hanson, *The Dawn of Apocalyptic*, 10. For more discussion of apocalyptic, see Collins, *The Apocalyptic Imagination*; Daly, *Apocalyptic Thought in Early Christianity*; Sacchi, *Jewish Apocalyptic and Its History*. Hanson assumes that the setting of this apocalyptic eschatology is a post-exilic community. However, it is not necessary to take Hanson's assumption because of different dating of the OT books.

99. Hanson, *The Dawn of Apocalyptic*, 73. Concerning these passages, especially the theme of the tabernacle, G. K. Beale's work is one of the finest. Here Beale meticulously works out how the concept of temple is developed through the OT and NT. In doing so, he relevantly compares it to a massive corpus of contemporary literature. Beale, *The Temple and the Church's Mission*. See also another great volume, Beale, *A New Testament Biblical Theology*, esp., 592–749.

100. These apocalyptic texts reveal the theme of reversal in a big picture since one of the important features of apocalyptic writings is social and eschatological reversal or upheaval. See §1.4.

101. Wright, *The New Testament and the People of God*, 282. Also see Beale, "General Use of Eschatological Language in Judaism," 117–28.

102. Wright lists the symbols of first-century Judaism within the Greco-Roman world as temple, land, Torah, and racial identity. Those symbols are related to the story of Israel that shapes their worldview and becomes the center of their belief and hope. Although not all those symbols and metaphors appear in first-century Jewish apocalyptic literature, they are subsumed under these four symbols and somewhat related to them. "The Jewish people of the first century, like all peoples, told themselves stories which encapsulated their worldview. One of the major differences between them and some other cultures, however, was that their controlling stories had to do with actual events in history: they were waiting for the last chapter in their story to begin" (Wright, *The New Testament and the People of God*, 149). Consequently, the setting of reversal is found here. The restoration of the temple, land, Torah, and racial identity is considered reversal of fortune of God's people. For more details on symbols and elements of Israel's

Wright insists that the reading of apocalyptic works cannot be literal since "the metaphorical language of apocalyptic invests history with theological meaning."[103] Wright suggests "a broad *historical* continuum" to understand the context of apocalyptic works: "We may expect to find it where intense longing for a reversal of current ill-fortune merges with intense devotion to the god [sic] who revealed secrets to his servants in former times and might be expected to do so again."[104] From this statement, it is reasonable to think that a longing for reversal of current ill fortune is an important feature of the Second Temple period.

The reason for this longing for reversal is that, according to Wright, Israel believed that the exile was not over yet:

> Most Jews of this period, it seems, would have answered the question "where are we?" in language which, reduced to its simplest form, meant: we are still in exile. They believed that, in all the senses which mattered, Israel's exile was still in progress. Although she had come back from Babylon, the glorious message of the prophets remained unfulfilled. Israel still remained in thrall to foreigners; worse, Israel's god had not returned to Zion. Nowhere in the so-called post-exilic literature is there any passage corresponding to 1 Kings 8:10f., according to which, when Solomon's temple had been finished, "a cloud filled the house of YHWH, so that the priests could not stand to minister because of the cloud; for the glory of YHWH filled the house of YHWH." Instead, Israel clung to the promises that one day the Shekinah, the glorious presence of her god, would return at last.[105]

Accordingly, for most first-century Jewish people, "the present age is still part of the 'age of wrath'; until the Gentiles are put in their place and Israel, and the Temple, fully restored, the exile is not really over, and the blessings promised by the prophets are still to take place."[106] To be sure, first-century

---

worldview, see ibid., 215–79.

103. Ibid., 284. In my opinion, the appreciation of apocalyptic language as symbol and metaphor works well in Wright's scheme but does not always work because sometimes or often times, apocalyptic language has literal meanings as well.

104. Ibid., 288.

105. Ibid., 268–69. This is one of the famous arguments of N. T. Wright. He tries to prove this argument with numerous texts from the second temple Judaism and the OT. Although there have been various counter-arguments on it, this thesis is very persuasive working in the second temple literatures. However, it is not as much as properly working in the context of OT in terms of fulfillment. For the critique of Wright's "Apocalyptic," see Newman, *Jesus, Paul and the People of God*, 170–74. In this volume, various scholars dialogue with Wright regarding many theological topics from his works.

106. Wright, *The New Testament and the People of God*, 270.

Jews were expecting the final restoration whether they believed their situation to be exile or not. They were looking forward to their fortunes being fully changed, hence, full restoration from their ill fortune. Reversal was their ultimate hope.

With an understanding of apocalyptic eschatology in mind, we will examine three important passages from the Second Temple literature in which weeping is reversed.

1 Baruch 4:23; 5:1

The book of Baruch is the only work among the apocrypha that was modeled after the prophetic writings of the Old Testament, since Baruch is the one who was secretary and friend of Jeremiah, the Old Testament prophet (Jer 36:27–32; 45:1–5). Most scholars think that the author of 1 Baruch is not Baruch.[107] The date of writing is disputed, but the most persuasive argument dates it during the Maccabean era.[108] First Baruch is distinguished from the non-canonical apocalypses titled *2 Baruch*, *3 Baruch*, and *4 Baruch*.[109] The focus of the book of Baruch is on the social suffering of Israel in exile and how this suffering came because of and will be resolved in Israel's history. Thus, the main themes of the book are sin, exile, repentance, and return.[110]

The book is divided into three sections. The introduction states that Baruch wrote the book five years after the destruction of Jerusalem by the Babylonians in 586 B.C. After this historical introduction, a prayer of confession and deliverance appears in 1:15–3:8. This long prayer is a national confession of sins.[111] In 3:9–4:4, a poem identifies God with universal wisdom, calls the Judaic Law God's gift of wisdom to the people, and praises Wisdom. Finally, consolation and help for Jerusalem are described in 4:5–5:9. These chapters portray Jerusalem as a widow who weeps for her lost children. However, the book ends not with a lament for Jerusalem, but

---

107. Burke, *The Poetry of Baruch*, 17–22; Dancy, *The Shorter Books of the Apocrypha*, 169; Harrington, *Invitation to the Apocrypha*, 93; Moore, *Daniel, Esther and Jeremiah*, 255–56; Tov, *The Book of Baruch*. The most recent work is by Adams, *Baruch and the Epistle of Jeremiah*. However, Moore also suggests the possibility that the author of 1 Baruch is Baruch himself by showing the moods and attitudes toward exile and toward their foreign masters in the book (1:1–14; 1:15–2:5; 3:9–4:4; 4:5–5:1). Moore, *Daniel, Esther and Jeremiah*, 256.

108. Burke, *The Poetry of Baruch*, 32. See pp. 26–33 for more details.

109. *2 Baruch* is in Syriac, *3 Baruch* is in Greek. For more information of 2, 3, 4 Baruch, see Charlesworth, *OTP 1 and 2*.

110. Harrington, *Invitation to the Apocrypha*, 99.

111. This prayer is also related to the lamentation in Daniel 9.

with an exhortation to her, comforting her by proclaiming that her children will return to her someday.

The passage in view is located in the last part of the book, which illustrates the restoration of Jerusalem and deals with the exile vividly. Baruch 4:23 is in the first section (4:21–26), beginning with "take courage" (θαρσεῖτε). This first section parallels the following section, vv. 27–29, which also presents restoration and salvation. Baruch 4:21–26 reads,

> Take courage, my children, cry to God, and he will deliver you from the power and hand of the enemy. For I have put my hope in the Everlasting to save you, and joy has come to me from the Holy One, because of the mercy that will soon come to you from your everlasting savior. *For I sent you out with sorrow and weeping, but God will give you back to me with joy and gladness forever.* For as the neighbors of Zion have now seen your capture, so they soon will see your salvation by God, which will come to you with great glory and with the splendor of the Everlasting. My children, endure with patience the wrath that has come upon you from God. Your enemy has overtaken you, but you will soon see their destruction and will tread upon their necks. My pampered children have traveled rough roads; they were taken away like a flock carried off by the enemy (Bar 4:21–26).[112]

Features of apocalyptic writing can be easily seen in the text of Baruch. Verse 21 tells of God's deliverance from the power and hand of the enemy. It is obvious that, in the context of the whole book, deliverance is return from exile.[113] The people of God are currently experiencing suffering as a result of their sin, but God will soon come to them with great glory and with the splendor of the Everlasting (v. 24). Here also dualism is clearly working. In the end, the God of Israel will restore his people. He will save them and destroy their enemies. Interestingly, the term "'salvation' would mean for a first century Jew 'Israel's rescue, by her god [*sic*], from pagan oppression. This would be the gift of Israel's god to his whole people, all at once."[114] If

---

112. Unless otherwise mentioned, the texts from Apocrypha are from New Revised Standard Version. Emphasis is added in v. 23.

113. Particularly, 3:9—4:4 demonstrate the topic of the exile and the next section (4:5—5:9) tells return from exile to Jerusalem.

114. Wright, *The New Testament and the People of God*, 334. The idea of Wright on exile is supported by others as well. Evans, "Aspects of Exile and Restoration," 299–328; Knibb, *The Qumran*, 20; Verseput, "The Davidic Messiah," 102–16. However, also see opposing argument. Marsh, "Theological History?," 77–94; Casey, "Where Wright Is Wrong," 95–103.

this is correct, the rescue from the enemies' control and restoration from exile is the hope for Israel.

Verse 22 portrays the joy of the people as having already come because mercy has come from the savior. We can find here the same principle of reversal as in the Old Testament, particularly in Isa 30:18–20: it comes from God. He only makes it happen (v. 21), and reversal comes from his goodness and mercy (v. 22). God's people expect him to turn their ill fortune into genuine joy (v. 23). Intriguingly, v. 22 uses the aorist ἦλθέν, ("joy has come")[115] in describing their hope for the future. They are convinced of the vindication of their God, so they are enjoying God-given joy in spite of the present evil situation.

This is followed by v. 23, which presents the reversal of weeping. The narrator of the book vividly contrasts past events with future ones. Although he experienced sorrow and weeping when his contemporaries were sent into exile, he is now assured that God will restore them once again. He emphasizes the grief and bitterness of exile by using the synonyms πένθους and κλαυθμοῦ. The sorrow and weeping symbolize calamity in v. 29: "For the one who brought these calamities upon you will bring you everlasting joy with your salvation." Once again, the bringer of good or bad is God; there is no other one like Him who brings the reversal. The weeping and sorrow will turn into joy and gladness when God restores his people. The interesting thing here is that joy and gladness are not temporary but will last forever (αἰώνιον εὐφροσύνην), implying that there will be no more suffering, pain, or exile. This joy and gladness is eschatologically fulfilled in the perfect salvation for which God's people have longed. Weeping and sorrow will turn into everlasting joy and gladness.

The outcome of this reversal extends to other nations in v. 24: "For as the neighbors of Zion have now seen your capture, so they soon will see your salvation by God, which will come to you with great glory and with the splendor of the Everlasting." All other people, personified as the neighbors of Zion, will also see the glory of the LORD in the Israelites' return in spite of their present captivity.

In sum, Israel's hope for restoration looks ahead to, but in terms of her belief, this restoration is already actualized. It is this future hope that leads them to endure the present situation. Now they are weeping, but they can tolerate and endure all agonies because of their belief in the vindication of God. Indeed, weeping turns to laughter, joy, and gladness.

---

115. Wallace, *Greek Grammar beyond the Basic*, 577.

1 Enoch 95:1–3

First Enoch is a pseudepigraphical work of the Second Temple period, having been composed by many writers over a long time, from the fourth century B.C. into the A.D.[116] The Ethiopic version of *1 Enoch* is the only complete version, while few Greek and Latin fragments exist.[117] The work is important not only for the information it gives regarding the development of Judaism but also as a "prime example of an apocalypse."[118] The significance of *1 Enoch* lies in its theology, as it "helps clarify the rich complexities of both intertestamental Jewish thought and early Christian theology."[119] *1 Enoch* includes several apocalyptic characteristics like its contemporary literature including reversal. Nickelsburg lists some important apocalyptic features of *1 Enoch*: the coming judgment as the focal point of the book;[120] the temporal and spatial dimensions of its worldview of *1 Enoch*;[121] its dualism and its temporal and cosmic dimension;[122] its presentation of salvation as the resolution of its dualism.[123]

---

116. *1 Enoch* is a complicated and composite work, which is highly debated. Scholars are different from each other to date the time of writing from 4th BCE to late pre-Christian era. See Charlesworth, *OTP*, 1:6–7. For intensive study of *1 Enoch*, see Nickelsburg, *1 Enoch 1*, 1–128; Barker, *The Lost Prophet*, 1–4; Knibb, *Essays on the Book of Enoch*, especially 1–198; VanderKam, *Enoch*, 17–18, 25–26.

117. Charlesworth, *OTP,* 1:6.

118. Knibb, *Essays on the Book of Enoch*, 17. See especially, Apocalypse of Weeks (91:12–17; 93:1–10) and Later Additions to Dream Visions (91:1–11, 18, 19; 92; 94–104).

119. Charlesworth, *OTP,* 1:9.

120. "There is scarcely a page in *1 Enoch* that is not in some sense related to the expectations of an impending divine judgment that will deal with human sin and righteousness, and the angelic rebellions that are in one way or another related to them" (Neusner and Avery-Peck, *George W. E. Nickelsburg*, 1:31).

121. "It views the present situation in terms of the past and the future; and, alternatively, it sets the locus of human activity in relationship to the heavenly ream and the rest of the cosmos" (ibid., 32).

122. On the one hand the temporal dimension is divided between the present and a new age to come. On the other, the cosmic dimension is characterized by vertical and horizontal aspects: Nickelsburg characterizes the former when he states "heaven is the realm of the divine and earth the habitation of humans" in *1 Enoch*, and the latter when he observes that "Enoch's journeys carry him across the face of earth's disk" (ibid., 36–37).

123. As most apocalyptic works depict, *1 Enoch* pictures future salvation as executed by God's intervention. However, the salvation in the present time is experienced by revelation. In other words, *1 Enoch* is "a corpus of texts that guarantee future salvation on the basis of a present reality to which the seer has been privy and which he now reveals" (ibid., 40–42).

Among the apocalyptic features identified by Nickelsburg, of particular interest is the heavenly Messiah, the Son of Man, especially as shown in chapters 45–57:

> The Messiah in 1 Enoch, called the Righteous One, and the Son of Man, is depicted as a pre-existent heavenly being who is resplendent and majestic, possesses all dominion, and sits on his throne of glory passing judgment upon all mortal and spiritual beings. This description of the Messiah is placed in the Similitudes in the context of reflections upon the last judgment, the coming destruction of the wicked, and the triumph of the righteous ones. This eschatological concept is the most prominent and recurring theme throughout the whole book.[124]

The Son of Man in *1 Enoch* is developed from Daniel 7.[125] As Wright appropriately argues, "there is no reason at all why different groups and individuals should not have made their own variations on a theme, returned to the original for fresh inspiration, or harked back to earlier interpretations behind current ones. Nor is there any need to postulate dependence, whether literary or otherwise, between *1 Enoch* on the one hand and *4 Ezra*, *2 Baruch* and the gospels on the other. What we have here is one more strand in the richly variegated tapestry of first-century Jewish messianic belief and re-reading of scripture."[126]

Another feature of *1 Enoch* is social concern for the weak, a similarity with the Gospel of Luke pointed out by Nickelsburg.[127] He compares *1 En.* 94:8–10; 96:4–6, 8; 98:1–3; 100:6; 100:10–13; 101; 102:4–104 to Lukan passages to show the reversal of the poor, marginalized, and weak and the rich, a reversal we discussed in the previous chapter. However, Nickelsburg concludes that these two books deal differently with the problem of the poor. While Luke urges the rich to share and give their riches to the poor without using strong words of woe, *1 Enoch* uses very strong words to pronounce the "inevitable doom" of the rich.[128]

The account of the Son of Man, as well as the concern for the marginalized in the context of reversal, are characteristics of apocalyptic that

---

124. Isaac, "1 (Ethiopic Apocalypse of) Enoch," in Charlesworth, *OTP*, 1:9.

125. It is not right place to discuss this huge topic here. Rather, I would like to point out that the Son of Man in *1 Enoch* is developed from Daniel 7 as Beale, Wright and many others do. For more discussion, See Beale, *The Use of Daniel in Jewish Apocalyptic Literature*, 108–11; VanderKam, "Righteous One," 169–91.

126. Wright, *The New Testament and the People of God*, 318.

127. Neusner and Avery-Peck, *George W. E. Nickelsburg*, 1:521–88.

128. Ibid., 541–42.

appear directly and indirectly throughout the text of *1 Enoch* and allow us to examine the reversal of weeping in the book. *First Enoch* 95 illustrates the reversal of weeping well:

> 1 Who would induce my eyes like a cloud of waters; that I may weep over you, pouring my tears over you like a cloud of waters, so I would rest from the sorrow of my heart!
>
> 2 Who permits you to engage in evil fight? Judgment will catch up with you, sinners.
>
> 3 You righteous ones, fear not the sinners! For the LORD will again deliver them into your hands, so that you may carry out against them anything that you desire.[129]

First Enoch 95 is located in the main body of The Book of the Epistle of Enoch (chs. 91–107), which consists of six woes and is the fifth of the five sections into which most scholars divide *1 Enoch*, the others being The Book of the Watchers (1–36), The Book of the Similitudes (37–71), The Book of Astronomical Writings (72–82), and The Book of Dream Visions (83–90).[130]

In his detailed discussion of the structure of the fifth section, Stuckenbruck identifies 94:6–100:6 as "Woe-Oracles and Words of Consolation." Chapter 95 includes both the end of the first woe oracle against the wicked (94:6–95:2) and the second woe oracle against the wicked (95:4–7). Verse 3, which is located between the first woe and the second, is about the consolation of the Righteousness."[131] Thus, *1 En.* 95:1–3 contains both consolation and woe, especially woe against the wicked.

Who, then, are the wicked? In 94:6–11, the wicked are depicted as those who build iniquity and violence, and lay deceit as a foundation (v. 1); sinners who acquire gold and silver (v. 2); the rich who have not remembered the Most High in their days of riches (v. 3); and blasphemers and doers of iniquity (v. 4). They are, in sum, the sinners and the wicked (v. 10). They are the powerful in this present world, and their foundation seems to be firm.

The woes are introduced with pronouncements of judgment in 94:6–11. These pronouncements are "picked up in Jewish and early Christian eschatological prophecies in which, as here, they are combined with or

---

129. The text is from Charlesworth's. Neusner and Avery-Peck, *George W. E. Nickelsburg*, 2:31.

130. Ibid., 7. Here Charlesworth thinks that the final chapter, 108 is a later addition. Nickelsburg and VanderKam have a similar structure except the five sections, which they see it from ch. 91–105. Then following two sections that they structure are: The Birth of Noah (106–107) and Another Book by Enoch (108). Nickelsburg, *1 Enoch: A New Translation*, and VanderKam, *Enoch*, 1–17.

131. Stuckenbruck, *1 Enoch 91–108*, 189.

interspersed among the pronouncement of blessing amongst the righteous (so *2 En.* 52:1; Luke 6:20-26—the poor righteous and wicked rich), or stand alone (as in *4 Ez.* 13:16b-20a; Jdt. 16:17; Mt. 24:19; Mk. 13:17; Luke. 21:23; 22:22; Rev. 8:13; 9:12; 11:14; 12:12)."[132] Their riches and their pride in their deceitful foundation will be overthrown by the Most High, the Creator, whom they have not remembered. The great day of judgment, which is characterized by bloodshed and darkness, is already prepared for them (v. 9). In other words, their fortune will be reversed by God.

Following these pronouncements, 95:1 clearly alludes to Jeremiah 9:1, which reads, "Oh that my head were waters, and my eyes a fountain of tears, that I might weep day and night for the slain of the daughter of my people!" (ESV). It also alludes to *2 Bar.* 35:2: "O that my eyes were springs, and my eyelids, that they were a fountain of tears."[133] However, we see a strange scene in v. 1: Why does the narrator ("I") weep? Why are the tears heavily poured out like clouds? While Jeremiah weeps for his contemporaries' sin and betrayal against God, the narrator in *1 Enoch* weeps for the wicked. What, then, makes the narrator weep for the wicked people?

Stuckenbruck rightly comments, "The reason for the writer's sorrow is not so much their punishment or destruction as it is their misdeeds."[134] Consequently, the weeping in 95:1 is not that of the oppressed, as it was in passages discussed in the previous section. It is the weeping of the righteous. It is the weeping that cannot endure or accept the misdeeds of the sinners and wicked. Thus, we have another element of reversal of weeping: not only are the oppressed weeping, but so are the righteous. This is why v. 3 is an exhortation to the righteous.

Verse 2 poses a rhetorical question to the wicked, who are described as blasphemers and evildoers: "The text assumes that the sinners are in a relationship of accountability to God, who provides no warrant for what they do."[135] At last, the judgment, as seen in v. 9, the great one, will overwhelm them. Interestingly, the expression "catch up" or "overwhelm" here is literally, "will find you."[136] This is a kind of language of retribution, demonstrating that sinners will be punished according to their deeds.

Change of fortune is not only for the wicked and sinners; in the exhortation of v. 3, which is located between the first woe with its pronouncements

---

132. Ibid., 260.
133. Klijn, "2 (Syraiac Apocalypse of) Baruch," in Charlesworth, *OTP,* 1:632.
134. Stuckenbruck, *1 Enoch 91–108,* 270.
135. Ibid., 271.
136. Ibid. See Deut 31:7; Num 32:23; 4Q378 3i3.

and the second, change of fortune also comes upon the righteous.[137] This implies that the punishment of the wicked is unavoidable. The righteous might be afraid of the sinners, who seem to be rich and powerful in this present world, and they have experienced bitterness as result of the deeds and iniquities of the wicked. However, the LORD *will again* deliver the righteous with his righteous hand. And the wish of the righteous, that the justice of the LORD will be established, is fulfilled by the destruction of the sinners. The LORD of the righteous will again vindicate his people in the imminent future.

From *1 En.* 95:1–3 we gain some important insights. First, those who weep are not only the oppressed, who are living in hard situations, as seen in the OT and the Book of Baruch. They are also exiles having a hard time with Israel's fate. Here in *1 En.* 95:1–3, those who weep struggle with the unfairness of this world, which is brought about by their wicked enemies. Whether the enemies here are other nations who oppress the Israelites or are inner enemies, those who weep are called righteous.[138] They are socially marginalized, economically exploited, politically powerless, and few in number, and they live in fear of powerful sinners. In the Gospel of Luke, this marginalized group is described as those who weep. They experience the reversal of weeping. In addition, the inner enemies in *1 Enoch* are similar to those who laugh in Luke 6:25b. As we will see, they are satisfied with what they have and what they are enjoying in this present world, but their fortune will be reversed by Jesus. *1 Enoch* depicts that they are upright in the eyes of the Most High, but not in the eyes of the people of this world, although they are weeping because of the iniquities and evil of this world. However, all tears will be dried up by God's intervention. The righteous will be delivered and vindicated by the righteous God, and their fortune will be reversed. The righteous, who are weeping, shall rejoice.

Second, the reversal of fortune is coming upon their enemies as well. The enemies are usually other nations that do not know Israel's God, YHWH. Although they seem to have permanent control over the world and their dominion is spreading, the Righteous God will reverse their fortune by punishing their wickedness and evil. Their foundation seems firm, but it will be torn down with God's intervention. The wicked, who are laughing, shall weep.

---

137. Stuckenbruck sees it as the "first, and most brief, direct address in the *Epistle* to the righteous" (ibid.).

138. It can be connected to the "righteous sufferer," which is one of the great themes in the Old Testament. Job is one of the representatives of the righteous sufferer. Also see, Ps 22. However, in the Old Testament and early Judaism, there is a development of this righteous sufferer.

4Q Apocryphal Lamentations A

Only five fragments of 4Q Apocryphal Lamentations A (4Q179) currently exist: two large portions and three small. The title alludes to the Book of Lamentations, and the text especially alludes to Lam 4, telling about the destruction of Jerusalem. However, it is not clear whether the destruction of Jerusalem is that of 586 B.C., when the first temple was destroyed, or the later destruction of A.D. 70. Maurya Horgan leans toward the former, but he allows room for the latter by saying it is possible that "more contemporary events inspired the work."[139] One of these events is described in 1 Macc 1:16–40, which describes the attack on Jerusalem by Antiochus IV Epiphanes around 169/8 and 168/7 B.C. Berlin has a counter argument against Horgan:

> In light of the fact that the theme of the exile is so prevalent in prayer of the Second Temple period, and that a text like ours can easily be related to the theme of exile, there is no need to seek a post-586 threat to Jerusalem to account for a Jerusalem lament. We know from Zech 7:5 and 8:19 that Jews commemorated the destruction of Jerusalem with fasts and lamenting.[140]

Lawrence Schiffman shares Berlin's view. "This text has no element in it peculiar to the Qumran sect and may represent the general sorrow of the Jewish people for the loss of the ancient glories of First Temple times."[141]
Berlin and Schiffman's view, along with N. T. Wright's argument that the exile is in the background of the worldview the common worldview among the Jewish people of the Second Temple period, is more reasonable than that of Horgan. If the destruction of the first temple is a symbolic event for people of the Second Temple period, the text does not describe the actual destruction of the temple and Jerusalem; rather, it is a reminiscence of that first destruction composed while the second temple was still standing or at the time of its destruction. Berlin points out that the image of the desolation and abandonment of Jerusalem, which is described as a wasteland, would be strange if it were written while Jerusalem was thriving. "As many Second Temple penitential prayers do, that even though the Jews have returned to Judah they are still spiritually in exile."[142]

---

139. Horgan, "A Lament over Jerusalem (4Q179)," 222.
140. Berlin, "Qumran Laments," 1–18.
141. Schiffman, *Qumran and Jerusalem*, 304.
142. Berlin, "Qumran Laments," 9.

As briefly mentioned above, 4Q179 does not display the typical Qumranian *pesher* ("interpretation" or "solution") exegetical method.[143] The emphasis of *pesher* interpretation is on the Qumranians themselves, but again, 4Q179 does not show evidence of this *pesher* method. Berlin admits that the text contains *pesher* method in a reductionistic fashion but concludes, "It is a prayer, not a *pesher*."[144]

Another feature of the text is that it does not contain exact citations of biblical passages, although it does have some allusions. Unlike other Qumran texts, in 4Q179, "there is a distinct tendency to add words to biblical expressions or to combine biblical citations."[145] This leads readers to interpret or view the text in a new light.[146] In this respect, 4Q179 is different from other Qumranian midrash.[147]

Understood as either prayer or lament, the first two fragments contain woes against the Israelites, not against enemies or other powerful people who are described as sinners or the wicked in *1 Enoch*. It is the second

---

143. *Pesher* is the "technical term for commentary on scripture used in the writings of the Qumran community. Typically, each interpretation is introduced by a formula featuring the word *pesher*. Exegetical techniques (allegory, puns, *notariqon*, analogy between verses, etc.) are used to apply the prophetic citations to the history and eschatological beliefs of the Qumran community. The interpretation reveals the mysteries of the end of days hidden in biblical prophecy and are held to be the product of divine inspiration granted to a chosen interpreter" (Chazon, "Pesher," 256–57). According to Davies, the purpose of *pesher* is not to reveal the future, but to show that what was predicted long ago in Scripture has already taken place: "The point of this claim is not just to demonstrate that the end times have already begun but also to emphasize the central role in these events played by the group authoring the *pesher*" (Davies, "Biblical Interpretation in the Dead Sea Scrolls," 158). He takes an example of *pesher* interpretation in 1QpHab 7:1–5.

144. Berlin, "Qumran Laments," 17. Hence, Berlin categorizes 4Q179 as prayer.

145. Ibid., 18.

146. Ibid.

147. The word midrash is multi-dimensional and hard to define. However, Neusner aptly narrows it into three categories. He points out that "by the word *Midrash*, the Hebrew word for investigation, people commonly mean one of three things": 1) the explanation of the meaning of individual verses of Scripture; 2) Midrash-compilations; and 3) the process of interpretation, for instance, the principles that guide the interpreter, is called the Midrash–method. Neusner, *Invitation to Midrash*, 4–5. He properly encapsulates the term as "the imaginative recasting of Scripture's stories in such a way as to make new and urgent points through the retelling" (ibid., vii). Bloch, in terms of genre, says that midrash "designates an edifying and explanatory genre closely tied to Scripture, in which the role of amplification is real but secondary and always remains subordinate to the primary religious end, which is to show the full import of the work of God, the Word of God'" (Bloch, "Midrash," 29). Here I use the term midrash in a simpler sense that it is to read the older text in light of contemporary concerns.

fragment rather than the first that concerns itself with the reversal of weeping. 4Q179 2 can be read as follows:

> $^{1-2}$ [. . .] . . . [. . .] ^{3} [. . .] in your tent [. . .] ^{4} [How] solitary [lies] the [l]arg[e] city [Jerusa]lem (once) f[ull] ^{5} [of pe]ople; the princess of all the nation[s] has become desolate like an abandoned woman; all her [daug]hters have been aban[doned,] ^{6} [like] a woman without sons, like a distressed and abandoned [woman.]. All her palaces and [her] squa[res] ^{7} are like a barren woman, [and her . . .]/like/ a bitter woman. ^{8} And all her daughters like those mourning for <for> [their] hu[sbands . . .] her [. . .] like those bereft ^{9} of their only sons. How Jeru[salem] must weep, [the tears will flow] down her cheek for her sons ^{10} [. . .] . . . and her sigh . . .^{148}

Additionally, the second fragment, which is continued from 4Q179 1, shows the result of the reversal of weeping. Although the text does not explicitly describe the people of Jerusalem as laughing, it is certain that they are living a much more peaceful life before the destruction. The main reason for this devastating destruction is shown in 4Q179 1:

> . . . because we have not listened at the time of the visitation, so that all these things will happen to us because of the evil . . . (4Q179 1 *col.*I. vv. 2–3)

> Woe to us, because the wrath of God against us and we have been defiled with the dead like a detested woman . . . for their sucklings. The daughter of my people is cruel . . . her youth . . . (4Q179 1 *col.*II. vv. 3–6).

From the first fragment, it is obvious that this tragedy comes from the evil behavior of the Israelites that defiled them in the eyes of God. According to Berlin, "4Q179 is too fragmentary for a close reading of individual lines, but we can see that along with the verbal conflation there is a corresponding tendency to conflate the imagery."^{149} The imagery in use here is an abandoned and barren woman, alluding to the book of Lamentations, especially 4:2–5, although there are also some differences.^{150} "Whereas Lam 1:1 speaks of a widowed woman dwelling alone, and then goes on to portray a faithless woman, 4Q179 2, calling on descriptions of destroyed cities from Isa 54:1–6 and perhaps Zeph 2:4, speaks of a woman abandoned, barren, and bitter. 4Q179 1 I introduces prophetic imagery of Jerusalem as a wasteland,

---

148. Martínez and Tigchelaar, *The Dead Sea Scrolls Study Edition*, 371.
149. Berlin, "Qumran Laments," 8.
150. See Lange and Weigold, *Biblical Quotations and Allusions*, 259.

a habitat for wild animals, a theme absent from Lamentations except for 5:18."[151]

The differences between Lamentations and 4Q179 demonstrate how the Qumran community understood what Jerusalem was like in their day. For Qumran, "the Temple was a place of impurity, unfit for sacrifice, and whatever sacrifice was done there would not be pleasing to God."[152] This is the *Sitz im Leben* of the Qumran community. Although the temple was still standing, they felt that it had already been destroyed spiritually, and they were in exile as a barren, bitter, and abandoned widow.

The expression "at the time of the visitation" in v. 2 of *col*. I is interesting because the divine visitation is one of the central theological themes in the Dead Sea Scrolls. It is sometimes interchangeable with the popular phrase "Day of the LORD"[153] or "Day of vengeance" (1QRule of the Community; 1QS IV.23; X.19; War Scroll, 1QM VII 5; 11Q13 2.13, and so on). Divine visitation is a two-edged sword: judgment for evil on the one hand, and refinement and vindication for the righteous (or chosen of God) on the other. The former appears in 1Qp Hab XII. 14, XIII 2-3 as "Day of Judgment," or sometimes "the time of distress" (1QM I. 11-12, XV.1), "time of vengeance" (1QM XV.6), or "the time of punishment" (CD XIX. 10-11), and so on. For the latter, the righteous, it is the day of vindication or reward (1QS IV.6-8; CD III.20; 4Q181 1.3-4; 4Q525 14.II.14, etc).

Accordingly, the expression "the time of visitation" in v. 2 of 4Q179 implies that the destruction is obvious evidence of God's punishment or judgment on the Israelites due to their misdeeds. Even at the time of visitation, they refused to listen to the Judge, but kept sinning against the LORD, and the end result was desolation and destruction. Here, the time of visitation functions as punishment according to Israel's wickedness and cruelty toward the weak. Since there is no explicit mention of a foreign enemy or exile, the situation in view implies criticism of "the city's elite who wore the clothing of Jerusalem the prostitute."[154] Hence, the elite of Jerusalem, who might have been the top class among religious leaders, are associated with powerful foreign enemies and as a result are the object of divine vengeance.

---

151. Berlin, "Qumran Laments," 8.

152. Ibid., 9.

153. This is one of the most popular themes in the Bible. Although the OT and NT do not explicitly use the phrase "Day of the Visitation" (the only two places to use "the day of visitation" in the OT and NT are Isa 10:3 and 1 Pet 2:12), it is a common concept that denotes the coming of God in the Day of the LORD (Isa 13:6, 9; Ezek 13:5; 1 Thess 5:2; 2 Pet 3:10, etc.). For more detail, see Vander Hart, "The Transition of the Old Testament Day of the LORD," 3-25.

154. Berlin, "Qumran Laments," 9.

The aftermath of divine vengeance is vividly described in v. 9. Jerusalem, personified as a barren and bitter widow, which symbolizes the elite group, must weep (4Q179 2. v. 9). Jerusalem's citizens are bereft, having had all their advantages and power taken away before the LORD. Their good fortune is significantly changed into tragedy. Therefore, the weeping that is described in 4Q179 2 v. 9 is the result of reversal. The temple elite have eaten the fruit of their disobedience and evil.

From 4Q179, we can see a negative version of the reversal of weeping; those who laugh turn to weeping. The text clearly shows apocalyptic eschatology by presenting the significant theme "Day of Visitation." In 4Q179, the temple elite do not listen, even in the time of visitation, which leads them to tragic destruction. The fact that YHWH is the bringer of the reversal of weeping, as we have seen before, shows fully the true nature this eschatological concept of divine visitation. If the texts of the OT that we have examined in this chapter lay out the change of the fortune of God's people in a positive direction—restoration from suffering or a hard situation—4Q179, along with *1 Enoch*, vividly portrays how the wicked are punished through God's intervention. While *1 Enoch* pictures the petition of the righteous, 4Q179 describes the sinners' fate.

Conclusion

Throughout this chapter, we have examined several important passages that deal with the reversal of weeping. Some display a positive reversal, but others a negative one. Although the theme of reversal is notable throughout the Old Testament and the Second Temple literature, the reversal of weeping is not prevalent. The reason for its infrequency is not that the reversal of weeping is insignificant or easily ignored; rather, "weeping" is characterized by imagery that illustrates the outcome or aftermath of reversal. In other words, the reversal of weeping is subordinate to the theme of reversal, as I have mentioned in chapter 1.

However, the reversal of weeping is significant because it emphasizes the situation of the recipients of reversal, whether the reversal is positive or negative. More to the point, the reversal theme *per se* can pertain to any category: the rich or poor, the full or hungry, those who laugh or weep, and so on. Based on the recipients (or objects) of the reversal, the expressions of reversal can change. For instance, people rarely say they "hunger" when a tragic situation comes upon them; rather, they say they "weep." The point is that while different expressions can illustrate different situations and result in diverse pictures, the principles that we have examined through this chapter can help us to understand how these expressions define the recipients of the reversal. Although all those insights and principles are not clearly illustrated in Luke, they provide helpful background for understanding of Lukan reversal of weeping.

The first principle is that YHWH restores people by intervening in their lives; this action is repeated throughout history, although the ultimate intervention eschatologically occurs on the last day, return of Christ. Second, the one who causes restoration is YHWH, who initiates everything to do with the reversal. Third, the reversal that changes the fortune of God's people comes in a sudden and unexpected way; while it may have been long awaited and hoped for, it seems to comes out of nowhere, and no one knows YHWH's timetable for it. Fourth, YHWH reveals himself to his people in reversal; God's people clearly know who he is and what he is doing in their change of fortune. However, fifth, they also experience God's goodness and gentleness or justice when God brings about reversal; God's characteristics are clearly shown in reversal. Sixth, one of the main motifs associated with the reversal of weeping, used repeatedly in the OT and Second Temple literature, is exile. Indeed, Israel's crucial and central story is exile and subsequent restoration. Seventh, the reversal of weeping is embedded within the exile/restoration motif in the Second Temple period, a time when apocalyptic eschatology and worldview governed. For this reason, the most Jewish people who lived in the Second Temple period naturally believed that the change of their fortune from weeping to laughter had already been actualized. It was their hope, their belief, and their worldview. Finally, the reversal of weeping operates not only in a positive direction, in which YHWH, the LORD of Israel, vindicates his people. As we have seen in *1 Enoch* and Qumran text, 4Q179, it also has another dimension: on the Day of the LORD, the reversal of weeping aims at sinners, the wicked, the powerful elite of the temple, and evildoers. It also includes foreign enemies and the foes within. All are described as rich, elite, people wearing beautiful clothes, and those who enjoy this present world. However, at the time of vindication, they end up being destroyed. Their fate will significantly change when reversal occurs: laughter to weeping, joy to mourning. By showing the desolation of Jerusalem, the Qumran text shows how the Most High will take vengeance upon the wicked. Here, the weeping is the aftermath of their misdeeds and sins.

All these observations shed light on how Lukan passages deal with the theme of the reversal of weeping by providing basic and contemporary contexts. They also help us to read Lukan reversals of weeping better in that they are in turn derived from Lukan passages.

In the next two chapters, we are going to identify how Luke utilizes some important insights and principles of the reversal of weeping from the OT and Second Temple literature.

CHAPTER THREE

THE REVERSAL OF WEEPING TO JOY

In this chapter, we are going to examine the reversal of weeping in the Gospel of Luke. Luke provides reversal of weeping that is both positive and negative. As we have seen in chapter 1, the positive reversal of weeping is an illustration of the Lukan Beatitude of 6:21b, μακάριοι οἱ κλαίοντες νῦν, ὅτι γελάσετε, whereas the negative reversal of weeping is illustrative of the Lukan Woe of 6:25b, οὐαί, οἱ γελῶντες νῦν, ὅτι πενθήσετε καὶ κλαύσετε. The former is to show how weeping people become people who laugh, while the latter shows the opposite, those who laugh become those who weep. This chapter will present the positive reversal of weeping: the fortunes of weeping people are changed so that they become those who laugh.

The Lukan Beatitudes and Woes are the programmatic statement of the reversal of weeping.[1] In other words, 6:21b and 6:25b provide the frame on which subsequent appearances of the theme are hung. Having begun with the Beatitudes and Woes, Luke presents the stories of the reversal of weeping in his travel narrative (9:51–19:44)[2] and in the passion narrative (Luke 22:1–24:53). Specifically, the positive reversal of weeping occurs mostly in the travel narrative, while the negative occurs most often in the passion narrative. Thus, in showing the positive reversal of weeping, Luke fits the stories of reversal of weeping into the places where he wants to emphasize his idea that those who weep will experience the reversal of their fortunes.

---

1. See chapter 1.

2. Luke 9:51–19:44 is often called the travel narrative. "The whole section gives the impression at first sight of a journey from Galilee to Jerusalem, for we are constantly reminded of the fact: 9:51–56, 57; 10:1, 38; 11:53; 13:22, 33; 17:11; 18:31, 35; 19:1, (11, 28)" (Marshall, *The Gospel of Luke*). For the travel narrative in Luke, see Bailey, *Poet and Peasant*, 79–85; Conzelmann, *The Theology of St. Luke*, 60–73; Moessner, *LORD of the Banquet*.

In this chapter, the first task is to examine Luke 6:21b. After that, four incidents of the reversal of weeping will be discussed.

Luke 6:21b as the Programmatic Statement of the Reversal of Weeping

Lukan Beatitudes (6:21b)

The Beatitudes of Luke and Matthew have a lot of similarities in literary structure and content.[3] However, the most important feature that the Sermon on the Mount in Matthew and the Sermon on the Plain in Luke share is that they are not just ethical teachings *per se*.

> The sermon—to take it for the moment as a whole—is not a mere miscellany of ethical instruction. It cannot be generalized into a set of suggestions, or even commands, on how to be "good." Nor can it be turned into a guide-map for how to go to "heaven" after death. It is rather, as it stands, a challenge to Israel to *be* Israel.[4]

Wright argues that this sermon can be a great answer for the peoples' question in the first century: "how to be faithful to YHWH in a time of great stress and ambiguity, a time when many thought the climax of Israel's history was upon them, It offers a set of specific kingdom-agendas, consonant with the rest of Jesus' message."[5]

Although Wright's argument is relevant from the first Jewish people's perspective because it emphasizes the corporate dimension of Israel as nation,[6] it is only one important dimension of both sermons. It is reasonable to see that it is the story about how Israel is to be Israel, which means a challenge to Israel to be Israel, but the way in which each evangelist presents his material shows that each has a different interest. In other words, Wright

---

3. A representative work that deals both Sermon on the Mount and Sermon on the Plain is Betz, *The Sermon on the Mount*. Also see Bock, *Luke*, 1:930–43. The differences between Matthew and Luke will be discussed later.

4. Wright, *Jesus and the Victory of God*, 288. For this reason, Wright thinks that there are not many actual differences between Matthew and Luke. Consequently, he is not interested in the problem of poverty (whether the poverty is spiritual or not). Rather, he focuses on the way of the powerful and powerless. However, for those who do not agree with Wright, see Hunter, *A Pattern for Life*; Turner, 141–56. These scholars think that Sermon on the Mount is teaching for a life-pattern or ethics.

5. Wright, *Jesus and the Victory of God*, 292.

6. For the corporate dimension of Israel or Israel as community, see Bailey, "Sermon on the Mount," 85–94.

grasps the big picture but might overlook the differences between Matthew and Luke.[7] Thus, the issue of poverty, for instance, cannot be almost completely ignored in the context of Luke, because it is one of the important themes in the Gospel of Luke.[8] On the whole, Wright's argument can be sustained only in his theological system of Israel's story–exile–restoration; it is less effective in dealing with others of the many theological themes and subjects, such as the issue of poverty, concern for the poor and rich, specific concern for the marginalized groups, found in the narratives of Matthew and Luke.

Nevertheless, he is correct that "those who are blessed" are the new and true Israel:[9] Jesus' main audience when he speaks the Beatitudes in Luke are his disciples based on 6:20a, Καὶ αὐτὸς ἐπάρας τοὺς ὀφθαλμοὺς αὐτοῦ εἰς τοὺς μαθητὰς αὐτοῦ ἔλεγεν, while Matthew's are to both disciples and crowds.[10] Although the addressees include the crowd in Luke 6:27a (ὑμῖν λέγω τοῖς ἀκούουσιν),[11] Jesus' message is primarily, not exclusively, for the disciples since the characteristics and the real condition of disciples are

---

7. In my opinion, this is one of the weaknesses of Wright's view. He successfully understands and depicts the big picture in the context of the grand narrative of Israel's story. However, sometimes he focuses so much on the big picture that he misses the details unique to each evangelist.

8. See Keesmaat and Walsh, "Outside of a Small Circle of Friends," 66–89. Keesmaat and Walsh have a valid critique of Wright's argument of Jesus' prophetic critique and hope. Specifically, their focus on Jesus' prophetic critique is that Wright puts too much emphasis on nationalistic perspectives on Israel, so that he misses the ethical teachings and theological practices that are shown in the Matt 5:38–48 and Luke 6:27–36. "The point is that while the abandonment of nationalist zeal is clearly one of the things Jesus is calling for in his ministry, loving your enemy is linked in these verses with a certain kind of *economic* practice" (ibid., 89).

9. Wright, *Jesus and the Victory of God*, 288. Blomberg also agrees with Wright. See Blomberg, "The Wright Stuff," 31–32.

10. Fitzmyer, *The Gospel according to Luke I–IX*, 627. Not only Fitzmyer but also many other scholars understand the differences between two sermons as the result of redaction. For instance, Fitzmyer calls the first of the Lukan sermon the "little Interpolation" that introduces material from Q and L as well as modifications from his own editorial pen. He also thinks that Matthew makes more use of Q than Luke (627–28). However, Bovon adds the importance of oral tradition as an element of making the difference, but he does not articulate who uses oral tradition heavily: "Redaction history has also taught us to recognize the freedom and coherence of each evangelist," although Luke is less "artistic and creative" (Bovon, *Luke*, 1:217–18). Bock also enumerates and summarizes the differences well. Bock, *Luke*, 1:548–53. Also see Betz, *The Sermon on the Mount*.

11. Many scholars think that it is not necessary to think that the disciples of Jesus are the exclusive audience. Bock, *Luke*, 1:571; Evans, *Saint Luke*, 327–28; Stein, *Luke*, 199; Nolland, *Luke*, 1:280. However, see Bovon, *Luke*, 1:223.

poverty, huger, weeping, hatred, and ostracism.[12] "Jesus regarded his followers . . . the eschatological people promised in the scriptures, through whom, in a manner yet to be explicated, the glory of YHWH would be revealed to the world."[13] In this respect, the Sermon on the Plain of Luke and the Sermon on the Mount of Matthew shed light on the characteristics of the true people of God, which includes reversed fortune.[14]

In spite of this overarching argument, the scholarly interest has often been in the differences between Luke's Beatitudes and Matthew's, rather than in the uniqueness of each evangelist.[15] There are obvious differences between Luke and Matthew that can be seen when the two passages are compared: First, Matthew uses the third person throughout the Beatitudes in 5:3–10, while Luke uses the second person. For instance, Matt 5:3 is Μακάριοι οἱ πτωχοὶ τῷ πνεύματι, ὅτι αὐτῶν ἐστιν ἡ βασιλεία τῶν οὐρανῶν. Here the third person plural, αὐτῶν ἐστιν is used. However, in Luke 6:20, Μακάριοι οἱ πτωχοί, ὅτι ὑμετέρα ἐστὶν ἡ βασιλεία τοῦ θεοῦ, the second person singular, ὑμετέρα ἐστὶν is used. This use of each evangelist is consistent throughtout the Beatitidues. Second, although in Matthew and Luke the blessed are distinguished by their condition: poverty, hunger, and mourning, Luke, for his part, shows an interest in contrasting the present with the future by using νῦν, which appears twice in 6:21."[16] In other words, Luke demonstrates the theme of reversal with emphasis on the present situation

---

12. "The Lucan beatitudes are addressed to the 'disciples' as the real poor, hungry, grief-stricken, and outcast of this world; they are declared 'blessed' because their share in the kingdom will guarantee them abundance, joy, and a reward in heaven. Luke has not spiritualized the condition of the disciples as Matthew has done (in adding to Jesus' words distinctions that would suit the members of his mixed community . . . Rather, poverty, hunger, weeping, hatred, and ostracism characterize the real condition of the Christian disciples whom the Lucan Jesus declares 'blessed'" (Fitzmyer, *The Gospel according to Luke I–IX*, 631).

13. Wright, *Jesus and the Victory of God*, 444. Also see Jeremias, *Jesus' Promise to the Nations*. Jeremias provides a more detailed explanation about this issue than does Wright.

14. Here, "the true people of God" means: those who are faithful Jesus. As Wright points out, the Sermon on the Mount can be seen as "the promise that would formerly applied to those who were faithful to Torah now applies to those who are faithful to Jesus" (ibid., 288).

15. Most commentators deal with the differences and make comparison of the two. Moreover, commentators on Luke allow smalls portions to 6:25b than to 6:25a. See Bock, *Luke*, 1:556–57; Bovon, *Luke*, 1:226–27; Fitzmyer, *The Gospel according to Luke I–IX*, 634; Green, *The Gospel of Luke*, 267–68; Marshall, *The Gospel of Luke*, 251. But here, it is better to narrow down to each beatitude for our purpose.

16. Bovon, *Luke*, 1:222.

of God's people. Third, the Lukan Beatitudes are paralleled to woes are not found in Matthew's Beatitudes.[17]

The most notable differences between Luke and Matthew can be shown when it comes to our passage, Luke 6:21b, and Matt 5:4:

Luke 6:21b: μακάριοι οἱ κλαίοντες νῦν, ὅτι γελάσετε.[18]

Matt 5:4: μακάριοι οἱ πενθοῦντες, ὅτι αὐτοὶ παρακληθήσονται.

First, the verbs in use are different. While Luke uses κλαίοντες, Matthew has πενθοῦντες. Second, as noted previously, only Luke uses νῦν ("now"). Finally, Luke uses γελάσετε ("laugh"), whereas Matthew adds αὐτοὶ and uses the different verb παρακληθήσονται. In other words, Luke and Matthew have different emphases according to their theologies.[19]

From this observation, we can see the distinctive interests of Luke. First, the use of the verb κλαίοντες instead of πενθοῦντες demonstrates that the use of κλαίω is Luke's purpose of introducing the idea that he develops in his seven illustrations in the following narrative that use the same verb. There is only one occasion in the Gospel of Luke in which πενθέω is used (6:25b), but it is used with κλαίω even there: οἱ γελῶντες νῦν, ὅτι πενθήσετε καὶ κλαύσετε. We will see in the next section how κλαίω is related to the reversal throughout the narrative of Luke.

Second, νῦν, used only in v. 21, shows not only the contrast of the present with the future, but also the concern for present life, which Fitzmyer rightly points out that the Lukan Beatitudes are "eschatological, perhaps less radical than the Matthean form, because Luke is less preoccupied with an imminent eschaton, but the dimension is concern for Christian life here and now."[20] Fitzmyer bases this claim on his observation that Lukan eschatology is determined by quality rather than by time: "To exist 'eschatologically' in this sense means that Christians always have to conduct their lives as if the Son of man is behind the door. From this follows: in terms of time,

---

17. However, Matthew has similar "woes" in Matt 23, not in his Beatitudes. Ibid., 222–23. There are several detailed differences between two Beatitudes. However, our interest lies in 6:21b. The "woes" are examined in the next chapter.

18. Note variant reading γελάσουσιν (W e sys sapt Marcion Origen Eusebiuspt). This is due to harmonization with the Sermon on the Mount. See also Betz, *Sermon on the Mount*, 577.

19. I think this is one of the positive merits of redaction criticism. By focusing on the different touches given to the original sources (although it is not always sure which one is the first or the second), the differences of each book's theology, interests, concerns, and emphasis can be demonstrated. For more in redaction criticism, see the "Methodology" section of chapter 1.

20. Fitzmyer, *The Gospel according to Luke I–IX*, 630. For Luke's emphasis on the present, see ibid., 231–35.

eschatology has been swallowed up by ethics; i.e., by the quest for the proper conduct in life."[21] Although the Lukan Beatitudes do not focus exclusively on Christian conduct or ethics, the significance of the present life is an indispensable element of them.[22]

This distinctive feature of Luke, the focus on the present, leads us to understand his concern for people who are suffering, marginalized, and isolated in this present world. They are *now* suffering and having a hard time, but their fortune to come will be totally different.[23] God will vindicate them in the near future. Thus, although one of theological interests of Luke is universalism, he shows in 6:21b that he is concerned with those who weep.[24] From this observation, it is apparent that Luke sympathizes with the weak, poor, and marginalized people of this world, or at least he tries to portray them with empathy. Hence, they are the ones whose fortunes will be reversed, which Luke wants to show from the following stories of the reversal of weeping. He shows them in his Beatitude to be the poor, the hungry, the ones who weep, the persecuted, and the powerless, but their fortune is soon to be reversed.

All these differences from Matthew show the distinctive perspective and theology Luke is trying to convey and illustrate though his accounts of the reversal of weeping. The following four of the seven stories of reversal of weeping demonstrate these emphases of Luke, which is based on 6:21b,

21. Wolter, "Eschatology in the Gospel according to Luke," 91 and 106.

22. The significance of the present is not based on the delay of the parousia, which is the famous concept of Conzelmann. Tuckett refutes Conzelmann position by saying that Luke already recognizes that Jesus coming is not imminent, as people expect. See note 13 in Introduction and Tuckett, "Luke," 280–81.

23. This is also a characteristic of being Jesus' disciple, as stated earlier. Wright gives a different option for here in terms of Israel's story. Regarding Matthew and Luke as not much different, Wright interprets Matt 5:4 (par. Luke 6:21b) as follows: "Israel longs for consolation, for *paraklesis* (5.4). But YHWH has in mind to give her, not the consolation of a national revival, in which her old wounds will be healed by inflicting wounds on others, but the consolation awaiting those who are in genuine grief" (Wright, *Jesus and the Victory of God*, 288). However, those who are in genuine grief are not clearly mentioned here yet, although Wright implies that they are the new Israel who is formed by Jesus.

24. Universalism is one of the predominant features in Luke-Acts. For instance, in Luke 21:29, Fitzmyer points out that the use of "all" is a trait of Luke: "It is a part of the Lucan stress on the universality involved in the new form of salvation being made available" (Fitzmyer, *The Gospel according to Luke X–XXIV*, 472). There are a number of passages to show this concern of Luke's; Simeon's word that God has prepared before *all* peoples (Luke 2:31–32); the genealogy that traces back from Jesus to Adam (3:23–38); Jesus' sending seventy, which implies the whole world, including the Gentiles (10:1), and so on. For more discussion on this issue, see Esler, *Community and Gospel in Luke-Acts*, 33–45.

the touchstone passage for all positive reversal of weeping in the Gospel of Luke.

Those Who Weep Now Shall Laugh

Based on his framework for the reversal of weeping (6:21b), Luke presents four stories of the reversal of weeping. The identity of those who weep now is very clear, since Luke vividly describes the causes of weeping and who weeps in the text. They are the widow of Nain (7:11–17), the sinful woman (7:36–50), Jairus (8:40–56), and Peter (22:54–62). What highlights this point is Luke's use of the technique of repetition, *Leitwort*. A problem can be raised, for there is no incident that anyone who weeps laughs in the stories of positive reversal of weeping. In other words, Luke gives no account that weeping people actually laughing.

We note that Luke does not use, first, γελάω as *Leitwort* the same way he uses κλαίω. This means that he does not stick to a specific word to describe the laughing people who weep now. Rather, Luke wants to show how the tragic situation of people weeping is reversed to the happy situation, which is shown in the reversal of weeping stories in following sections. In other words, the emphasis lies on weeping rather than laughing. Consequently, second, the programmatic statement of "those who weep now shall laugh" in 6:21 means that the situation of weeping people will end happily. In this sense, the weeping to actual laughter (or vice versa) is one specific way of referring the reversal of weeping, but not every incident of the reversal of weeping has actual laughing. In other words, the stories of the reversal of weeping in positive direction do not have actual laughing. The widow of Nain, the sinful woman, Jairus, and Peter do not actually laugh but all the stories, as we will see, show that their miserable fortunes are reversed to joyful ones, which signifies laughter. However, in negative direction of the reversal of weeping, the laughter is used as a synecdoche[25] to indicate those who are satisfied with this present world.[26]

This claim is supported by the meaning of the word γελάω ("to laugh") in Luke 6:21b and 25b. Both verses use γελάω as it is used in the LXX, where it has two different meanings. It has the negative connotation of looking

---

25. Synecdoche is a literary device in which a part of something represents the whole or it may use a whole to represent a part. Synecdoche may also use larger groups to refer to smaller groups or vice versa. It may also call a thing by the name of the material it is made of or it may refer to a thing in a container or packing by the name of that container or packing. For detatiled discussion, see Bullinger, *Figures of Speech Used in the Bible*, 612–56.

26. More details will be discussed in § 4.1.

down on the fate of enemies and being in danger of becoming boastful and self-satisfied (Gen 17:7; 18:12, 13n, 15, Esth 4:17; Ps 51:6; Jer 20:8; Lam 1:7),[27] but it also can indicate an expression of joy (Gen 21:6; Ps 126:1–5).[28]

Concerning those who will laugh in v. 21b, K. H. Pridik states, "To laugh here is a picture of a carefree and unencumbered life in joy (οἱ γελῶντες νῦν in v. 25b is near οἱ πλούσιοι in v. 24 and οἱ ἐμπεπλησμένοι in v. 25a) that believers possess only as an eschatological promise, not as a way of life in this world."[29] However, it is evident that γελάω refers to joyful laughter that is not solely future.[30] Craddock thinks that reversals in the Lukan Beatitudes and Woes are drawn from an eschatological frame of reference, but they are not exclusively future:

> Does this mean that this entire passage is descriptive of a condition still in God's future? Luke's answer is yes and no. Both the blessings and the woes are anchored in the present. Notice: "Blessed are you poor, for yours *is* the kingdom of God" (v. 20) and "But woe to you that are rich, for you *have received* your consolation" (v. 24). Both of these conditions are realized, not promises for the future. However, in blessings and woes two and three, "now" is contrasted with "you shall," clearly indicating future fulfillment. This joining of present and future reminds us that the eschatological reality is already beginning with the advent of Jesus.[31]

In this respect, Pridick's explanation has a serious weakness in that it leaves out the Lukan use of νῦν, making laughter for believers only in the eschaton. Thus, γελάω in Luke 6:21b involves the present and future reality of the people who weep.[32]

---

27. Marshall, *The Gospel of Luke*, 256. See also Johnson, *The Gospel of Luke*, 107. The details of the other, negative, meanings of γελάω will be discussed in chapter 4.

28. Evans, *Saint Luke*, 330; Nolland, *Luke 1:1–9:20*, 284.

29. Pridik, "γελάω," *EDNT*, 1:240.

30. The recent publication of Inselmann is a great study of joy in Luke. Inselmann presents the idea that joy is not a mere literary motif but is theology based on God's plan and intervention. Inselmann, *Die Freude Im Lukasevangelium*. Also see Wenkel, "The Emotion of Joy and the Rhetoric of Reversal in Luke–Acts: A Socio-Rhetorical Study." Weknel examines Lukan joy with related to some reversal passages based on York's work, *The Last Shall be First*. Wenkel thinks that the rhetoric of reversal is empowered by the emotion of joy in Luke–Acts; De Long, *Surprised by God*. De Long discusses the response of people to Jesus' words and deeds.

31. Craddock, *Luke*, 88.

32. Note that this concept is an aspect of Lukan eschatology, which I showed in note 13 in Introduction.

If this is the case, it is reasonable to think that those who laugh in 6:21b are those who will receive God's consolation in this world,[33] as well as the future world; Luke shows this through describing God's comfort given here and now to weeping people in all four stories.[34] Although the word γελάω is not used explicitly in these stories, the reversal of weeping assumes that the objects of reversal are the those who weep now but later will laugh.

The Weeping Widowed Mother of Nain (Luke 7:11–17)

The story of Jesus' raising the widow's son at Nain (7:11–17) is the first incident of positive reversal of weeping after the Lukan Beatitudes. The story is only recounted in the Gospel of Luke. Before delving into the story, it is necessary to examine several features and characteristics of the story.

First, it is follows the story of a centurion whose servant was healed by Jesus, which is a normal Lukan presentation of a male–female pair.[35] There are contrasts between the two accounts:

> These two accounts reflect Luke's pattern of alternating complementary episodes with male and female characters. The gap between the two could not be greater. The centurion was wealthy and had influence and power; he had a deathly sick slave. The woman, by contrast, is a poor and powerless widow whose only son is dead. She has no one to fend for her and no hope for her future.[36]

Although there are several similarities between two accounts, the story of the widow of Nain is more dramatic in that Jesus raises the dead rather than the sick. Moreover, the centurion regains his slave from disease while the widow receives her beloved only son from death. In addition, Luke shows his concern for women by presenting two healing stories involving women (7:11–17 and 13:10–17) that are not shown in other Gospels, although the male–female parallelism in healing is common practice of the Synoptics.[37] Thus, the story of the widow of Nain has less in common with other such stories and is more dramatic than the story of the centurion's servant.

---

33. This "realized eschatology" is supported by Dodd. It will be discussed more fully in chapter 5. See Dodd, *The Parables of the Kingdom*.

34. Stein says, "Although this verb is not a passive, it functions like a divine passive for 'God will cause you to laugh'" (Stein, *Luke*, 201).

35. Green, *The Gospel of Luke*, 289.

36. Garland, *Luke*, 299.

37. Green, *The Gospel of Luke*, 289; Witherington, *Women in the Ministry of Jesus*, 51. Also see Drury, *Tradition and Design in Luke's Gospel*, 71.

A similar reversal of weeping story appears at 8:52, the healing Jairus' daughter. This has parallels with the story of the raising of the widow's son: 1) it is at the death of the μονογενής ("only") child that the people are weeping; 2) Jesus bids the persons weeping to stop; 3) Jesus raises the dead in the presence of the parents. The most salient of these parallels is Luke's use of μονογενής, which is intended to link the two stories through pathos.[38] In addition, the pericope of the raising of the widow's son and of Jairus are the only two in which Jesus raises the dead in the Gospel of Luke.[39] Thus, these two stories' reversal of weeping demonstrates that Jesus can change even the most frustrating, miserable, and difficult situations that make humans weep. Therefore, the best story to pair with the raising of the widow's son is not of the centurion's servant but of Jairus' daughter, which shows the intention of Luke's treatment of the reversal of weeping.

Second, it is reasonable to think that the story of the widow of Nain is an answer to the disciples of John the Baptist who asked whether Jesus is the one to come (7:18-23). Luke puts 7:11-17 before the question that came from John the Baptist to provide an answer for the question in advance.[40] Along with other miracles that are described before the question is asked—the cleansing of the leper (5:12-16) and the healing of the paralytic (17-26)—this story of the widow of Nain provides an answer to John the Baptist.[41] "Clearly, Luke has placed the two miracle stories of the centurion's servant and the widow's son just before the Baptist's question to provide Jesus with a clear basis for his reply."[42] Accordingly, the story of the widow of Nain explicitly shows that Jesus is the one who is to come, the Messiah, who was promised in the OT, especially in Isaiah.[43] Whether the contemporaries of John the Baptist understood the identity of Jesus or not, Luke tries to show that Jesus is the coming Messiah by answering the inquiry of John the

---

38. Meier, *A Marginal Jew*, 2:791; Albert, *Literary Patterns*, 39-43. Meier thinks that μονογενὴς is distinctively Lukan.

39. The raising of Lazarus is another one in John's Gospel (11:1-44), not shown in Luke.

40. Bovon asserts that the "reason for including vv. 11-17 at precisely this point is obvious: Jesus is about to emphasize to the disciples of John, who will arrive in 7:22, that the dead are raised. Since Luke has not yet described any resurrections from the dead, he is now filling this lacuna, as 7:21 shows, a verse summarizing the healing activity of Jesus" (Bovon, *Luke*, 1:266).

41. Ibid., 267.

42. Meier, *A Marginal Jew*, 2:789.

43. Isa 61:1 (LXX only); 29:18-19; 35:5-6; 26:19.

Baptist.⁴⁴ Therefore, the story of the widow of Nain demonstrates the messianic activity of Jesus by reversing the weeping widowed mother's fortunes.

Third, the story of the widow of Nain has a clear allusion to 1 Kgs 17:7-24, in which Elijah encounters a widow of Zarephath. Parallels between two episodes are obvious.

The LXX of 1 Kings 17		Luke 7	
v. 9	χήρα	v. 12	χήρα
v. 10	τὸν πυλῶνα τῆς πόλεως	v. 12	τῇ πύλῃ τῆς πόλεως
v. 20	τοῦ θανατῶσαι τὸν υἱὸν αὐτῆς	v. 12	τεθνηκὼς μονογενὴς υἱός
v. 23	καὶ ἔδωκεν αὐτὸν τῇ μητρὶ αὐτοῦ	v. 15	καὶ ἔδωκεν αὐτὸν τῇ μητρὶ αὐτοῦ
v. 24	ἰδοὺ ἔγνωκα ὅτι ἄνθρωπος θεοῦ	v. 16	προφήτης μέγας ἠγέρθη ἐν ἡμῖν

Both accounts have widow as one of the main characters (7:12; 1 Kgs 17:9, χήρα); the death of her son (7:12; 1 Kgs 17:12⁴⁵); the meeting of the widow at "the gate of the city" (7:12, τῇ πύλῃ τῆς πόλεως); 1 Kgs 17:10, τὸν πυλῶ να τῆς πόλεως]; the same clause, ἔδωκεν αὐτὸν τῇ μητρὶ αὐτοῦ "he gave him to his mother" (καὶ ἀνεκάθισεν ὁ νεκρὸς καὶ ἤρξατο λαλεῖν, καὶ ἔδωκεν αὐτὸν τῇ μητρὶ αὐτοῦ 7:15; καὶ κατήγαγεν αὐτὸν ἀπὸ τοῦ ὑπερῴου εἰς τὸν οἶκον καὶ ἔδωκεν αὐτὸν τῇ μητρὶ αὐτοῦ καὶ εἶπεν Ηλιου βλέπε ζῇ ὁ υἱός σου 1 Kgs 17:23); and the miracle-worker is recognized as God's messenger (7:16; 1 Kgs 17:24).⁴⁶

---

44. To be sure, Luke portrays that John the Baptist is a credible figure throughout the narrative. By depicting his birth, growth, and ministry in detail, sometimes paralleled with those of Jesus, Luke highlights his greatness, although the focus is always on Jesus. See Jesus' assessment of John the Baptist in Luke 7:28. Moreover, that the story of the widow of Nain also illustrates that Jesus is the Messiah is supported by the response of the people in Nain, "God has visited his people," which I argue at the end of this section. The response of Jesus in 7:22 surely accentuates his mission that is proclaimed in 4:18-20. York relevantly argues that "the poor" (πτωχοῖς) in 4:18 is not just socioeconomic poor. Rather, in the context of 4:18-20, they are "grouped with the captives (αἰχμαλώτοις), the blind (τυφλοῖς), and the downtrodden (τεθραυσμένους). What characterizes these term is the helpless condition of each, and it suggests that primarily physical circumstances are to be reversed." It is no doubt the messianic activity as well, as Jesus designates himself as a prophet (4:24). See, York, *The Last Shall Be First*, 97-99.

45. LXX reads τοις τεκνοις μου ("for my sons"); MT reads וְלִבְנִי "and for my son."

46. Pao, "Luke," 99. Also see, Fitzmyer, *The Gospel according to Luke I–IX*, 656. The second half of each verse is verbatim. I am using the LXX version of Alfred Rahlfs, *Septuaginta* (Stuttgart: German Bible Society, 1935).

Brodie is the most enthusiastic supporter of the idea that the two episodes are closely connected. He maintains that the close relationship of the two stories is the result of a "sophisticated and coherent process of dramatization and christianization."[47] Based upon the Hellenistic literary technique of *imitatio*, which is the basic element of the rhetorical training method of that time, Luke adopts the OT story of Elijah's raising the widow's son in 1 Kgs 17.[48] By employing this technique,[49] what Luke aims at is threefold: First is *positivization*, in which the NT brings a positive image of the LORD, giving hope and salvation in opposition to the OT's negative image of a God who brings death. Second is *universalization* by using "all" ($\pi\acute{\alpha}\nu\tau\alpha\varsigma$ in 7:16); Luke demonstrates that God's saving visitation is for everybody. Third is *christianization*: "The entire OT text has been so taken over and reworked that it fits into the fabric of the Gospel narrative and into the NT message which sees Jesus as LORD of life and as a source of hope for all."[50] In other words, Luke utilizes the tradition of Elijah in the OT for a christological purposes.[51]

Brodie's points are mostly convincing, except the first one. He simplifies and limits the image of God into two dimensions. Although the image of God is presented as strict and harsh in the OT, there are many passages that show God's compassion and love (e.g., Exod 34:6; Ps 103:8). Kavin Rowe's argument elaborates Brodie's last point that Jesus is the LORD and source of life and hope for all people. Commenting that Luke's authorial use of of ὁ κύριος in v. 13 shows Luke's particular idea of Jesus as the LORD, Rowe asserts that Luke deliberately chooses the word in order to present Jesus as the LORD who is not only the anticipated prophet but also God.[52] As Brodie and Rowe both insist, one of the central focuses of the story is to highlight Jesus as Christ, who gives life and God's healing.

In this line of the argument, Bovon points out that the story of the widow of Nain is greater than the OT narrative in 1 Kgs 17:

> (1) The time elapsed between the death of the young man and the intervention of the miracle-worker becomes longer (cf. 1

---

47. Brodie, "Towards Unraveling Luke's Use of the Old Testament," 247.

48. Brodie thinks that Luke prefers to use Hellenistic literary approaches and techniques rather than Jewish. Ibid.

49. According to Brodie, the main techniques that Luke uses for adapting the OT text are simple rewording, geographic adaptation, compression, elaboration, dramatization, explication or clarification, complementarity, and contrast. Ibid., 257–58.

50. Ibid., 258–59.

51. For the tradition of Elijah in Second Temple times, see Brodie, *The Crucial Bridge*; Shaver, "The Prophet Elijah"; Molin, "Elijahu der Prophet," 256–58.

52. Rowe, *Early Narrative Christology*, 118. Also See Bovon, *Luke*, 1:269.

Kgs 17:17–18 and 2 Kgs 4:18–21); (2) Jesus takes the initiative, whereas in 1 Kgs 17:18 and 2 Kgs 4:22, the widow turns to the prophet for help; (3) the resurrection occurs more spontaneously (cf. 1 Kgs 17:19–22 and 2 Kgs 4:31–35); (4) in the Lukan account, and additional acclamation by the crowd follows the account (7:16).[53]

Whether Luke adopts the techniques of Hellenistic *imitatio* or not, it is quite certain that he utilizes the OT account of the widow of Zarephath in order to show the greatness and supremacy of the LORD Jesus Christ. "Luke created the Nain story out of the building blocks of other stories of revivification known to him. The disparate building blocks would have been selected and put together according to Luke's vision of Jesus as the merciful LORD, the prophet like—but greater than—Elijah, a 'greater prophet,' mighty in word and work, through whom God has definitively 'visited' his people Israel."[54] Therefore, it is not an overstatement to say that Luke portrays Jesus as the greater (the greatest) prophet as a bringer of reversal.[55] Moreover, as we have seen in the previous chapter, the similar principles of reversal of weeping can be found here as well.

From the above, it is Jesus who takes the initiative as YHWH does in the OT passages discussed in chapter 2. In addition, as the previous OT texts demonstrate, the reversal is YHWH's work and his people recognize it, so do the people in this Lukan account recognize who Jesus is.

With these observations, it is time to focus on the story of the widow of Nain in the context of the reversal of weeping. The story begins with Καὶ ἐγένετο ἐν τῷ ἑξῆς,[56] usually translated as "soon afterwards." This is a connection to the previous episode, the healing the centurion's servant, which happened in Capernaum. The expression denotes temporal and chronological transition, and it expects that a new episode has begun. Jesus and his disciples went to a city named Nain (v. 11). This city is mentioned only in this episode. Nain is located in Galilee three miles west of Endor, twenty

---

53. Bovon, *Luke*, 1:268.

54. Meier, *A Marginal Jew*, 2:792. When Meier says Luke "creates" the story of the widow of Nain, the focus of Meier is not historicity of the account itself. Rather, in my opinion, Meier might have been stressing the Lukan redaction or utilization of the Elijah tradition.

55. For discussion on Jesus as the prophet like Elijah, see Miller, "Luke's Conception of Prophets." See especially, 42–52; 191–235.

56. See MSS such as C D, which read the feminine form τῇ with ἐν. However, this is found nowhere else in Luke. Thus, the preferred reading is ἐν τῷ ἑξῆς shown in P75 A B Θ f1 *et al.*

miles southwest of Capernaum, and six miles southeast of Nazareth.[57] As Jesus is drawing near to the gate into the city of Nain, many people are accompanying him. He meets a funeral procession coming out the gate, as burials were typically done outside of city walls.[58]

Interest lies in the expression that Luke uses in v. 12b, καὶ ἰδοὺ ("behold"), which is used to introduce a worthwhile event that happens in the context of habitual activities.[59] The focus of Jesus is not only the dead son, who is his mother's only child, but it is also on his widowed mother. More descriptions are attributed to the mother than the dead son: the dead man is the only son of his μήτηρ (mother); αὐτὴ (she) was widow; and, a considerable crowd from the city was with αὐτῇ (her). More importantly, Jesus also had compassion on her, not only her boy. Hence, the funeral procession is for the dead young man but the main focus of Jesus is on his mother.[60]

The funeral procession now meets Jesus and his disciples. As stated previously, the attention is paid to the widowed mother, who has lost her only son and been left alone. The situation that the mother confronts is desperate and frustrating. Now she does not have any hope at all.[61] Luke adds μονογενής in order to describe her miserable situation, since the loss of her only son implies that she does not have any support for living. "She is a widow who has lived since her husband's death in relation to her son, himself a young man. With his passing, she is relegated to the status of dire vulnerability—without visible means of support and, certainly, deprived of her access to the larger community and any vestiges of social status within the village."[62] However, Luke's interest does not lie in that the widow is de-

57. Bock, *Luke*, 1:649.

58. McCane gives good information about how Jewish funeral processions fit into the Jewish burial and funeral process. According to Jewish custom, funerals usually took place soon after death, most often before sunset on the same day. Thus the preparation, the so called "wrapping and binding" found in numerous rabbinic texts, is normally done once death was certain. This wrapped and bound corpse was carried out in a procession accompanied by friends, neighbors, and relatives. Jewish funeral processions started at the home of the family of the deceased and went to the family tomb. See McCane, *Roll Back the Stone*, 31. Bock adds more evidence: "A family tore their garments as a sign of mourning and closed the eyes of the corpse to show that death had come" (Bock, *Luke*, 1:651).

59. Bovon, *Luke*, 1:271.

60. See Vogels, "A Semiotic Study of Luke 7:11–17," 282–83. Vogels thinks that the focus of the story is the widowed mother, but this story is a sub-genre of miracle stories, which focuses on Jesus. More details on miracle story and its genre, see Theissen and Mertz, *The Historical Jesus*, 281–315.

61. Bock describes the widow as an "orphaned parent" (Bock, *Luke*, 1:649).

62. Green, *The Gospel of Luke*, 291. For more details about widows, see Finger, *Of Widows and Meals*.

pendent on her son. Rather, in parallel with the story of Jairus' daughter (8:41–42, 49–56), Luke wants to highlight her grief for her only son.[63] The point is the mother's grieving over losing her son.

Jesus keeps focusing on the widow in v. 13 as well. καὶ ἰδὼν αὐτὴν ὁ κύριος ἐσπλαγχνίσθη ἐπ' αὐτῇ καὶ εἶπεν αὐτῇ μὴ κλαῖε. Jesus saw *her*, had compassionated on *her*, and spoke to *her*.[64] Here Luke deliberately uses the christological title ὁ κύριος to present Jesus as the LORD, who gives the life.[65] This LORD had compassion on the widow, who had lost her only son. From this the most important element of the reversal of weeping in the OT can be recalled: reversal of weeping occurs due to the compassion and mercy of God,[66] who is the initiator of the change of fortune. The words ἐσπλαγχνίσθη ἐπ' αυτη (7:13) establish the point of the story that Jesus starts to reverse death and sorrow into life and joy.[67] More specifically, the moment that Jesus had compassion on her is the point of departure for the reversal.

Another principle of the reversal of weeping is also work at here. As seen in chapter 2, there is to be no doubt that the bringer of reversal is YHWH. No other can bring true reversal of fortune to his people. Thus, Luke makes the important proclamation that Jesus is identified with God by using the christological title ὁ κύριος,[68] which is used exclusively by YHWH.[69] Luke also shows the initiative of Jesus in this incident. *He* first saw her, *he* had compassion on her, and *he* spoke to her. Although the focus of Jesus is on the widow of Nain, the initiative is all centered on Jesus. He is the beginning of the reversal. The story is about Jesus, which has christological focus.

---

63. Stanford, *Luke's People*, 252–53. Stanford thinks that Luke could have followed the "Septuagintal stereotype of widows and orphans by continuing with his model of the widow of Zarephath, who had young children."

64. Italics are mine.

65. In my opinion, Rowe's view that Luke intentionally uses the christological title κύριος throughout his narrative is very convincing. Rowe not only persuades the readers by accurate and appropriate exegesis of the text but also argues that the Lukan use of ὁ κύριος is *Leitwort* for the Lukan narrative. See Rowe, *Early Narrative Christology*. For *Leitwort*, see chapter 1. There is a textual variant that reads κύριος as Ιησοῦς. However, the preferred reading is κύριος. κύριος is a distinctive Lukan title for Jesus: Luke 7:13,19; 10:1, 39, 41; 11:39; 12:42; 13:15; 16:8; 17:5, 6; 18:6; 19:8a; 22:61a, b; 24:3, 34.

66. See the previous chapter, especially, §2.2.3.

67. Menken, "The Position of ΣΠΛΑΓΧΝΙΖΕΣΘΑΙ and ΣΠΛΑΓΧΝΑ in the Gospel of Luke," 109.

68. Some mss (D W *f*1 700. 1241 f vgmss sys.p bo) have ὁ Ἰησοῦς instead.

69. This is thoroughly discussed by Rowe throughout his book, *Early Narrative Christology*.

THE REVERSAL OF WEEPING TO JOY

Now the LORD Jesus said to her, μὴ κλαῖε. This expression of Jesus is extraordinary in that it was customary for the Jewish people's grieving process to last thirty days and involve loud wailing.[70] However, this is a word not of rebuke but of comfort, hope, and mercy, which will bring a totally new situation. "Jesus does not forbid a mother's grief, but counsels the woman in view of his coming action."[71] Followed by vv. 14–15, the command of Jesus not to weep is a reminder of 6:21b, μακάριοι οἱ κλαίοντες νῦν, ὅτι γελάσετε. Thus, it is a foreshadowing of what will come after, "a transparent reminder to Luke's audience that the good news of salvation will turn weeping into laughter (6:21b)."[72] The widow is weeping *now*, but she will laugh. Jesus will keep his word. By saying to the widow the word of comfort, Jesus begins turning the tide for the widow.

In v. 13, Luke uses κλαίω for the first time in his narrative since the Sermon on the Plain (6:21b and 25b), the point of departure from which he illustrates the reversal of weeping throughout the Gospel of Luke. In portraying the reversal of weeping, the Lukan Jesus takes one of the most marginalized people in the society, a widowed mother who has lost her only son, as his first choice. Although her weeping implies that her future is precarious because she has no protector or provider, it represents the grief of her loss of her only son. Thus, the main focus is on her grief over the loss of son.[73] Certainly, she is now going through the hardest time of her life, but Luke implies that the reversal is coming shortly by having Jesus say to her, μὴ κλαῖε.

Jesus now shows his compassion and accomplishes his word to the widow. He comes up and touches the bier. He stops the procession. The bearers stand still (v. 14). When the term προσέρχομαι is applied to Jesus, it heralds his acting with authority (Mark 1:31; Matt 17:7; 28:18; Luke 9:42).[74] For instance, when Jesus heals a boy with a demon in Luke 9:42, προσέρχομαι is used before Jesus heals the boy (ἔτι δὲ προσερχομένου αὐτοῦ ἔρρηξεν αὐτὸν τὸ δαιμόνιον καὶ συνεσπάραξεν· ἐπετίμησεν δὲ ὁ Ἰησοῦς τῷ πνεύματι τῷ ἀκαθάρτῳ καὶ ἰάσατο τὸν παῖδα καὶ ἀπέδωκεν αὐτὸν τῷ πατρὶ αὐτοῦ). Hence, the action of Jesus' approaching the bier implies that something unexpected is going to happen under his authority. Touching the bier is, however, a forbidden action according to the law (Num 19:1, 6). Accordingly, the action

---

70. Witherington, *Women in the Ministry of Jesus*, 178.

71. Fitzmyer, *The Gospel according to Luke I–IX*, 659.

72. Green, *The Gospel of Luke*, 291–92.

73. Spencer, "Neglected Widows," 724. Also see Spencer's recent volume, Spencer, *Salty Wives, Spirited Mothers, and Savvy Widows*.

74. Bock, *Luke*, 1:651. Marshall defines it as messianic action. Marshall, *The Gospel of Luke*, 286. Also see *TDNT*, 2:683.

of Jesus is surprising in the eyes of the people. However, Jesus touches the bier to stop the procession.

Now Jesus says to the dead young man, νεανίσκε, σοὶ λέγω, ἐγέρθητι. Bovon translates this clause, "Wake up!" by taking the primary meaning of ἐγείρω as "to wake," rather than "to raise." This translation makes good sense when this story is compared to that of the raising of the daughter of Jairus (8:40–56), especially vv. 52–56. When Jesus tells them the girl is not dead but sleeping (v. 52), they laugh at him.[75] However, Jesus calls and says to her, ἡ παῖς, ἔγειρε. The usage of ἐγέρθητι in 7:14 shows that the dead son wakes up from death. Nevertheless, the verbs in 7:14 and 8:52 differ in tense and voice: the former is aorist passive imperative and the latter is present active imperative. The aorist imperative indicates a statement that is fulfilled at the moment of speaking. "Such usage is reserved for passives that cannot be fulfilled by the recipient of the imperative."[76] Although the verb is used to denote the dead "being raised" in Lukan narrative (7:22; 9:7, 22; 20: 37; 24:6, 34), which can be read as passive,[77] it is reasonable to sees the command of Jesus in 7:14 as a messianic action that highlights Jesus' authority rather than a command for the young man respond. Green supports this point as well. "Jesus speaks, not in prayer to God (as Elijah had done), but directly to the corpse, commanding it to be revived. This is the act of healing, and with this speech-act Jesus evidences striking dimensions of his apparent authorization, status, and institutional role in the salvific purpose of God."[78] The fortune of the dead young man is totally reversed under the authority of Jesus. He now sits up and begins to speak. At first Luke intentionally calls him not "young man" but ὁ νεκρὸς (dead man), thus giving a background to which Jesus' healing provided vivid contrast, since the dead man could not sit up or speak. Surely, life flows in another direction.

After the young man has come to life, Jesus gives him to his mother (v. 15b). Luke maintains his focus on the widowed mother from the beginning to the end. Jesus has already seen her, had compassion on her, spoken to her, and raised up her son; now at last he gives her her son. By regaining her son from death, the widowed mother also regains her life. The reversal is not

---

75. Here the word "laughing" is significant. It will be discussed later in section. §3.4.

76. Wallace, *Greek Grammar Beyond the Basics*, 492–93. Bovon more clearly states that "the aorist imperative emphasizes less the passivity of the young man in contrast to, let us say, the action of God, than the fact that the subject—the young man—realizes and manifests his awakening" (Bovon, *Luke*, 1:272).

77. Fitzmyer, *The Gospel according to Luke I–IX*, 659. Fitzmyer thinks that this is an added Christian theological connotation.

78. Green, *The Gospel of Luke*, 292.

just the restoration of the son but also the restoration of the mother and the reversal of her fortunes.

After witnessing the resurrection of the dead young man, the crowd that was following Jesus and those accompanying the procession are seized by fear, which is a typical response to God's great deeds.[79] Luke shows the fear and amazement of the crowds elsewhere who experience the amazing deeds of God (Luke 1:12, 65; 5:26). They not only are seized by fear, but also glorify God, saying, "A great prophet has arisen among us!" and "God has visited his people!" Here are two important sentences. On the one hand, "a great prophet," which is reminiscent of Elijah, who did a similar thing in 1 Kgs 17. It is also reminiscent of Deut 18:15–18, which is the prophecy that God will raise up a prophet like Moses. On the other hand, "God has visited his people" is a typical apocalyptic concept. The response of the people can be said in this way: "God has visited his people through a great prophet who has arisen among us." In other words, Luke portrays Jesus as the anticipated prophet through whom God visited his own people.

There has been a debate whether the title "a great prophet" is christological or not. Rowe argues that this prophetic element in v. 16b is an expression of the Lukan christological thrust.[80] However, Kingsbury does not relate the passage to a Lukan christological title because it is based on the crowds' response, which is different in different situations. For instance, the crowds have a very good attitude toward Jesus; they accept his message and him (Luke 5:26; 13:27) but at other times, they are hostile to and ignorant of Jesus (11:14–16; 11:29; 12:54–56). Thus, since the characterization of the crowds in Luke's narrative is not fixed, Kingsbury does not give credit to "a great prophet" in v. 16 as christological title.[81] Accepting the fact that the use of "a great prophet" as a christological title in v. 16b is not sufficient, Rowe argues that this title should be examined under the context of the following incident, in which John the Baptist sends his disciples to Jesus and ask who he is.[82]

---

79. De Long, *Surprised by God*. De Long extensively examines the response of praise in Luke-Acts, including Luke 7:11–17 in the miracles and healing stories. De long argues that this response of praise reveals the identity of Jesus as Messiah, Son, King, and Risen LORD.

80. Rowe, *Early Narrative Christology*, 119.

81. Malherbe and Meeks, "Jesus as the 'Prophetic Messiah' in Luke's Gospel," 37–40. Bovon also claims that "a great prophet" is not a Lukan christological title at all. Bovon, *Luke*, 1:273.

82. "The people's prophetic-christological appraisal in 7:16, then, should be interpreted in light of Luke's own christological judgment with which he introduces consecutive scenes. In this light, we can see that Luke preserves the widespread view of Jesus as a prophet (cf. esp. the ὁ λόγος οὗτος of 7:17) but also directly introduces his own

Bovon has a position different from those of Rowe and Kingsbury, arguing that the crowds recognize Jesus as an eschatological prophet: "In brief, the author allows the audience to express a not yet complete confession of faith, but also implies that, according to his own opinion, Jesus is the eschatological prophet (Deut 18:15) and Elijah redivivus (Mal 4:5–6 [LXX 3:23–24])."[83] However, Bock criticizes Bovon's position by relying on Cullmann, who notes that προφήτης is anarthrous.[84] He contends that the "crowd has responded to the event they have seen, which recalls the great prophet of old and points to the renewal of God's miraculous activity for his people. They are no more specific than that."[85]

In spite of the differences in the views, the most significant words are found in the latter part of verse 16, ἐπεσκέψατο ὁ θεὸς τὸν λαὸν αὐτοῦ. This clause gives information important to the debates whether or not "a great prophet" is a christological title and whether or not the phrase is intended to refer to the eschatological prophet. The point that Luke wants to make in this story is that God has visited his people through Jesus. Visitation of God is His salvific and redemptive activity in the OT as well (Exod 4:31; Ruth 1:6; Ps 80:14; and 106:4) as in the Second Temple literature.[86] In the Gospel of Luke, ἐπισκέπτομαι ("visit"), is used only four times: 1:68, 78, 7:16, and 19:44. The three uses of ἐπισκέπτομαι exclusive of 7:16 indicate messianic visitation, "God's gracious activity for his people as he utilizes his power on their behalf."[87] Jesus' time, the Second Temple Period, was dominated by the apocalyptic worldview, so the crowds might have understood that "a great prophet" raised up by God would be the eschatological prophet, an idea taken from Deut 18:15.[88] Moreover, if the story of the widow of Nain is to show that Jesus is greater than Elijah, who was also considered an eschatological figure by the contemporaries of Jesus, the "great prophet" that God

---

basic christological judgment of κύριος, thereby qualifying the category of prophet as christologically insufficient" (Rowe, *Early Narrative Christology*, 120).

83. Bovon, *Luke*, 1:273–74.

84. Bock, *Luke*, 1:653. Also see Cullmann, *The Christology of the New Testament*, 30.

85. Bock, *Luke*, 1:653–54.

86. See the discussion in chapter 2. Although the Qumran community's notion is that God will raise up the Teacher of Righteousness, the meaning of "visitation" is very like Luke's in that God will take care of his people and vindicate them.

87. Bock, *Luke*, 1:654. Bovon clearly understands the concept of ἐπισκέπτομαι within three dimensions. The first is soteriological: the raising up of a prophet represents salvific visitation. The second is ecclesiological: Jesus' action is valid for the entire people of God, who experience and recognize in the saving of one of its members the recovery of the whole. The last is christological: what Jesus does is nothing less than the fulfillment of God's will. It is God's personal action. Bovon, *Luke*, 1:274.

88. Miller, *Luke's Conception of Prophets*, 236–58.

has sent is Jesus. Luke, then, puts Jesus in the seat of that "great prophet." People might have recognized Jesus as the eschatological prophet, although they had not fully known who he was. In this respect, Luke uses ὁ κύριος in v. 13 to support the point christologically. Jesus, who is the eschatological prophet, the Messiah, can bring reversal. He can turn weeping to laughter.[89] Thus, the clause ἐπεσκέψατο ὁ θεὸς τὸν λαὸν αὐτοῦ implies that Jesus is the long-awaited prophet who brings true reversal.

Luke closes the story of the widow of Nain by mentioning that this word about Jesus spread through Judea and all the surrounding country (v. 17). There is, however, ambiguity in the verse: ὁ λόγος οὗτος. Does it denote the story of resuscitation itself or include the crowd's response? Green rightly says, "'This word about him' undoubtedly includes not only reports of his miraculous activity, but also its significance in the form of news of a great prophet in whose ministry God's salvation was being made available."[90] The news about Jesus' being the eschatological prophet spreads out from this time on.

The story of the widow of Nain tells many significant elements of the reversal of weeping. First, it is the first incident that Luke wants to choose as a story of the reversal of weeping. The Lukan Jesus keeps his eye on her. This disadvantaged and marginalized character shows the Lukan concern for the powerless and the least. She has even lost her son. Hence, the object of the reversal of weeping, in other words, those who need or experience the reversal of weeping, are those who suffer in this present age, νῦν. If the blessings in 6:21 and other Beatitudes are applied to the true Israel or the true people of God, this widow is blessed and a member of the true people of God. Second, Luke portrays Jesus as *the* bringer of the reversal of weeping. Not only as a great prophet of God but also as the LORD, Jesus is the bringer of the reversal of weeping. Only he can change the destiny of people, even a dead man. In the OT context, only YHWH can change the fortunes of his people. In this regard, Jesus is identified with God. He is the LORD, ὁ κύριος.[91] This LORD has compassion on his people and brings the reversal to those who weep. However, we should not lose sight of Luke's portrayal of Jesus as a prophet. He is the eschatological prophet whom many people are anticipated for a long time. Finally, all initiatives are taken by Jesus as it

---

89. See §3.1.2 for "laughing."

90. Green, *The Gospel of Luke*, 293.

91. Rowe relevantly says, "The narrative itself is the theology: the coming of the κύριος Χριστός is the coming of the κύριος ὁ θεός. The opening of the Gospel thus narrates, in the move from promise to active fulfillment, the presence of the God of Israel in the life of Jesus." He further connects Jesus to κύριος. See Rowe, *Early Narrative Christology*, 199–207.

was with YHWH. Jesus stops the procession, approaches the widow, comforts her, tells her not to weep, touches the bier and raises the dead young man. Now the widowed mother is given her son back. Those who weep shall laugh.[92]

In this regard, the story of the widow of Nain is focused on Jesus as well as on the widow's reversal story. It is a doubly focused story. Thus, the reversal of weeping in the story is christological. Also, Luke's focus and interest in the marginalized, especially in women, continues to the next story, in 7:38. Indeed, the story of the widow of Nain reminds us of the power of Jesus to defeat the most notorious enemy that causes weeping, and changes weeping into true laughter.

The Weeping Woman (Luke 7:36–50)

The story of a sinful woman who is forgiven in 7:36–50 has been considered one of the most difficult passages in Lukan narrative because of its complexity and the many interpretive issues mingled in it. First, although Luke 7:36–50 is considered parallel to Matt 26:6–13, Mark 14:3–9, and John 12:1–8, Luke is different from the other two in many ways. How can these differences be explained? Second, many different interpretations of the woman's action, the washing and drying of Jesus' feet with her unbound hair, have been suggested in various ways throughout the history of interpretation. Third, there have been different views of the reason for her weeping. Is her weeping an expression of gratitude, or is it an expression of repentance? Finally, what is the focus of the passage? What is Luke trying to say? In other words, what is Luke intending to provide in this story?

It is not the purpose of this work to answer all these questions fully, nor is to focus on every aspect of these texts.[93] Rather, we will pay attention to

---

92. Note that laughter is not literally used in telling the reversal of weeping stories. See §3.1.2.

93. Concerning the many differences between Luke 7:36–50 and parallel passages in other Gospels, different settings in terms of chronology and locale are discussed; Luke and John depict that woman anoints Jesus' feet, not head that Matthew and Mark do; the identity of woman by Luke is sinner while John identifies woman as Mary; the reaction to the event differs. Luke focuses on the sinner not wasting of perfume as in Matthew and Mark; unique Lukan parable appears in vv. 41–42; Luke does not say about Jesus' burial in related to woman's action; the conclusions differ. Matthew and Mark present that woman's act will be memorialized while Luke focuses on the forgiveness. Bock, *Luke*, 1:670–71. See Resseguie, "Luke 7:36–50," 286. Also, there is an issue that all accounts refer to one incident or not. Some think that each evangelist fixed the tradition from a single memory (Although Bovon argues that it came from a single memory, he admits many counter arguments against his position. Bovon, *Luke*,

selected verses and exegesis that provide general information; the focus will be primarily on the reversal of weeping, especially as it relates to determining the primary message of the passage. We will examine other questions in order to support our conclusion that the weeping of the sinful woman is that of repentance and remorse, which is reversed by Jesus to joy and laughter.

Regarding the nature and cause of the woman's weeping, it is necessary to examine the structure of the pericope. Bailey structures the story as follows:

Introduction (the Pharisee, Jesus, and woman)
    The outpouring of the woman's love (in action)
        A dialogue (Simon judges wrongly!)
            A parable
        A dialogue (Simon judges rightly)
    The outpouring of the woman's love (in retrospect)
Conclusion (the Pharisee, Jesus and the woman)[94]

Bailey's chiastic structure shows that the parable that Jesus tells to the Pharisee is the focal point of the pericope and helps readers see that the focus on the reversal of weeping should be interpreted under the context of the parable. Through the parable, Jesus articulates and gives his opinion of Simon and the woman.

The story begins with an unnamed Pharisee's invitation (later his name is shown, Simon) to Jesus to eat with him (v. 36). Interestingly, Luke gives specific names to none of the characters before v. 40, neither the name of the Pharisee who asks Jesus to eat with him nor that of the sinful woman. Even Jesus is not mentioned by name. Moreover, Luke does not provide the name of the city, referring to is as "the city" (v. 37). In other words, the narrator veils the characters of the story. As the story goes on, however, Luke unveils

---

1:291–92); others think that it is an account totally distinct from others. Ibid.; Marshall, *The Gospel of Luke*, 304–6. However, Bock is not sure of Marshall's argument that the incidents are distinct and that the two traditions have crossed at points. Fitzmyer argues that Luke's story comes from his own source, L, and Luke adds oral tradition to it. Most scholars except Bock and Marshall think that the story of the sinful woman comes from the same incident and Luke touches it according to his source, oral tradition, and so on. Fitzmyer, *The Gospel according to Luke I–IX*, 684–88. Here, it is reasonable to hold that Luke's presentation of the story of the sinful woman is distinct from that described by the other evangelists. The story of the sinful woman is Luke's unique story.

94. Bailey, *Jesus through Middle Eastern Eyes*, 239. See also Van Til, "Three Anointings," 77–78. Van Til thinks the parable shows that the authority of forgiveness is the focal point of the story.

the characters' identities. This is one of Luke's literary devices to highlight surprises.⁹⁵

As mentioned in the previous section, ἰδού in v. 37 is a means of attracting readers' attention by introducing a new or noteworthy event. In this case, it is unconventional act of an unnamed woman of an unnamed city. The identity of the woman is stated only as ἁμαρτωλός. According to BDAG, ἁμαρτωλός refers to (one who engages in) behavior or activity that does not measure up to moral or cultic standards, and so the ἁμαρτωλός is a social outsider because of failure to conform to certain standards. Persons engaged in certain occupations such as herding and tanning that jeopardized cultic purity would be considered by some as "sinners," a term tantamount to "outsider."⁹⁶ From this definition, it is easy to recognize the woman's identity as a sinner or outsider, which means she is marginalized and cast out from her community. Luke does not provide the specific sin or failure of the woman. However, many scholars think that she is guilty of prostitution or other sexual misconduct on the basis of the definition of the word ἁμαρτωλός or her washing Jesus' feet with unbound hair. Plummer thinks that she is a prostitute, connecting this pericope with Matt 21:32.⁹⁷ Bovon also renders her a prostitute, inferring from ἐν τῇ πόλει that her sin is a social one.⁹⁸ Witherington is another proponent of this view, saying that the context confirms that the woman is a prostitute.⁹⁹

However, not all commentators share this view. Fitzmyer thinks that she can only be considered a prostitute on inference from the Pharisee's thought. It is thus only "implied, not being said openly in the text."¹⁰⁰ Marshall and Bock are also reluctant to accept that the woman is a prostitute. Rather, they rightly note that the woman is a sinner, but not a prostitute because her action does not show that of prostitute.¹⁰¹

Accordingly, the focus of v. 37 is not solely on the identity of the woman, whether she is a prostitute or not, but on her action.¹⁰² This woman had most likely not been invited to the meal because she learned (ἐπιγνοῦσα) that Jesus reclined the house of the Pharisee. If she had been invited, it

95. Section §3.5 deals in more detail with anonymity.
96. "ἁμαρτωλός," BDAG, 51.
97. Plummer, Gospel according to St. Luke, 210.
98. Bovon, Luke, 1:293.
99. Witherington, Women in the Ministry of Jesus, 54–55.
100. Fitzmyer, The Gospel according to Luke I–IX, 689.
101. Marshall, The Gospel of Luke, 308. Also see Bock, Luke, 1:696–97.
102. I agree with Marshall and Bock that she is not a prostitute because the text does not provide the details of her being prostitute. Bock, Luke, 1:697. Marshall, The Gospel of Luke, 308.

would not have been necessary to use the verb ἐπιγινώσκω, which denotes that she found out.[103] The woman must have known Jesus' reputation, that he eats and has fellowship with sinners.[104] Bailey confirms by saying, "The story assumes that before the drama opens, the woman had heard Jesus proclaiming his message of grace for sinners. The entire account makes no sense without this assumption."[105]

The woman enters the house. Witherington explains that the woman had unrestricted access because of the openness and hospitality of Jewish homes. It was not considered uncommon for a poor or disadvantaged person to come into a house during a banquet to be with the people or even to grab something to eat.[106] However, when the Pharisee, who thinks one of the most important things is purity, holds the banquet, he considers the approach of the woman to Jesus as that of an intruder. Marshall comments that for this woman "to dare to enter the Pharisee's house was particularly objectionable in the eyes of people in general—except for Jesus."[107] Thus, this sinful woman takes access to Jesus, which implies that she bears shame from others in order to enter the Pharisee's house to see Jesus. But she is now standing behind Jesus.

What the woman does to Jesus is somewhat puzzling. All her actions are described in 7:37-38. She has brought an alabaster flask of ointment, and standing behind him at his feet weeping, she begins to wet his feet with her tears and wipe them with her hair and kiss his feet and anoint them with the ointment (vv. 37-38). Luke here shows that the woman's actions contrast with those of the Pharisee before Jesus mentions them in 7: 44-45. This is why there is no description of the welcoming process for Jesus when he enters the house of the Pharisee. By not mentioning that the Pharisee did not show any welcoming courtesy for Jesus, Luke wants to maximize the woman's devoted action here.[108] To omit all these customs was regarded as rude and insulting. Hence, the woman's actions are the opposite of those

---

103. "ἐπιγινώσκω," *BDAG*, 369.

104. Bock, *Luke*, 1:695. For the sinners in the Gospel of Luke, see Neale, *None but the Sinners*.

105. Bailey, *Jesus through Middle Eastern Eyes*, 242.

106. Witherington, *Women in the Ministry of Jesus*, 55.

107. Marshall, *The Gospel of Luke*, 308.

108. Bailey explains the traditional custom of welcoming: "Custom required a kiss of greeting, usually on the face. After the guests were seated on the stools around the broad U-shaped dining couch, called a *triclinium*, water and olive oil would be brought for the washing of hands and feet. Only then could the grace be offered. Finally, the guests would recline on the couch (or couches) and the meal would begin" (Bailey, *Jesus through Middle Eastern Eyes*, 242).

of the Pharisee. She is now washing Jesus' feet with her tears and giving him the alabaster flask of ointment instead of water and olive oil to wash. She even wipes Jesus' wet feet with her unbound hair. She kisses Jesus' feet. She does every welcoming custom by herself. Instead of giving olive oil, she provides her alabaster flask of ointment, which is one of the most precious things for her. The word ἀλάβαστρος denotes "a vase for holding perfume/ointment, often made of alabaster, hence *alabaster vase*, a vessel with a rather long neck which was broken off when the contents were used, or a container for spikenard ointment"[109] Luke tells not the price of the anointment but its value: "Aromatic and expensive, such perfume was not the less expensive olive oil normally used for anointing."[110] She puts oil better than olive oil on Jesus. She washes Jesus' feet by weeping and dries them with her unbound hair.

Concerning these actions of the woman, several issues have been discussed intensely in Lukan scholarship. On the one hand, the reason for the woman's weeping has been questioned. On the other is the question of the implication of woman's unbound hair. On the whole, why does this woman do these things to Jesus? What is her motivation?

For the issue of her weeping, Luke uses βρέχω with κλαίω. The verb βρέχω denotes "to make wet (through immersion or flooding)" then "rain or cause to rain," so the implication is that she shed many tears, enough to wet and wash Jesus' feet. The weeping of the woman is great. Some scholars think that her weeping is an expression of joy to honor Jesus or of her thankfulness and love for her forgiveness.[111] One strong proponent of the idea that her weeping is for joy and gratitude is C. F. Evans, who affirms that she already knew herself "to be one of the company with whom Jesus, the Son of man, associates, that he had already declared her sins forgiven and that her actions were expressions of gratitude for this (not of penitence; the title The Penitent Woman for the story is a misnomer)."[112] However, even Evans has some reservations about his argument: "That is, the woman's actions can only be accounted for by reference to something the story does not itself contain."[113] Evans assumes that her sin was forgiven (by Jesus) already sometime in the past, but this is not in the text; however, the forgiveness of her sin is declared by Jesus in v. 47.

109. ἀλάβαστρος, BDAG, 40. It is "a flask carved from the expensive soft alabaster which was believed to help preserve ointment and perfumes" (Nolland, *Luke*, 1:354).

110. Bock, *Luke*, 1:695.

111. Ibid., 697. Fitzmyer agrees with Bock. See Fitzmyer, *The Gospel according to Luke I–IX*, 686–87.

112. Evans, *Saint Luke*, 362.

113. Ibid.

Bailey gives another interpretation: "It is clear that her tears are not for her sins but for his public humiliation. She is in anguish because, before her eyes, this beautiful person who set her free with his message of the love of God for sinners, is being publicly humiliated. . . . The woman was deeply dismayed at the insult to Jesus, and said to herself, '*They* will not offer these courtesies! Very well, *I will offer them* instead!'"[114] However, Bailey's point is not persuasive, even if Jesus does mention the Pharisee's omission of courtesy in vv. 44–46. Bailey puts too much focus on ancient Middle Eastern hospitality, so he does not properly identify the meaning of Jesus' parable in vv. 41–42. In other words, the parable of Jesus in vv. 41–42, along with v. 47, shows that the woman's love comes from the fact that her many sins are forgiven (ἀφέωνται αἱ ἁμαρτίαι αὐτῆς αἱ πολλαί, ὅτι ἠγάπησεν πολυ), not from some desire to be hospitable. It is the importance of love from forgiveness of sin.[115] Of course, woman's action to show Jesus all the omitted signs of welcome can be viewed as an expression of love. However, the focus of this story is forgiveness and the love that comes from it.

In order to identify the weeping of the sinful woman, Charles Cosgrove has engaged in intensive study of the unbinding of women's hair in ancient contexts. He explores various ancient Jewish and Hellenistic documents and provides the connotations of unbound hair. He lists six situations in which women unbound their hair: (1) to show sexual availability; (2) to express gratitude; (3) to religious devotion, a gesture of humility and reverence or self-offering to a god; (4) to signify guilt or ritual or legal (quasi-legal) proceeding, or grief, or impending disaster; 5) to engage in conjury; (6) to prepare for baptism.[116]

Cosgrove concludes by combining two seemingly contrary interpretations that he thinks the most relevant in the text into one: the unbound hair of woman in Luke expresses either her gratitude and devotion or her quest for forgiveness and acceptance. "Perhaps these two interpretations can be combined by imaging that the woman approaches seeking acceptance from Jesus but also assuming that he will give it, that she belongs to the class of people to whom he has already extended God's forgiveness. In that case, she is grieving, supplicating, and grateful."[117] Thus, it is not easy to decide whether woman's actions, especially her weeping, are expressions of grief and repentance or of gratitude.

114. Bailey, *Jesus through Middle Eastern Eyes*, 247, italics are original. However, Nolland is not sure to understand that woman's action is due to conscious gestures of hospitality omitted by Jesus' Pharisaic host. Nolland, *Luke*, 1:354.

115. Bailey himself puts the parable at the center of story.

116. Cosgrove, "A Woman's Unbound Hair," 675–92.

117. Ibid., 692.

Her kissing on Jesus' feet has also two interpretations. "Marks of honor are accorded to one who is recognized as God's agent of salvation. She spares no lavishness."[118] Fitzmyer thinks that the woman already knows that Jesus is the Messiah and is giving him proper honor. However, these actions express not only honor and gratitude but also deep humility.[119]

Green appropriately grasps the whole point of the problem and explains it in the context of the reversal of weeping:

> We are given no unambiguous guidelines for understanding the cause of her tears. Do they identify her as a recipient of eschatological blessing (cf. 6:21b)? Are they symbolic of her (new?) reliance on God (cf. Psalm 126; Isa 25:8; 35:10; 65:17–25)? Are they tears of remorse or repentance? What we do know is that actions are rooted in the disposition of the heart, that actions divulge one's fundamental allegiance (cf. 3:10–14; 6:43–49). What do these actions disclose about this woman? Luke's account provides two, mutually exclusive interpretations.[120]

Although Green takes an ambiguous position here, all the causes of the woman's weeping that he provides are relevant to an explanation of the reversal of weeping. Her weeping is that of eschatological blessing at last because she is one of those who weep *now* (Luke 6:21b). Her weeping also reveals her reliance on God, who will forgive (or has already forgiven) her sins and does not just have fellowship with sinners. This must be the weeping of remorse for her past sins.

However, there is no clear evidence that it is the weeping of repentance. Although the woman's weeping is that of repentance, which can be supported by use of the perfect tense in v. 47 (ἀφέωνται) and 48 (ἀφέωνταί) when Jesus declares forgiveness of her sins after telling the parable, the perfect tense is used not only to indicate the past action but also to denote emphasis on the fulfillment of action.[121]

All these actions of the woman have no conclusive interpretation. Scholars have provided two dominant interpretations and mixed them into one, thus paying attention to the fact that the woman's actions are disgraceful, shameful, and unconventional.

The reason for weeping of the woman becomes clearer when the time of her forgiveness is known. In other words, when exactly was her sin forgiven

---

118. Fitzmyer, *The Gospel according to Luke I–IX*, 689.
119. Snodgrass, *Stories with Intent*, 82.
120. Green, *The Gospel of Luke*, 310.
121. See especially Kilgallen, "Forgiveness of Sins (Luke 7:36–50)," 677. Also see Applegate, "And She Wet His Feet with Her Tears,'" 76.

by Jesus? As said previously, the reason for or type of the sinful woman's weeping cannot be identified only by her actions or through grammatical analysis. It is better to argue this issue from the perspective of the reversal, especially the reversal of weeping, since the main concern for this study is to examine how reversal of weeping is illustrated throughout the narrative.

Most of all, the beatitude in 6:21b should be remembered. It reads μακάριοι οἱ κλαίοντες νῦν, ὅτι γελάσετε. The attention must be paid to the word νῦν. Throughout the narrative, Luke wants to illustrate this point: those who are weeping *now* will laugh at last. "Those who weep now" denotes people who have not already been restored from their miserable situations or sufferings; they are those who are eagerly waiting for the reversal of their fortunes. Thus, it makes more sense to think that those who weep in Luke 6:21 are still suffering now. From this consideration, the woman in this story weeps because of suffering from her sin that she has *now*. In this regard, her weeping is that of repentance, grief, remorse, and regret rather than that of joy, gratitude, and so on. If Luke consistently uses κλαίω throughout his narrative to show the reversal of weeping, the weeping of the woman here is doubtlessly that of repentance or remorse. In this respect, the comment of Judith Applegate is appropriate: "The woman enters with mourning and repentance for her sins (which in Jesus' words 'are many,' 7.47), with love for Jesus, and with faith in Jesus' connection to the One who forgives."[122]

The reversal of weeping begins with the word of Jesus. In showing the reversal of weeping, Luke provides two different reactions to woman's action, the reaction of Simon the Pharisee and that of Jesus. By presenting two different reactions, Luke wants to demonstrate the true interpretation of the event. Luke provides a terse description of what Simon thinks in v. 38: Simon's reaction is not just to question the woman's action but also to wonder about Jesus' identity.[123]

Bovon aptly grasps the Lukan intention to increase the Simon's anger by catching the meaning of καλέσας. "By recalling the invitation (καλέσας, 'who had invited'), Luke heightens the degree of outrage on the part of the Pharisee, who promptly reacts to the events in the form of an interior

---

122. Applegate relates this story to the immediate context before, especially 7:32. "The weeping of those in verse 7.32 depicts a funeral wake, and the woman obviously illustrates those who weep in that verse, in contrast to the Pharisee who is not weeping" (Applegate, "And She Wet His Feet with Her Tears," 76. See also my discussion on the perfect tense and its various usages above.

123. Luke also contrasts the way in which Simon and Jesus express their thought. Jesus openly speaks and commends the woman's action, while Simon thinks and criticizes it internally.

dialogue."[124] His analysis that Simon is only interested in Jesus rather than the woman is right. However, there is another angle to ponder, which is how Luke skillfully presents this story according to his intention. More to the point, Luke wants to show that the true host and guest in this story are not who they first appear to be. Simon the Pharisee thinks that he is the host of the banquet, and in one sense he is. He has invited Jesus to be his guest and held the banquet. However, he is not the real host from the perspective of the Lukan Jesus, who has a very different interpretation of the woman's action. The true host is Jesus, who has invited the sinful woman to forgiveness. In this regard, the real guest is the sinful woman, who treats Jesus like host. York sees that this story is about a reversal of the roles.

> In the beginning the Pharisee is the host, the woman is a sinner. He is inside; she is outside. He has honor; she is shameless. As the story develops, she acts hospitably; he fails to show any special kindness toward Jesus. She understands him to be a prophet; he rejects Jesus' prophetic character. She is forgiven much and loves much; he is forgiven little and loves little. Her faith saves; by implication, Simon's lack of faith means the rejection of salvation. She now has honor; Simon is shamed. The outsider has become an insider; Simon, the supposed insider, has become an outsider.[125]

Now the focus of the story shifts to Jesus, who tells the parable. Simply speaking, the parable is about forgiveness and love. It is about the cancellation of debt. The main point of the parable is that the one who is forgiven much loves much. Of interest is that Jesus lets Simon answer the question, "Which of them will love him more?" Simon answers, "The one, I suppose, for whom he cancelled the larger debt." The significant point is Jesus' interpretation of the parable in v. 44–47. After agreeing with Simon in v. 43, Jesus explains the meaning of the parable that he just told to the Pharisee. He commends the woman's action of pouring the oil and precious ointment on him while Simon the Pharisee did not provide him with anything. The woman's action can be seen as symbolizing the temple ritual, since it follows the sacrificial system in Leviticus: a priest makes the sacrifice and offering; a male makes an offering, and a priest makes the offering on the altar in the Temple.[126] However, the woman's action is in contrast to the Levitical system

---

124. Bovon, *Luke*, 1:295.
125. York, *The Last Shall Be First*, 125–26.
126. Van Til, "Three Anointings," 79.

in that she, not a priest, makes an offering and she pours herself at the feet of Jesus, not on an altar.[127]

The more persuasive point can be made by Jesus' interpretation of this parable. Although Luke does not include any statement that her action is to prepare Jesus for burial, as they are in Matthew and Mark, he highlights the importance of the forgiveness of sin. As said previously, v. 47 is important since Jesus finally declares the forgiveness of sins of the woman.[128] Her weeping of repentance, grief, and remorse turns to joy and freedom. Reversal of weeping once again happens to a sinful woman who is marginalized from the community. Jesus' final word confirms it: "Your faith has saved you; go in peace."

The response of the people around the scene is much similar to that at the previous reversal of weeping at Nain, but here the people are surprised to the point of asking who Jesus is. Luke leaves the answer to his readers through the comment of the people. Van Til makes an important point on this under the context of the sacrificial offering. "It is the priest, not the king, who announces forgiveness. . . . The woman came to Jesus with the confidence that she was approaching the true source of forgiveness. She brought appropriate offerings (precious ointment and tears of genuine repentance) and poured them out at Jesus' feet. She then received the expected announcement of forgiveness."[129] This is confirmed by Jesus' mention of her faith. If her weeping is that of joy or gratitude, Jesus' mention of faith is not quite relevant or persuasive in the context of the story, since her sin was forgiven by Jesus after his proclamation rather than before she came to Jesus.

Several points about the reversal of weeping can be inferred from the story of sinful woman. First is the importance of "now," which is in 6:21b. The sinful woman, who is *now* weeping, comes to Jesus and experiences the reversal of weeping, which turns her weeping to joy and forgiveness. Those who suffer in this present world experience God's reversal of fortune. Thus, the reversal of weeping not only occurs only in the far future, but also happens now and presently, which means some eschatological events, i.e., reversal of weeping, is actualized in this present world.[130] As does the

---

127. Van Til interprets the woman's actions as sacrificial offering, which intends to be forgiven of sin. This interpretation also fits the Lukan theology of forgiveness as he insists. Ibid.

128. The question, "when is her sins forgiven?" is constantly debatable one among scholars. See, Kilgallen, "Forgiveness of Sins." Kilgallen leans toward that she was already forgiven her sins before Jesus' declaration. Thus, the weeping of the woman is that of gratitude based on love instead of remorse or repentance.

129. Van Til, "Three Anointings," 80.

130. This is an aspect of Luke's eschatology, which I discussed which I discussed in

widow of Nain, the sinful woman who suffers from her sin in this world experiences the reversal of weeping.

Second, the reversal of weeping comes from Jesus and his words. He reverses the fortunes of those who weep. By declaring the forgiveness of her sins, Jesus turns her fortunes around: the sinner becomes the righteous one. Therefore, Jesus is the bringer of reversal.

Third, the story of the sinful woman not only shows the woman's restoration but also the fault of the Pharisee, who is the confident host of the feast. One can easily see the fact that Simon the Pharisee is described as the one whose laughter is turned to weeping, as in 6:25b. Although Simon does not actually laugh, the portrayal of those who laugh in 6:25b is shown in this account. Thus, Luke shows the double message through the story: those who weep shall laugh, but those who laugh shall weep. Finally, Jesus is not identified only as a prophet. Rather, he is described as the king and priest. Although there is no explicit expression to indicate that Jesus is the king and priest, such as "the LORD," Luke shows that Jesus is the king and priest by showing that he forgave the sinful woman and gave her salvation (7:50). The story of the sinful woman has many other issues that should be discussed, but under the context of reversal of weeping, we can see those insights that Luke provides.

The Weeping Father (Luke 8:40–56)

Luke 8:40–56 contains another reversal of weeping story: Jesus' raising of Jairus' daughter from death. This pericope consists of two episodes: Jesus heals a sick woman and raises a dead girl. The unique feature of the pericope is the intercalation of the two accounts. Numerous linguistic and topical commonalities between the two passages of levels, such as falling before Jesus (vv. 41, 47), daughter (vv. 42, 48, 49), twelve years (vv. 42, 43), heighten the dramatic effect of the girl's healing that is interrupted by the healing of the sick woman.[131] Many scholars have thought that these commonalities between two episodes come from Markan tradition, especially based on a "sandwich" (or "sandwiching") technique that Mark uses to highlight the

---

Introduction].

131. For more similarities, see Green, *The Gospel of Luke*, 343–44. Also see Culpepper, *The New Interpreter's Bible*, 190. Bock comments that these are the only intertwined miracles in the Gospels. See Bock, *Luke*, 1:785.

major themes in the narrative.[132] Here, Luke also uses a sandwich technique for the same purpose.[133]

However, Luke is different from Mark in several ways. Fitzmyer lists eight differences of Luke from Mark, arguing that they come from Lukan redaction: 1) Luke has shortened the stories and joined them to what precedes them more closely than does Mark. 2) He introduces the age of the girl early into his form of the story. 3) He adds that she was an "only child." 4) He softens the criticism of the physicians, omitting that the woman "had suffered much from many of them." 5) In 8:45 Peter becomes the spokesman for the disciples in expostulating about the crowds. 6) In 8:46 Jesus is made to say that power has gone forth from him, whereas it is the evangelist's comment in Mark 5:30. 7) Luke explains why the crowd ridicules Jesus when he says that the girl was only sleeping in v. 53. 8) In 8:55, Luke adds "her breath returned," making clear that the resuscitation involved a return to former life.[134]

Among these eight points, the most notable insights are the third and seven, which are closely related to reversal of weeping, especially in parallel with the story of the widow of Nain in chapter 7, which this pericope parallels in several ways. First, Luke adds that Jairus' daughter is his only child. Tannehill points out that the narrator of the Gospel of Luke intends to heighten pathos for his readers by "specifying that the child is an *only* son or daughter" in the story of the widow of Nain and Jairus' daughter.[135] Interestingly, these two stories are closely related to each other in terms of reversal of weeping, and we have seen that the two stories are thematically and literally symmetrical.[136] Fitzmyer summarizes the similarities between the two and carefully connects two episodes to Jesus' resurrection: "The resuscitation of the girl has to be related to the earlier resuscitation of the son of the widow of Nain (7:11–17). There it concerned a son and his mother; here it

---

132. See Marshall, *The Gospel of Luke*, 341. Also see Schramm, *Der Markus-Stoff bei Lukas*, 126–27. For "sandwiching" technique, see Edwards, *The Gospel according to Mark*, 11–12. The two stories are related by parallel motifs such as "daughter" (θυγάτηρ, Luke 8:42, 48/ θυγάτριόν, Mark 5:23; θυγάτηρ, Mark 5:34), "twelve years" (ἐτῶν δώδεκα, Luke 8:43/ δώδεκα ἔτη, Mark 5:25), and "saved/well" (σέσωκέν, Luke 8:48/ ὑγιὴς, Mark 5:34).

133. "The intercalation fills in time in the narrative and serves to heighten the dramatic tension and the miracle's magnitude. During the delay with the woman, the daughter dies. The compositional technique also allows the two intersecting stories to make a similar point. It is wrong, therefore, to treat these two miracles separately. They are tied together" (Garland, *Luke*, 365).

134. Fitzmyer, *The Gospel according to Luke I–IX*, 743–44.

135. Tannehill, *The Narrative Unity of Luke–Acts*, 1:91–92, 94.

136. See §3.2 above.

is a daughter and her father. Lucan parallelism is again at work, but with contrast. Both of the resuscitations, moreover, are not without foreshadowing elements for the resurrection of Jesus himself."[137] Here, the importance of the parallel of two passages is well explained.

Second, Luke gives the reason for the crowd's laughing at Jesus. They laugh because they know the girl is already dead. Moreover, Jesus says that the girl is not dead but sleeping. This additional information provides the detailed context for what is going to happen, the reversal of weeping. "Capitalizing on the wordplay available to him in the use of the term 'sleep' as a euphemism for 'death,' Jesus asserts that her condition is more temporary than the crowds might think."[138] Not only the euphemism but also Jesus' words foreshadow what is going to happen soon. Jesus' saying "Do not weep" (μὴ κλαίετε) in v. 52 reminds the reader of the account of widow of Nain in Luke 7. In both accounts, Jesus tells someone not to weep and performs a miracle of raising the dead. Thus, Luke attempts to show what is going to happen by providing details and parallels with the story of the widow. Green encapsulates the point in terms of reversal of weeping by stating that the narrator has reorganized the story for the purpose of dramatic effect: "Who is weeping and wailing? Who laughs? This confusion is resolved when it is realized that the narrator has again reorganized his account for dramatic effects, ordering the events outside of chronological time so as to focus separately on two distinct discourses"[139] By displaying these differences, Luke portrays his theme more dramatically, not just by intercalating the story of the bleeding woman into that of Jairus' daughter but touching Markan sources with his theological emphasis, which is the reversal of weeping. The intention of Luke can be found more clearly through exegesis of the passage. The differences that Fitzmyer speaks of can shed useful light on the exegesis. Since the main subject of this pericope is the story of Jairus' daughter, the focus of the exegesis will be on this story.[140]

Verse 40 tells that Jesus has returned to Galilee. Here the crowd welcomes Jesus, and Luke underscores the positive response and attitude of the crowd throughout his narrative.[141] Specifically, Luke uses the word

---

137. Fitzmyer, *The Gospel according to Luke I-IX*, 744. However, he notes that the same verb used in resurrection account (24:6) has different nuance, which is not a resuscitation, a return to physical, earthly existence.

138. Green, *The Gospel of Luke*, 351.

139. Ibid., 350.

140. This story is also a sub-genre of miracle stories like the story of the widow of Nain (7:11–17), which focus on Jesus.

141. Stein, *Luke*, 260. For the role and function of the crowd in Luke (and Acts), see Ascough, "Narrative Technique," 69–81; Tyson, "The Jewish Public in

προσδοκάω to denote the crowd's waiting for Jesus in v. 40. Along with ἀποδέχομαι, which means "to welcome or to receive," which is used only in 9:11, προσδοκάω is used to indicate a positive acceptance or reception.[142] However, the crowd in the Gospel of Luke is not always presented as having a positive attitude or response to Jesus. Rather, they are like spectators since "when Jesus gets serious about teaching his disciples how to live after his departure, references to the crowd are lacking."[143] Moreover, an unspecified group of people in vv. 51–54 laughs at Jesus when he claims that the dead girl is not dead, although they are not the same crowd as that in v. 40. Thus, the attitude and response of the crowd toward Jesus and his teaching are ambivalent. The reason for the ambivalence of the crowds can be understood in the context of first-century Jewish eschatology. Bovon explains that the waiting of the crowd in v. 40 is not just the usual waiting; rather, "one 'awaits' (προσδοκάω) the Messiah.[144] In this regard, Bovon extends his argument to the fact that the crowd's reception is related with joy,[145] which is a result of encountering and experiencing the Messiah and his work. At the same time, they "still have to learn how to go to meet someone."[146] In other words, the crowds do not have clear recognition of who the Messiah is and how to respond properly. The point that Luke wants to make by providing the ambivalent response of the crowd is that whether the response is positive or negative, not all people are going to follow or believe in him, only those who have faith in him and acknowledge him as the Messiah. Those who have faith in him can experience the reversal of fortune that the Messiah, Jesus, will give. The story of Jairus and the bleeding woman clearly exhibit this point.

Luke–Acts," 574–83. Tyson shows that crowds, especially the Jewish in Luke–Acts are described as antagonistic to Jesus and his teaching. Minear has more extensive study of people as audience in the Gospel of Luke. Minear, "Jesus' Audiences," 81–109. The word λαός in the passion narrative of Luke is well explained in Kodell, "Luke's Use of *Laos*," 327–43. For a study of the crowd in the Gospels, esp., Matthew, Cousland's work is one of the finest. Although he shows the distinctiveness of the crowd's identity, role, and narrative functions in the Gospel of Matthew from what they are in the other Synoptic Gospels, this work includes and compares each Synoptic Gospel with good balance. Cousland, *The Crowds in the Gospel of Matthew*.

142. Bovon says that in Luke's time Christians are awaiting his parousia. Bovon, *Luke*, 1:333.

143. Bock, *Luke*, 1:790.

144. Bovon, *Luke*, 1:336.

145. For joy and laughter in the Gospel of Luke, see Inselmann, *Die Freude Im Lukasevangelium*. See also Wenkel, *The Emotion of Joy*; De Long, *Surprised by God*. De Long includes this story of Jairus in particular in the category of praise after healing

146. Bovon, *Luke*, 1:336.

The story of the reversal of weeping begins when Jairus, a ruler of the synagogue, comes to Jesus in v. 41. Luke, along with Matthew, uses ἄρχων τῆς συναγωγῆς (ruler) instead of Markan ἀρχισυναγώγων (leader/head of the synagogue). Luke's use of ἄρχων is intentional since he uses ἀρχισυναγώγου later in v. 49.[147] By using ἄρχων τῆς συναγωγῆς, Luke attempts to demonstrate Jairus' dignity rather than his role or particular office. The point is that Jairus is "an official representative of Judaism who here prostrates himself before Jesus."[148] Thus, Jairus is without doubt an honorable, well known, and respectable man in his time. And this man is now falling at Jesus' feet to implore Jesus to come to his house and heal his only daughter. By showing one of the noblest men kneeling down to Jesus, Luke wants to magnify the greatness and dignity of Jesus. This scene of Jairus' kneeling down to Jesus echoes the Magnificat, especially in 1:52: καθεῖλεν δυνάστας ἀπὸ θρόνων καὶ ὕψωσεν ταπεινούς. However, Jairus does not claim his high positions in order to ask Jesus' coming to his home. Rather, he kneels down with humility and submits himself to Jesus.[149]

The tension is intensified when Luke adds more detail in v. 42 about the girl. She is Jairus' only daughter and her age is only twelve. As noted previously, the word μονογενής ("only") intensifies the urgency of Jairus.[150] The daughter's age is of interest as well. A twelve-year-old girl in ancient times was eligible for marriage.[151] In other words, twelve was the age for when a female could begin giving birth. "The tragedy is intensified by the fact that the daughter who lies dying has just become nubile, and is thus at an age at which she can give life to others."[152] A girl who can give a life to others is now under the risk of losing her own life. For the sake of the dying girl, the noble man is now falling at the feet of Jesus. Moreover, the use of the imperfect tense παρεκάλει, which indicates uncertainty of the result,[153] displays the urgency and humility of Jairus as well. Jairus might next have acknowledged that his high status cannot solve the problem that he confronts. He needs to rely entirely on Jesus now. There is no other option for him but Jesus.

147. Usually there were three to seven leaders in Jewish synagogues and their responsibility was to arrange services or serve as a synagogue board member (Acts 13:15).

148. Nolland, *Luke*, 1:419.

149. For more discussion, See Green, *The Gospel of Luke*, 345.

150. See the same word used in the story of the widow of Nain, 7:12. Also note that μονογενὴς is not used in either Matthew or Mark.

151. Strack and Billerbeck, *Kommentar zum Neuen Testament*, 3:374. Also see, *Gospel according to St. Luke*, 234.

152. Bovon, *Luke*, 1:336.

153. BDF, §328. Also Barton, *Syntax of Mood and Tenses*, 15.

Luke's use of the phrase παρὰ τοὺς πόδας (at the feet of) not only indicates that Jairus is a would-be disciple,[154] but also is used throughout the narrative when there is healing of disease or forgiveness of sins (7:38; 8:35; 17:16). All those who appear in stories where παρὰ τοὺς πόδας is used experience healing and forgiveness of sin; 17:16 is different from the other two in that the Samaritan leper falls at Jesus' feet to express gratitude rather than to ask for something. However, all stories show that the person who fell at Jesus' feet show great humility, recognizing Jesus as the Messiah. Hence, the use of παρὰ τοὺς πόδας foreshadows that Jairus' daughter will be healed. Differently speaking, Jairus who is now experiencing a status reversal, from greater to lesser, will experience another reversal. Luke intends his readers to realize that the reversal can happen not only for those who are in lower position but also for anyone who suffers.

To increase the tension, Luke provides another story of an incident that blocks Jesus from accomplishing Jairus' urgent ask. The crowd's pressing on Jesus in v. 42 also heightens the tension.[155] Jairus might have been perplexed since the incident delayed Jesus' progress to his home. While the crowd surround and press on Jesus, somebody touches him. A seriously ill woman blocks the way of Jesus and Jairus. Jesus immediately knows that somebody has touched him, but no one knows who did it, since there were so many people pressing on Jesus. When Jesus asks who touched him, a woman who has had a discharge of blood for twelve years comes up and shows herself to Jesus. She has suffered from this illness for twelve years, and no doctor could heal her. To Jairus, this is a bad delay and a serious interruption.[156] The juxtaposition of the two stories gives dramatic tension and heightens the crisis. Not only the juxtaposition but also the healing stories give suspense. According to Tannehill, "the narrator of Luke has various ways of increasing this sympathy and adding suspense, thereby heightening interest in the afflicted person's fate."[157] In other words, the purpose of inserting another healing story is to provide suspense and tension to the story of Jairus. Thus, the appearance of the bleeding woman leads readers to focus on Jairus' daughter and her fate.

---

154. Ibid.

155. Bovon thinks the use of plural of "crowd" (οἱ ὄχλοι) is intentional to underscore the pressing. Bovon, *Luke*, 1:336.

156. Full commentary on the story of the hemorrhaging woman is beyond the scope of this dissertation.

157. For more detail, see Tannehill, *The Narrative Unity of Luke–Acts*, esp. 1:89–96. Tannehill explains how the exorcism and healing stories of Jesus play the narrative function in the Gospel of Luke.

While Jesus is spending his time with the hemorrhaging woman, the girl dies. Verse 49 clearly shows connection between the time taken with the woman and the girl's death by the use of the adverb ἔτι: "The opening phrase underlines the fact that the delay caused by the episode with the woman is the immediate cause of Jesus' not reaching the sick girl before she dies."[158] The news that someone from Jairus' house brings is that his daughter is already dead. Everything seems to be over for Jairus. The messenger confirms that she has died. Luke uses perfect tense rather than Mark's aorist, which indicates the finality of Jairus' daughter's death with the messenger's saying: μηκέτι σκύλλε τὸν διδάσκαλον.[159]

However, the tension that comes from the death of Jairus' daughter begins to be resolved when Jesus' responds to the news that the messenger has brought. Luke wants to portray that Jesus became actively involved in conversations by using the verb ἀκούω rather than Mark's παρακούω.[160] Jesus is still attentive to Jairus' request and what has happened to his daughter. He is not overhearing but focusing on Jairus' daughter. Accordingly, he answers, "Do not fear, only believe, and she will be well." This answer of Jesus "encapsulates the whole of the larger section constituting Luke 8 of the Gospel. Fear must give way to a faith that encompasses a proper recognition of Jesus' identity and concomitant trust in his ability to provide salvation."[161] Jesus proceeds to Jairus' home to prove his words.

When Jesus arrives at Jairus' home, he brings three disciples and the parents of the dead girl into the room where the girl is. There is much debate over the reason for Jesus' allowing only a limited number of people to attend the resurrection, but it is likely that the point that Luke wants to make is simple: "to mention the witnesses who were present during the raising from death."[162]

There is an ambiguity at the beginning of v. 52, for the referent of πάντες is not clear. The ambiguity comes because Luke shortens Mark's account. In Mark 5:38–39, the mourners were already inside of Jairus' house and Jesus put them all outside (Mark 5:40). Luke does not explain this,

---

158. BDF, §340, 341; Burton, *Syntax of Mood and Tenses*, 176; Wallace, *Greek Grammar*, 572–77. Here the perfect tense is used to emphasize the completed action.

159. Bock, *Luke*, 1:799.

160. According to *BDAG*, παρακούσας in v. 50 is "to listen to something when one is not personally addressed, *hear what is not intended for one's ears, overhear*."

161. Green, *The Gospel of Luke*, 350.

162. Bock, *Luke*, 1:800. As Nolland points out, the secrecy motif is not dominant in Luke; it is a feature of Mark. Thus, the discussion of the secrecy motif, including v. 56, is not of interest to Luke. For this secrecy motif, see Theissen, *The Miracle Stories of the Early Christian Tradition*, 149–51.

so the mourners seem to be outside and they come into the place where the girl is lying down with Jesus and his company. However, the problem is whether the referent of πάντες includes Jairus or not, because it surely includes the mourners and possibly the family apart from the parents of the girl.[163] It might not include Jairus and Jesus' three disciples, Peter, John, and James.[164] However, it is important to distinguish the identity of ἔκλαιον δὲ πάντες from that of κατεγέλων αὐτοῦ. They are not necessarily the same group. Those who weep for the girl's death do not all ridicule Jesus. Jairus, who has already put his trust in Jesus (Matt 9:18) wept over his only daughter's death.[165] In this sense, the weeping of Jairus among all mourners is true weeping.

The presence of the mourners implies that the girl has been dead for some time. After the death, one calls for mourners, which can be professional mourners or friends and relatives. Weeping and wailing with beating of breasts is typical Jewish custom for expressing grief, especially mourning of death (Luke 23:27, 48). It is an intense expression of mourning.

To those who weep because of the death of Jairus' twelve-year-old daughter, Jesus says, μὴ κλαίετε, the same words that he has spoken previously to the widowed mother in Nain.[166] Since the story of Jairus is parallel to that of widow of Nain, μὴ κλαίετε is an intentional device Luke uses to alert his readers to expect the same occurrence, the raising up the dead, which has happened in Nain. "Verbal repetition links similar stories, inviting comparison of the narratives."[167] The repetition not only links the stories, it also emphasizes the author's theology.[168] Thus, Luke's repetition here of μὴ κλαίετε strongly echoes the reversal of weeping in the story of the widow of Nain as well as foreshadows the same thing happening again soon. Moreover, the act of mourning through weeping and wailing, especially as standard practice at funerals, can be understood in the context of reversal. "The emotional heaviness that the terminology of mourning draws from funerary practices underlines the importance of the reversal of mourning

---

163. Morris, *Luke*, 177; Card, *Luke*, 117.

164. Evans, *St. Luke*, 392.

165. Matthew records this account as ἡ θυγάτηρ μου ἄρτι ἐτελεύτησεν· ἀλλὰ ἐλθὼν ἐπίθες τὴν χεῖρά σου ἐπ' αὐτήν, καὶ ζήσεται, showing that Jairus' daughter is already dead, but Jairus trusts in Jesus to raise her up.

166. The only difference is that the plural is used, since the mourners were weeping.

167. Resseguie, *Narrative Criticism of the New Testament*, 43. The technique of repetition in Bible narrative is well explained in Alter, *The Art of Biblical Narrative*, 88–113. The repetition technique is not limited to verbal repetition. Rather it includes motif, theme, sequence of actions, and type-scenes, and so on.

168. Resseguie, *Narrative Criticism of the New Testament*, 44.

promised in the advent of salvation, both during the career of Jesus of Nazareth and anticipated in the eschaton."[169] Therefore, μὴ κλαίετε is a sign that the reversal of weeping is imminent.

After Jesus tells the mourners not to weep, he gives them the reason to stop weeping: "She is not dead but sleeping." The word for "sleeping" is καθεύδει, a metaphor for death that can be found in the OT (2 Kgs 4:31, 13:21, Job 3:13, 14:12, Ps 13:3, Jer 51:39, etc.).[170] Those who attend inside Jairus' house take Jesus' word literally and so begin laughing at him (κατεγέλων αὐτοῦ). καταγελάω usually denotes "to laugh" but it also has strong sense of "ridiculing."[171] Here, the latter is more plausible since the use of imperfect κατεγέλων vividly describes that the mourners mock and ridicule Jesus. As Bovon points out, their laughter is "reminiscent of the doubt."[172] However, Jesus' command μὴ κλαίετε is not only for the mourners who ridicule Jesus. The true recipient of Jesus' command is Jairus (and his wife). Of all of them he is the person who truly weeps. Although the text does not say that he weeps and wails, he is the one who experiences genuine grief. He cannot help crying because of his precious only daughter's death. Him Jesus commands, "μὴ κλαίετε." For him, Jesus' words that she is not dead but sleeping must be a glimpse of light. Only Jairus can hope that Jesus' word is literal, not figurative.

In this light, the true meaning of "sleeping" in v. 52 does not match the mourners' understanding. Rather, "the point is the contrast between death and sleep; death is not final, for it is possible to be wakened from it. Thus, death is reinterpreted from the point of view of God, which is different from that of men, and cannot be appreciated by them."[173]

> In Luke, the girl is not beyond Jesus' power to overcome death. Where God is active, death need not be the end of existence nor

---

169. Green, "Mourning," 162.

170. For the OT background study of death and the metaphor, see McAlpine, *Sleep, Divine and Human in the Old Testament*. McAlpine also provides information that the metaphor for death as "sleep" was common and found in Mesopotamian and Egyptian literature (esp. 117–53). N. T. Wright's work has much more information on the Jewish and pagan views of life after death. See, Wright, *The Resurrection of the Son of God*. In particular, chapters 1–4 deal extensively with the ancient understanding of death and hope beyond death. Wright makes use of a great amount of information from very ancient paganism to postbiblical Judaism, on the topic. In spite of its consistent focus on the topic of resurrection, this volume is a great resource for study of Jewish views of death and the afterlife.

171. We can see the glimpse of those who laugh (6:25b), which will discuss in the next chapter. They are doubtful on what Jesus does and live according to their belief.

172. Bovon, *Luke*, 1:452.

173. Marshall, *The Gospel of Luke*, 347.

need it nullify the reality of a future before him. The raising is a sign of God's power to resurrect and makes the point that death is not the end of existence for humans. The "sleep" of the child is not a premature death, but rather a temporary rest that allows Jesus through resurrection to show his power.[174]

Indeed, describing the girl's death as sleeping implies a new beginning of the experience of God's power. Jairus and his wife, as well as the mourners, would witness this great power of God's through Jesus.

Now, Jesus raises the girl. He takes her hand to help her sit up, calling out, "Child, arise" (ἡ παῖς, ἔγειρε). Luke uses the word ἐφώνησεν rather than more general λέγει found in Mark. Jesus' calling out is not just normal speaking to the dead girl but is a wake up call from sleep. It also indicates the active power of the word.[175] The verb ἔγειρε used here is the same verb in 7:14 (ἐγέρθητι).[176] Luke avoids Mark's use of ταλιθα κουμ, which is a Greek transliteration of Aramaic in order to fulfill his intention of showing plainly that the girl's rising up is the same as that of the young man in the Nain.[177]

Jesus raises the dead girl and gives her life. As soon as her spirit returns, she gets up. The return of the girl's spirit (ἐπέστρεψεν τὸ πνεῦμα) is an expression unique to Luke. It is shown in Luke 23:46, which Jesus calls out the Father to commit his spirit. In addition, Stephen's death in Acts 7:59 has the same one. According to Bovon, the idea behind returning of the spirit of the dead comes from Jewish thought. "The spirit or soul of a dead person remains for a while (the Jews usually thought of three days) in the vicinity

---

174. Bock, *Luke*, 1:802. Meier has a sophisticated comment on the "sleeping," although his focus is on Mark, not Luke: "Put more properly, Jesus is taking a well-known euphemism and twisting it to a different end. The frightening difference of death, the very essence of death as opposed to sleep, is its inexorable permanence. Now, a Pharisaic Jew might have understood girl's death can be seen as transitory sleep because on the last day God will raise the girl to eternal life. But Mark's story is concerned with something more specific and immediate. The good news Mark means to proclaim by the Jairus story is that, in the presence of Jesus, not only must demons flee and sickness give way, but even death loses its permanent grip on human beings. In Mark 5:39 death is declared mere sleep not because of a cagey medical diagnosis or a comforting euphemism or a general eschatological hope but because Jesus wills in this particular case to make death as impermanent as sleep by raising the girl to life" (Meier, *A Marginal Jew*, 2:844).

175. Bovon, *Luke*, 1:340.

176. The differences are the tense and voice of the verbs: 8:54 uses the present active, while 7:14 uses the aorist passive. For the latter, see §3.2.

177. Green explains that Jesus' command is for two parties. On the one hand, it is for the crowds, and on the other it is for the girl, her parents, and the three disciples. Green, *The Gospel of Luke*, 350–51.

of the corpse, before it departs forever for the world of the dead."[178] Wright also says, "The idea of a soul separable from the body, with different theories as to what might happen to it thereafter, was widespread in the varied Judaisms of the turn of the eras. Several inscriptions bear witness to this kind of belief."[179] If this is the case, the return of girl's spirit is, for those who lived in the times of Jesus, perfect restoration. Moreover, Jesus commands that food be given to the girl, clear evidence that there is no hallucination or vision at work here.[180] Now we can see that the reversal of weeping has occurred. The true weeper, Jairus, the girl's father, weeps no more. The weeping father receives the greatest comfort because his only daughter is alive now.

After the resurrection, Luke reports the response of the girl's parents. They are surprised. However, Luke does not provide editorial comments similar to those in 7:17 that tells that Jesus is the greatest prophet in which the people call him a great prophet. The reason for the difference can be found in Jairus' faith. As said earlier, Jairus has put his trust in Jesus (Matt 9:18). Also, throughout Luke 8, the significant theme is faith. Not only Jairus but also the hemorrhaging woman has faith in Jesus. Although the theme of faith is dominant in the Gospel of Mark, it is more clearly shown in the story of Jairus and the hemorrhaging woman.[181] In the midst of extreme hardship, their trust in Jesus led them to healing and resurrection. "The faith that is intended is the confidence of the individuals in the power of Jesus; that the woman is cured and the girl is raised did not happen as mode of deliverance or salvation without faith. In both stories, Luke has introduced this relationship."[182] From these words an important principle of the reversal of weeping can be identified: faith plays a significant role in the reversal of weeping. In other words, Jesus can make reversal of weeping happen without any other human effort, but he can bring the reversal of weeping to those who have faith in him. In this sense, faith itself is not the power to move God to act.[183] Rather, faith is an important pathway along which God's salvation and reversal take place.

---

178. Bovon, *Luke*, 1:340.

179. Wright, *The Resurrection of the Son of God*, 142. See Nolland, *Luke*, 1:421 for a counter argument against Bovon and Wright that the return of the spirit is not exclusively Jewish.

180. Bock, *Luke*, 1:804.

181. For more detail, see Marshall, *Faith as a Theme in Mark's Narrative*. Most commentaries on Mark deal with the theme as a significant one. Also see Dunn, *Jesus Remembered*, 500–503.

182. Fitzmyer, *The Gospel according to Luke I–IX*, 744.

183. *Contra* Bock, *Luke*, 1:805.

Luke concludes the story with Jesus' charge to Jairus and his wife not to tell what had happened. No clear reason has been stated for this silence in Luke.[184]

The story of the raising of Jairus' daughter provides some insights into the reversal of weeping. First, Luke makes Jairus' story parallel to that of the widow of Nain rather than to the intercalating story of the hemorrhaging woman. The intention of the evangelist is clear: to highlight the reversal of weeping as an important theme in the narrative. One can easily see that Luke arranges the stories according to his narrative intention, which is to show the reversal of weeping as an illustration of 6:21. The verbal repetitions are clearly found in the two stories, such as the use of μὴ κλαίετε and ἐγείρω. These repetitions make clear the narrator's intention and theology. Thus, the focus of the stories is none other than the reversal of weeping.

Second, as seen in the story of the widow of Nain, Jesus is the bringer of the reversal of weeping. He also the initiator of the reversal of weeping. He initiates and brings the reversal to those who are weeping *now*. Of significance is *now* as shown in 6:21b. The reversal is not solely future or exclusively eschatological. It is certain that the present reversal of weeping points to a future fulfillment, but it happens in this present age as well. At the center of the reversal of weeping is Jesus. Where Jesus is, weeping is no more. Jesus is the visitation of God (Luke 7:16), which is one of the points of the story.

Third, the noteworthy point in the story of Jairus is faith. In the story of the widow of Nain, faith is not explicitly mentioned, but it is clearly shown in Jairus' story. Jesus makes the reversal of weeping happen to those who have faith in him. The story of the hemorrhaging woman emphasizes the point that her consistent faith is what Jesus is looking for. In this regard, faith has an important role in the reversal of weeping. Faith is to recognize who Jesus is and to place one's whole trust in him. One can weep now, but one will laugh at last.[185] Jairus' story is a great example of this reversal.

The Weeping Disciple (Luke 22:54–62)

The story of the weeping disciple is that of Peter, one of the core members among the twelve disciples. This story is well known for Peter's denial of Jesus three times within the passion narrative of Luke. All four Gospels have

---

184. Here Luke is just following his Markan source.

185. Jairus does not laugh actually as the widow of Nain and the sinful woman. However, his happy ending demonstrates that he is the one of those who weep shall laugh. See §3.1.2.

the same story (Matt 26:57–58; Mark 14:53–54; John 18:12–18, 25–27), though with some differences. Accordingly, much scholarly discussion has been focused on sources and the issue of dependence among them.[186] In spite of many similarities, the Lukan account has unique elements different from the other three. Bock identifies six major differences of Luke based on the work of Creed.[187] However, the notable singularities in Luke are found in vv. 61–62, which are not in Bock's list. Thus, the focus of this section will be vv. 61–62, which deals with Peter's weeping. There is a textual issue concerning v. 62, which is missing from 0171^{vid}, a, b, e, ff^2, l, and r^1. The question is whether this omission is accidental or not. It is most likely accidental since it is hard to understand why Luke, who uses the verb κλαίειν nine times, would choose to leave out this verb.[188] Other details in the pericope (vv. 54–62) will be discussed as necessary.[189]

The pericope begins with Jesus being taken to the high priest's house (v. 54). The focus of narrative suddenly shifts from Jesus to Peter in v. 54b. Peter is following at a distance (μακρόθεν), which may indicate his fear or is an "ominous anticipation of the coming failure of Peter's 'following' of Jesus."[190] However, Luke, at the same time, shows that Peter still follows

---

186. Neyrey, *The Passion according to Luke*. As title indicates, Neyrey's work is based on the assumption that Luke redacted his sources according to his theological intention, which is christological. For the special material of Luke, see Soards, *The Passion according to Luke*. Soards intensively analyzes the Lukan passion narrative, chapter 22, and compares it to other Gospels. He thinks that Luke uses special material other than Mark and arranges his materials with compositional intention. In so doing, Luke has much freedom to use the traditions before him. See also Karris, *Luke*. For commentaries, see Bovon, *Luke*, 3:225–29. Bovon briefly summarizes the views of Luke's use of special material, possibly including oral tradition. Also see for commentators' discussion of the issue, Bock, *Luke*, 2:1775–78; Fitzmyer, *The Gospel according to Luke X–XXIV*, 1452–63; Marshall, *The Gospel of Luke*, 838–89; John Nolland, *Luke*, 3:1091–94. Furthermore, there have been various attempts to explain the uniqueness of Luke's passion narrative, e.g., Rice, "The Rhetoric of Luke's Passion," 355–76. Rice suggests that Luke used an ancient rhetorical technique, "Common-Place" to show the guilt of Jerusalem's leaders in Jesus' death.

187. Creed, *The Gospel according to St. Luke*, 275–76. First, Luke has only one meeting rather than two. Second, Luke does not record the charge about the temple. Third, in Luke the Sanhedrin does not explicitly condemn Jesus. Fourth, in Luke, Peter's denials are all together and preceded the trial. Fifth, in Luke the soldiers' mocking precedes the trail. Finally, the Gospels differ about who elicits Peter's denials; the slave girls are more prominent in Matthew and Mark than in Luke. Bock, *Luke*, 2:1775–76.

188. Nolland, *Luke*, 3:1092; Fitzmyer, *Gospel according to Luke X–XXIV*, 1465; Bock, *Luke*, 2:1804–5. Marshall is not certain. Marshall, *The Gospel of Luke*, 844.

189. In this dissertation, the focus will be on Lukan uniqueness and differences from others, whether those come from redaction, compositional arrangement, or other possibilities such as oral tradition.

190. Nolland, *Luke*, 3:1094. I also think that the adverb μακρόθεν is a marker that

Jesus by using imperfect tense, ἠκολούθει; all the other disciples who were following Jesus have disappeared.[191] So Bock comments that Peter's following may also be "curiosity or a timid attempt to be at Jesus' side."[192] Since Luke does not provide a detailed explanation of Peter's following, it is not clear what Peter's motivation is. But Peter may be following Jesus at a distance with mixed feelings, such as fear or curiosity, as Bock suggests above.

After following Jesus at a distance, Peter sits down among those who have arrested Jesus in the middle of (μέσῳ) the courtyard of the high priest's house. Luke again focuses on Peter by not naming anyone in the group sitting with him except Peter. Indeed, Peter is the center of attention not only in the courtyard of the high priest's house but also in this pericope.[193] If Peter's sitting together with them implies that he is one of those who will be against Jesus, Luke's naming him clearly indicates what he is going to do. Unfortunately, the kindled fire allows the other people to recognize who Peter is. It is a servant girl who acknowledges Peter at first. The fire might enable her to recognize Peter (v. 56). She stares at Peter and tells others that he was with Jesus. The word for "stared," ἀτενίσασα, is an expression unique to Luke, appearing only in Luke and Acts (Luke 4:20; Acts 1:10; 3:4, 12; 6:15; 7:55; 10:4; 11:6; 13:9; 14:9; 23:1).[194] It denotes "to look intently at" or "to stare at."[195] Luke uses it rather than Mark's ἐμβλέψασα (14:67, "to look at") to express looking at someone with a specific purpose. "In most instances it expresses a steadfast gaze of esteem and trust."[196] In v. 56, the verb expresses the servant girl's conviction that Peter is one of those who were with Jesus. Peter's first denial follows after the girl's saying, "This one (man) also was with him." Luke uses σύν with ἦν instead of Mark's μετά to show that Peter is one of the companions of Jesus.[197] Furthermore, Luke's use of the third person singular οὗτος has a pejorative sense, which is one variation of the purely deictic idiom due to the relation of the persons in question. According to BDF,[198] the pronoun οὗτος is used in a contemptuous

---

shows Peter's fear.

191. While Matthew and Mark give the same description as Luke, John does not. See John 18:15: there was another disciple who was known to the high priest. Luke, along with Matthew and Mark, wants to focus on Peter only.

192. Bock, *Luke*, 2:1781.

193. Marshall, *The Gospel of Luke*, 841, also thinks that the repetition of Peter's name may be for emphasis.

194. The only two cases in the NT are 2 Cor 3:7 and 13.

195. "ἀτενίζω," BDAG, 119.

196. Fitzmyer, *The Gospel according to Luke I-IX*, 533.

197. Bovon, *Luke*, 3:230. See also Schneider, *Verleugnung*, 80-81.

198. Bovon, *Luke*, 3:230. For contemptuous use of οὗτος, see Robertson, *A Grammar*

sense of a person present (cf. Luke 15:30). The selection of all these nuanced words and expressions heightens the tension of the pericope and reveals Peter's uneasiness and fear. Peter has kept silent until the servant girl began speaking.

Peter's first denial begins with strong affirmation in v. 57. Evans points out that the first denial of Peter is the strongest and the most emphatic among the three.[199] The use of the strong word ἠρνήσατο as well as οὐκ οἶδα demonstrates how serious Peter's denial is, since the expression οὐκ οἶδα means "we no longer know you" as in the phrase like the Jewish ban formulas used against those dismissed from the synagogue.[200] Thus, "it refers to the attitude of those who refuse to put their confidence in God and who reject the messengers who speak to them. This is the meaning that Luke's Christian readers give to v. 57."[201] If this is the case, Peter has spoken the opposite thing to his confession at Caesarea Philippi that Jesus is the Christ of God (Luke 9:18). Peter acknowledged that Jesus is the Son of God at Caesarea Philippi, but now he denies Jesus. Additionally, the word of Jesus in v. 34 that Peter would deny Jesus three times is here fulfilled.

It does not take long for Peter to make his second denial, which takes place "a little while" (μετὰ βραχὺ) after his first denial. There is another one (ἕτερος) who recognizes—the aorist participle ἰδὼν denotes "catching sight of"[202]—Peter, saying, "You are also one of them." Peter's second denial is very short: "Man, I am not," which denies his association with the other disciples as well.

Peter's third and last denial happens an hour (διαστάσης ὡσεὶ ὥρας μιᾶς) after the second one. Different from Mark, who puts the second and third denials together, Luke reports that the first and second denials occur one after another. "Luke, who is aware of no interrogation and nighttime trail, waits for morning and prepares for the crowing of the cock."[203] Luke attempts to describe the denial briefly. Thus, "Nicht nach kurzer Zeit (so Markus und Matthäus: μετὰ μικρὸν), sondern nach einer Stunde ritt die Frage nach der Jüngerschaft erneut an Petrus heran. Lukas will offenbar ausdrücken: die Verleugnung war keine kurze Episode. Die galiläische

---

of the Greek New Testament in the Light of Historical Research, 697. Also see BDF, §290 (6). Robertson's explanation is more detailed than the one in BDF.

199. Evans, *Saint Luke*, 825.

200. Marshall, *The Gospel of Luke*, 842.

201. Bovon, *Luke*, 3:231. He distinguishes Christian understanding of denial from that of pagans. "The pagan readers read a refusal in that verse: He denied him, locating the fault on the moral rather than the theological plane" (ibid.).

202. "ὁράω," BDAG, 719. See also Johnson, *The Gospel of Luke*, 357.

203. Bovon, *Luke*, 3:231.

Herkunft des Petrus, die nach Matth. 26.73 an der Sprache erkennbar ist."[204] There is another person, different from both the slave girl and the person in the second denial, who recognizes Peter. Luke does not identify who he is, while Mark tells that they are bystanders.[205] Luke tries to show in the pericope that the second and third accusers are insignificant, marginalized characters, so that Peter, who is named, is threatened and fearful even of insignificant characters.[206] Peter is at the center of the narrative, and his denial is the focus of interest. Another man is confident that Peter was with Jesus, since διϊσχυρίζετο denotes "to be emphatic, resolute about something, insist, or maintain firmly."[207] This man adds specific proof that Peter is Galilean; the Galilean accent must have been different from others.[208]

Luke's description of Peter's third denial is different from the other evangelists', especially that of Mark. Luke describes it simply, while Mark describes it dramatically, saying that Peter begins to invoke a curse on himself and deny Jesus (Mark 14:70). Also, Peter in Mark denies Jesus by saying that he does not know "this man" (Jesus), but in Luke Peter says, "Man, I do not know what you are talking about." This is evidence that Luke has painted Peter sympathetically throughout the narrative.[209] This is to say that Luke's focus is not Peter's denial. Luke adds to the tension by providing a detailed description of what happens at the moment of Peter's third denial: "And immediately, while he was still speaking (καὶ παραχρῆμα ἔτι λαλοῦντος αὐτοῦ), the rooster crowed." This is the fulfillment of Jesus' prediction in v. 34. The description of the rooster's crowing gradually leads the story of Peter's denial to its denouement, which is vv. 61-62.

204. Wiefel, *Das Evangelium nach Lukas*, 383.

205. John reports that he was one of the servants of the high priest, a relative of Malchus (John 18:26).

206. Resseguie summarizes the effects of anonymity. First, an overfull sobriquet may describe a character that literally and figuratively fills up the narrative. Second, anonymity may emphasize a character's traits. Third, it may also accent a character's marginalization. Finally, anonymity allows readers to identify with a character's traits. For more details, see Resseguie, *Narrative Criticism of the New Testament*, 129-30. For more depth on the issue of anonymity in the Gospels, see Malbon and Berlin, "Characterization in Biblical Literature," 3-227.

207. BDAG, 246. Thus Marshall thinks that the narrative reaches its climax here in this man's firm statement. See, Marshall, *The Gospel of Luke*, 843.

208. Matthew provides the specific reason for Peter's being Galilean in 26:73. With regard to the Galilean accent, there is a famous anecdote of a man from Galilee who went to the marketplace and was ridiculed by merchant because of his Galilean accent. See, 'Erub 53b. See also Vermès, *Jesus the Jew*, 52-54.

209. Fitzmyer, *The Gospel according to Luke X-XXIV*, 1465, thinks that the omission of detail is due to Luke's high esteem for Peter. For more details, see ibid., 564. Also see, Wiarda, *Peter in the Gospels*, 99-105 and 133-36.

Verse 61 is found only in Luke. As most commentators point out, the Lukan christology is shown plainly in v. 61. Rowe explicitly maintains that Luke's use of κύριος twice in v. 61 functions as an *inclusio* to emphasize that Jesus is more than prophet.

> Peter is allowed to waver in his faith to the point of a threefold denial of Jesus, and yet the Jesus whom he acclaims as κύριε in 5:8 and 22:33 remains the κύριος whom he rejects in 22:54–62. Jesus' identity as κύριος, that is, is not threatened by human fallibility for christological truth (κύριε) depends not upon permanence in human perception or depth of human faith but instead upon the ongoing story of the LORD.[210]

Rowe finds that no human work can change Jesus' identity as the LORD, which truth Luke wants to show throughout the narrative. Thus, Peter's failure in his denial cannot change the status of Jesus as the LORD because LORDship is not contingent on man's confession. The word ἐνέβλεψεν denotes, along with ἀτενίσασα in v. 56, "look intently" or "gaze." Whether this gaze of Jesus is reproach or not, it leads Peter to turn to Jesus as predicted in v. 32.[211]

The important point is that Jesus' look reminds Peter of the word of the LORD, which later leads him to turn to Jesus again. With the expression τοῦ ῥήματος τοῦ κυρίου ("the word of the LORD") Luke reveals his christology as that of the κύριος; Matthew uses τοῦ ῥήματος Ἰησου. As Johnson points out, "Luke's use of 'word of the LORD' gives a special *prophetic* coloration to the incident. The literal fulfillment of Jesus' prediction is in Luke's narrative just another of many prophecies that reach fulfillment."[212] It is important that this word of the LORD leads Peter to experience reversal. Green's point makes relevant sense on Peter's reversal in relation to Jesus' word and the previous stories of reversal of weeping that we have examined: "in this case,

---

210. Rowe, *Early Narrative Christology*, 178–79.

211. Nolland thinks that the intent look is reproach, while Bovon argues that Luke simply does not specify what the look means Bovon's argument is more plausible in that Luke does not give any detailed description of Jesus' look: "The readers know that he has lost his freedom of movement. What they learn is that Jesus uses his last remaining right, the right to turn his head and look at his disciple. The evangelist does not describe this look. All that once can say is that Jesus is concerned not about himself but about his disciple. Does he reveal sadness? Or does his look contain a reproach? Or does he want to be right? We do not know. Luke merely shows the effect the look produces" (Bovon, *Luke*, 3:232–33). See also Nolland, *Luke*, 3:1096.

212. Johnson, *The Gospel of Luke*, 358. Johnson thinks that "word of LORD" is the signature of the prophet, which is seen elsewhere in the Prophetic books such as Isa 1:10; 28:14; Jer 1:4; 2:31; Hos 1:1; 4:1; Joel 1:1; Amos 5:1; 7:16; Jonah 1:1; Mic 1:1; 4:2; Zech 1:1; Hag 1:1; Zeph 1:1.

to the sort of lament known earlier in Luke as an acknowledgment of one's own sinfulness or a precursor to the reversal that comes with divine restoration (6:21; 7:13, 38; 8:52)."[213] In other words, Peter's status shifts from denial to restoration. The word of the LORD can make it happen.

The reversal of weeping is now shown in v. 62. Peter goes out and weeps bitterly (καὶ ἐξελθὼν ἔξω ἔκλαυσεν πικρῶς). The weeping of Peter is clearly that of repentance since he has already remembered the LORD's word and gone out to weep bitterly. Thus, "'Weeping' mars the beginning of Peter's 'turning' (cf. v. 32), even if, on account of his particular focus on Jesus, Luke now dismisses Peter from the scene."[214] Moreover, the adverb πικρῶς emphasizes that Peter's weeping is that of remorse and repentance.[215] Indeed, the restoration has already begun for Peter. Thus, Peter's weeping is not just the beginning of reversal. His restoration is not explicitly told in the Gospel of Luke, but in John's narrative, Peter's true restoration comes later. Luke also shows the restoration of Peter, but it is in Acts, where he provides the contrast to his denial by describing his powerful preaching to the Jews (Acts 2: 14–42), his healing of the lame beggar (Acts 3:1–10), and bold speech before the Council (Acts 4). However, the focal point of the reversal of the weeping of this disciple is shown in vv. 61–62. The reversal of weeping begins when Peter encounters Jesus, which is described as Peter being stared at by Jesus, the LORD who fulfills his word. Luke wants to show that Jesus is more than the prophet depicted in 7:16. He is the God-sent Messiah. He is God, who vindicates his weeping people. Although his people betray and deny him, he restores them from their sin.

From the story of Peter's denial, some insights into the reversal of weeping can be obtained. First, the result of the reversal of weeping does not always happen immediately. It can happen in the intermediate future, one that is neither immediate nor eschatological. Peter's complete restoration does not come immediately, but it comes after Jesus meets him and restores him. Like the hope of those who weep in the OT and Second Temple literature, so is Peter's change of fortune coming up in the future.

---

213. Green, *The Gospel of Luke*, 788–89. Also see Bovon's comment. "More important than a physical movement, it is a matter of an inner reversal (see ἐπιστρέψας, 'once turned around,' 'once converted,' (v. 32). With this 'conversion' the apostle appears to be the model of the believer. And Luke is concerned to make clear that the one who speaks the word to Peter, then looks at him, is not simply 'Jesus,' but 'the LORD'" (Bovon, 3:233.)

214. Green, *The Gospel of Luke*, 789.

215. The expression "weep bitterly" is found in the LXX to denote a response to defeat, failure, ruin and loss (Isa 22:4; 33:7 and Ezek 27:30) See Fitzmyer, *The Gospel according to Luke X–XXIV*, 358.

Second, the starting point of the reversal of weeping is when one encounters the LORD. In the OT, those who encounter the LORD God experience significant change. Luke also shows that though Peter has already confessed that he is a sinner (5:8), he definitively confirms that he is a sinner by his denials. But Peter encounters Jesus once again and begins to experience the reversal of weeping at the moment Jesus turns to him and looks at him to remind him of Jesus' word. Thus, an encounter with the LORD is the beginning of the reversal.

Third, the reversal of weeping is christological, as seen in the stories of the widow, the sinful woman, and Jairus. It reveals Jesus as the LORD, not just one master among many. As pointed out earlier, Jesus not only fulfills his word but also changes his people's fortunes. Weeping cannot keep them from him. Rather, the weeping of God's people is the beginning of the reversal.

Conclusion

In this chapter, we have examined the reversal of weeping in the positive direction: those who weep shall laugh. The passages discussed illustrate this. Those who weep for various reasons, such as loss, death, sin, and denial of the LORD, experience the reversal of their fortunes. Their suffering and hardship, which is expressed through weeping, is compensated for by Jesus. They laugh at last.

However, their laughter is not necessarily to be understood literally because it implies their satisfaction and joy. This may be why Luke does not use γελάω as *Leitwort*. Rather, he focuses on κλαίω to highlight the theme of the reversal of weeping. To provide different examples of people weeping, Luke illustrates his interest in marginalized groups, such as widows, sinful women, and Gentiles. He attempts to show that Jesus focuses on this marginalized group. Also, by emphasizing the present situation of those who weep ("now" in 6:21b), Luke shows how their destiny will be reversed by the bringer of reversal, Jesus, who is portrayed as the promised prophet. The focus is christological and the reversal of weeping is Christ centered.

CHAPTER FOUR

THE REVERSAL OF JOY TO WEEPING

This chapter will examine the reversal of joy to weeping in the Gospel of Luke: οὐαὶ οἱ γελῶντες νῦν, ὅτι πενθήσετε καὶ κλαύσετε (Luke 6:25b). Luke's use of this reversal *to* weeping is consistent with his use of the reversal *of* weeping. They both use the word κλαίω and present the idea of reversal. As the reversal of weeping is an illustration of the Lukan beatitude found in Luke 6:21b, so also the reversal to weeping is an illustration of the Lukan woe in Luke 6:25b.

Luke also achieves his portrayal of 6:25b throughout the narrative; reversal to weeping functions as a significant and distinctive theme. While the reversal of weeping occurs in the contexts of Jesus' miracles and in the travel narrative, the reversal to weeping is alluded to in Jesus' discourses, especially in the passion narrative.

In this chapter, three stories that illustrate the reversal to weeping will be discussed after an examination of Luke 6:25b.

Luke 6:25b as the Programmatic Statement of the Reversal of Weeping

Luke 6:25b belongs to the "woe" section (6:24–26) of the Sermon on the Plain.[1]

Unique to Luke, this series of woes parallels the series of blessings found immediately before in 6:20–23. Both blessings and woes remind readers of God's final act of justice.[2] Both the reversal of weeping in 6:21b

---

1. For detailed discussion on the Sermon on the Plain, see chapter 3.
2. Bock, *Luke*, 1:566. Bovon thinks that they came from Lukan redaction rather than from a pre-Lukan source, listing five evidences of Lukan redaction: (1) Luke's

and the reversal to weeping in 25b use the word νῦν ("now") to show that the reversal of weeping occurs in the present life. Both state the subject using the present participles (κλαίοντες, γελῶντες) and state the predicate using the finite future (γελάσετε, κλαύσετε), one in v. 21 and two (πενθήσετε and κλαύσετε) in v. 25b.[3] However, the significant difference lies not in the verbal aspect or usage but in those whose fortunes will be reversed: those who weep in 6:21b and those who laugh in 6:25b. In other words, just as Luke portrays those who weep as those who are marginalized from the community or society but whose fortunes shall be reversed by Jesus, so he also portrays those who laugh as those who are self-satisfied but whose fortunes Jesus will also reverse. As seen in chapter 3, those who laugh in 6:25b are not identical as those who shall laugh in 6:21b. In this regard, it is necessary to examine the word γελάω first.[4]

In the NT, the word γελάω ("laugh") can only be found here in Luke 6:21b and 25b. Its use in the LXX, however, is abundant, with not only a positive connotation of joy and satisfaction, but also a negative association with looking down on the fate of enemies and being in danger of becoming boastful and self-satisfied (Gen 17:7; 18:12, 13, 15; Esth 4:17; Ps 51:6; Jer 20:8; Lam 1:7).[5] Here Jesus is borrowing the idea from OT Wisdom literature that laughter is the mark of a fool (Sir 21:20; 27:13; Eccl 7:6).[6] Thus, there is an ontological difference between those who laugh in 6:25b and 6:21b. The former are people experiencing worldly ease and are indifferent because of self-satisfaction, while the latter are those who are currently experiencing tragedy and poverty.[7] If this is the case, it is reasonable to think that those who laugh in v. 25b are enjoying their self-satisfied status apart from God and other people in this present age, whereas those who laugh in 6:21b are those who will receive God's consolation. Regarding the former, Luke illustrates in three separate pericopes how the fortunes of those who laugh now will be reversed to weeping (7:31–35; 19:41–44; 23:27–31). Although the word γελάω is not used explicitly in these passages, the reversal

---

familiarity with the genre of woes that can be found elsewhere in Luke (10:13; 11:42–52; 17:1; 21:23; 22:22); (2) the contras of rich and poor, which is typically Lukan; (3) the unique Lukan expressions such as πεινάω that appear next to ἐμπίμπλημι and καλῶς λέγω, and so on; (4) the match of the second person plural of the woes with the Lukan beatitudes. Bovon, *Luke*, 1:223.

3. Goulder thinks that Luke already knew Matthew's beatitudes and so added πενθήσετε to κλαύσετε. Goulder, *Luke*, 354–55.

4. As said in chapter 3, Luke does not use this term as *Leitwort*.

5. Marshall, *The Gospel of Luke*, 256. See also Johnson, *The Gospel of Luke*, 107.

6. Fitzmyer, *The Gospel according to Luke I–IX*, 636–67.

7. Bock, *Luke*, 1:584.

to weeping principle shows that those whose fortune will be reversed are those who laugh now.

One more thing to note is that Luke also uses κλαίω, but not γελάω, repetitively as a literary device, a *Leitwort*. This use of κλαίω implies that Luke wants to develop his reversal of weeping stories with κλαίω rather than γελάω. In other words, it is important to understand not only who those are who laugh but also how their fortunes will be reversed and that they will weep. Put differently, an important task is to grasp what is meant by their weeping in the stories of reversal of weeping. In this case, we will focus on those who laugh: how their fortune is reversed in this present world and the near future, and what the end result of their reversed fortune is.

The Weeping Generation (Luke 7:31–35)

Luke 7:32 is located within the third section (7:31–35, which parallels Matt 11:16–19) of the larger unit 7:18–35 (par. Matt 11:2–19). The first section begins with Jesus responding to John the Baptist's disciples and stating through OT prophecy that he is the promised Messiah (7:18–23). The second section has Jesus looking at the crowd, describing John the Baptist as the greatest among those born of a woman, and ending by saying that the least in the kingdom of God is greater than John (7:24–30). The third section is Jesus' evaluation of this generation. Green summarizes the contents of the section's three subunits as "the nature of Jesus' ministry, his identity, and the response he engenders."[8] According to this description, the passage in view is included within the response Jesus provokes.

Luke 7:31–35 consists of a parable, its interpretation, and a proverb-like maxim. This pericope is difficult to interpret for two reasons: The first difficulty is identifying the referent of the "children" (παιδίοις) in the marketplace and the second person plural (ὑμῖν), which seems to denote another group of children in vv. 31–32 and can be interpreted in two ways: Are we to understand that it is John and Jesus who do the calling, and it is 'this generation' who will not respond? Or should we understand the opposite, that is, that 'this generation' calls and it is Jesus and John who will not respond?[9] Second, the meaning of v. 35 is hard to understand and has long been debated. How one resolves these two interpretive and exegetical issues will determine the meaning one assigns to the pericope. Thus, a careful examination of the two issues is critical. The reversal of weeping principle

---

8. Green, *The Gospel of Luke*, 294.
9. Cotter, "The Parable of the Children in the Market-Place," 294.

enables us to identify the referent of children and "you" in vv. 31–32, and so to interpret the maxim in v. 35.

Many scholars believe that the pericope that features the parable of vv. 31–35 begins with vv. 29–30. For instance, Bovon argues that vv. 29–30 is a Lukan redactional summary that "narratively prepares a prophetic accusation of the hard heartedness of the leaders of Israel."[10] Bock's comment is more detailed and persuasive: "Luke contrasts people and tax collectors with the Pharisees in anticipation of Luke 7:31–35. Thus, the parenthesis is a bridge between Jesus' remarks about John (7:24–28) and Jesus' evaluation of the current generation based on their response to the Baptist (7:31–35)."[11] It is reasonable to see, following Bovon and Bock, that vv. 29–30 are the introduction to the pericope of vv. 31–35 because they are closely connected in content to what follows.[12]

Jesus begins his parable in v. 31 with a familiar OT formula, Τίνι οὖν ὁμοιώσω, which is used in the Prophets and the Book of Lamentations (Lam 2:13; Isa 40:18, 25; 46:5; Ezek 31:2).[13] The expression γενεᾶς ταύτης ("this generation") is sometimes used as neutral (Luke 1:48, 50; 21:32), but Luke uses it against those who opposed the prophet's message (Luke 9:41; 11:29, 30, 31, 32, 50, 51; 16:8; 17:25; Acts 2:40).[14] At first sight τῆς γενεᾶς ταύτης seems to refer to the specific group Jesus was addressing, especially the Pharisees in v. 30. However, Luke's addition of ἀνθρώπους broadens the boundary of the referent; this may be an instance of Lukan universalism.[15] Thus it is more likely that the referent of τῆς γενεᾶς ταύτης is not just the Pharisees but all those who oppose Jesus and his message. "In the role played by γενεά in

---

10. Bovon, *Luke*, 1:284. Nolland also includes vv. 29–30 in the pericope. He admits that vv. 29–30 have a transitional role, but concludes that they are part of the pericope because v. 29 has an obvious link with v. 35. Nolland, *Luke*, 1:341. See also Johnson, *The Gospel of Luke*, 123. See the long discussion in Green, *The Gospel of Luke*, 199–302. However, see Fitzmyer, *The Gospel according to Luke I–IX*, 673.

11. Bock, *Luke*, 1:677.

12. Wolter, *Das Lukasevangelium*, 284. Wolter also sees vv. 29–30 as a narrative introduction: "Der dritte Teil besteht aus einem Bildwort mit Einleitung und Anwendung (V. 31–34; Parallele in Mt 11, 16–19) und einer narrativen Einleitung (V. 29–30), auf die sich das Schlusswort in V. 35 bezieht."

13. This expression is used mostly by to describe the kingdom of God (Luke 13:18, 20; Matt 13:24; 18:23; 22:2; 25:1). See Schneider, "ὁμοιόω," *TDNT* 5:189.

14. Johnson, *The Gospel of Luke*, 123. The expression is also used as a biblical idiom in the OT (Deut 32:5; Judg 2:10; Ps 78:8; Jer 2:31; etc.); it has a negative connotation of an unbelieving, disobedient, and undisciplined people.

15. For Luke's universalism, see the previous chapter. In v. 31, the addition of "people" is not strictly seen as Lukan universalism as it is in other passages, but it can be understood as universalism in that the addition broadens the boundary of the target group that Jesus intended.

the sayings of Jesus we can see His comprehensive purpose—He is aiming at the whole people and not at individuals—and His view of solidarity in sin."[16] The referent of τῆς γενεᾶς ταύτης includes the Jews who oppose Jesus, not just that specific group of Pharisees and Jewish authorities.

The interpretation of the parable in v. 32 depends on how one identifies the referent of the children in the marketplace.[17] Some interpreters propose that the children sitting in the marketplace represent Jesus and John. The "game" that Jesus offers is to lead people to dance with joy by playing the flute, while John's "game" is to get people to weep by singing a dirge.[18] In this case, the other group of children, "you," denotes the people of this generation listening to the message of Jesus and John. "The children who invite the others to play (first at wedding, then at funeral) would represent John and Jesus and their followers. The children who sulk and refuse to join are their Palestinian contemporaries, 'the people of this generation,' rejecting both the asceticism of John and the unhampered attitude of Jesus."[19] This interpretation is influenced by vv. 33–34, where John and Jesus are the subjects.[20] According to this interpretation, the parable is teaching that while Jesus and John call this generation to dance and weep—perhaps symbolizing fellowship with sinners through eating and drinking, and repentance through weeping, respectively—they do not respond. The parallel structure of this parable supports this interpretation.

A. We played the flute for you (v. 32a)

B. And you did not dance (v. 32b)

A'. We sang a dirge (v. 32c)

---

16. Büchsel, "γενεά," *TDNT*, 1:662–65.

17. A more complex identification of the referent of the children sitting in the marketplace is to identify the first children as suggesting wedding play and the second children as offering funeral play. In this case, one group of children changes the mode of the game because the other group of children, "you" in v. 32b and 32d, do not accept and join the game that the first group offers. This option is based on Luke's use of ἀλλήλοις. See Hoffmann, *Studien zur Frühgeschichte der Jesus-Bewegung*, 226. See also, Jeremias, *The Parable of Jesus*. However, the general thrust of the parable is that "flightiness, moodiness, and desire to have [one's] own way (however that desire may change from moment to moment) are the objects of Jesus' rebuke" (Meier, *A Marginal Jew*, 2:147).

18. For more detailed and vivid description of this game in the first-century context, see Jeremias, *The Parable of Jesus*, 161. He discusses the version in Matt 11:16 rather than the Lukan version.

19. Fitzmyer, *The Gospel according to Luke I–IX*, 679. See also Zeller, "Die Bildlogik," 252–57; Meier, *A Marginal Jew*, 2:148–49.

20. Cotter, "The Parable of the Children in the Market-Place," 295.

> B′. And you did not weep (v. 32d)

A′. John the Baptist has come eating no bread and drinking no wine (v. 33a)

> B′. And you say, "He has a demon" (v. 33b)

A. The Son of Man has come eating and drinking (v. 34a)

> B. And you say, "Look at him! A glutton and a drunkard, a friend of tax collectors and sinners (v. 34b)

In this chiastic structure, the responses to John the Baptist and Jesus are parallel—though the order of Jesus and John are reversed, joy–sorrow–sorrow–joy, in antithetical parallelism—and the logical sequence clearly fits. In other words, v. 32 and v. 33 correspond to each other by logical order: the dirge is the preaching and asceticism of John the Baptist, and the lack of weeping is the refusal to repent.[21] Jesus does explain the meaning of the parable by picking up on the latter, but the weakness of this option is that the comparison is between "people of this generation" and "children sitting in the marketplace."[22]

Others suggest that the children in the marketplace are "this generation," people who have not received the messages of Jesus and John. In this case, the children sitting in the marketplace are "this generation," who complain that John and Jesus do not follow their desires. Bock identifies "the children" more specifically as the Jewish leaders: "From the leaders' perspective, God's messengers are at fault for not listening to them. The leaders do not wish to enter the game unless it is played according to their rules. This generation is like children who will play only if they can make the rules."[23] However, the weakness of this option is: "In this understanding, the complaints of the sulking children find even a chronological order. The last mode of interpretation may be allegorizing the passage more than is called for."[24]

---

21. Garland also sees vv. 32–34 as a chiastic structure. However, his structure has no center in it. Thus, it is better to see the structure of these verses as a parallel. See Garland, *Luke*, 317.

22. See, Green, *The Gospel of Luke*, 302–3. See also Cotter, "The Parable of the Children in the Market-Place," 295.

23. Bock, *Luke*, 1:681. Most recent scholars adopt this position. See Plummer, *Gospel according to St. Luke*, 207; Marshall, *The Gospel of Luke*, 301; Bovon, *Luke*, 1:180; Nolland, *Luke*, 1:299–301.

24. Fitzmyer, *The Gospel according to Luke I-IX*, 679. Meier also opposes this interpretation because "the intricate intersection created by the chiasm might lead one to expect a tighter fit in interpretation as well as in structure" (Meier, *A Marginal Jew*, 2:148).

Indeed, both these interpretive options above have strengths and weaknesses, but the first option fits better in logical sequence (joy-sorrow-sorrow-joy, in antithetical parallelism) and chiastic structure than the second: to see Jesus and John as the children in the marketplace offering the game of wedding and funeral, and "you" as "this generation" opposed to the message Jesus and John deliver.

This evaluation is confirmed when the parable of the children in the marketplace is seen as an example of the reversal of weeping. This pericope is sandwiched between two stories of the reversal of weeping: the story of the widow of Nain (7:11–17), and the story of the sinful woman (7:36–50). In these two stories of the reversal of weeping, Jesus is the protagonist, bringing a reversal of fortune to those who weep. The widow of Nain and the sinful woman both experienced a change of fortune by *responding positively* to Jesus and his word. Thus it is not Jesus who responds to their message; it is rather those who weep who respond to the message of Jesus. For this reason, the referent of "you" is "this generation" who do not respond to Jesus and the John the Baptist' offering games.

If Luke 7:31–35 is seen in line with the examples of the reversal of weeping that precede and follow it, the referent of "children in the marketplace" is Jesus and John, who convey the message, and "this generation" refers to those who do not respond to God's messengers. If Luke is illustrating his reversal of weeping theme in three consecutive stories, these three passages have thematic unity.[25] Moreover, vv. 29–30 mention two groups of people who have responded to John the Baptist: "all the people," including tax collectors, who have been baptized by John, and the Pharisees and the lawyers (v. 30), who had not. The former group is those who wept, which means responded to the message of repentance of John, while the latter laughed, which means satisfied with their present life. Thus, the focus of Luke is the response of "this generation" to the message of Jesus and John, not the people's desire to control the message of Jesus and John the Baptist. Therefore, it is reasonable to take the first interpretive option in light of the reversal of weeping stories as well as in light of the logical sequence and chi-

---

25. Neale also thinks that Luke 7:28–35 and 7:36–50 have a thematic unity in that both passages focus on sinners by excluding the Pharisees. See Neale, *None but the Sinners*, 135–37. See also Kilgallen, "John the Baptist," 675–79. Kilgallen shares the same understanding with Neale: "Indeed, in the light of this relationship between 7:24–35 and 7:36–50, one can see that the story of the woman and the Pharisee is not really a story of forgiveness to prove Jesus' power to forgive; it is rather concerned with the tragic irony that those who are sinners are accepting the plan of God, whereas the religious leaders, the 'men of this generation,' are not." For more broad information of sinners in the first century A.D., see Sanders, *Jesus and Judaism*, 174–211. Sanders argues that sinners were those who rejected God's commandments intentionally.

astic structure. For this reason, the parable of children in the marketplace is addressing the unresponsiveness and hardened heart of "this generation." In this respect, the expression "the people of this generation" is "reminiscent of the frustrating portrayal of the people of God as stubborn, stiff-necked, [and] rebellious."[26]

One more thing worth observing in the parable is the game that the children play. Cotter carefully examines the words used to describe this game and their ancient backgrounds to clarify the meaning and imagery of the parable. He first focuses on the verb προσφωνέω. After surveying its usage, especially in Luke, he concludes that the meaning of the verb is not simply "to call out." Rather, more precisely, the verb is used to express the action "to address" or "give speech to," used often to refer to a dignified and formal speech.[27] Cotter's second interest lies in the word "marketplace," ἀγορᾷ. He reminds readers that the marketplace not only was the center of everyday life, e.g., social fellowship, religious festivities, and the like, but also played a major role in the court system. The use of ἀγορᾷ would also echo the sense of "court" in the minds of the first-century audience.[28] Finally, Cotter deals with the expression τοῖς ἐν ἀγορᾷ καθημένοις ("sitting in the marketplace"). Building from his understanding of ἀγορᾷ, this phrase expresses the action of sitting in the court waiting to hear the judgment rendered by the judge.[29]

Cotter's study of backgrounds gives an insight.[30] Jesus and John the Baptist are sitting in the courtroom and giving a formal address to the unresponsive generation: ηὐλήσαμεν ὑμῖν καὶ οὐκ ὠρχήσασθε, ἐθρηνήσαμεν καὶ οὐκ ἐκλαύσατε. The parable is about judgment against "this generation," represented by the Pharisees and scribes in v. 30. Those who do not respond to Jesus and John the Baptist are like "those who laugh" in Jesus' woe of 6:25b since they are satisfied with their present situation and do not attempt to respond positively to the message from God. In other words, "those who laugh" in 6:25 is a synecdoche.[31] They will, however, obey the call to weep of v. 32. Their present happiness will turn into real weeping. The reversal to weeping will be actualized. They do not accept the true joy and happi-

---

26. This echoes the Exodus story, which tells of the unresponsiveness of the Pharaoh and the Israelites. See Green, *The Gospel of Luke*, 302.

27. Cotter, "The Parable of the Children in the Market-Place," 296–97.

28. Ibid., 298–99.

29. Ibid., 299–302. Cotter gives a second interpretive option, but that would take us beyond the scope of this dissertation.

30. Although Cotter seems to overinterpret through focusing on one kind of activity in the marketplace, the courtroom setting is still persuasive to see that the parable is about judgment.

31. For synechdoche, see §3.1.2

ness that Jesus offers. Jesus explicitly tells of this reversal in the passage that follows.

In vv. 33–34, Luke describes the hardness and unresponsiveness of this generation more plainly. Both verses use the same verb ἔρχομαι in the perfect tense, different from Matthew's use of aorist.[32] In other words, it links the past with the present situation. Luke is known to engage in prophetic commission by using the perfect tense.[33] Moreover, "the use of the second-person λέγετε shows that some rejecters are in the crowd."[34] What is the content of Jesus and John's proclamation? Without doubt, the message of John the Baptist focuses on repentance (Luke 3:7–17). Jesus' description in v. 33 speaks of John's life and message as a whole. Some of the people responded to the message of John the Baptist (Luke 3:10, 12, 14), but Luke does not record that Pharisees or leaders of the Jewish people were among them. The responsive people included tax collectors and soldiers, whom Luke's readers would have considered the worst of sinners. The unresponsive group reacts to John the Baptist by saying, "He has a demon."[35] Thus, Jesus in Luke symbolizes John's command to repent as weeping, and the rejection of that message by "the people of this generation" as their refusal to weep.

As Luke shows in 3:3, the message of John the Baptist is that of repentance.[36] John says to those who come to be baptized, ποιήσατε οὖν καρποὺς ἀξίους τῆς μετανοίας ("therefore bear fruits worthy of repentance," 3:8). Thus the message he offers to "this generation" is that they need to repent of their sins. The weeping symbolizes the repentance that "this generation" does not want to do. In this sense, "this generation" rejects the command to weep, but they will eventually engage in true weeping as the result of judgment.

Unlike John, Jesus "manifest[s] no ascetic restraints in taking ordinary sustenance, as a token of the freedom of the kingdom that he was proclaiming."[37] Jesus' dining with sinners and tax collectors is "a part of his campaign to restore sinners."[38] Against this message of freedom the people

---

32. The perfect tense has the theological advantage of combining the action of the past (the event) with the meaning for today. See Wallace, *Greek Grammar*, 579–80.

33. Bovon, *Luke*, 1:287.

34. It can refer to "you" in v. 32. Bock, *Luke*, 1:682.

35. According to Garland, people might have been saying that John the Baptist had a demon because only supernatural beings can live without food or water. Garland, *Luke*, 317.

36. καὶ ἦλθεν εἰς πᾶσαν [τὴν] περίχωρον τοῦ Ἰορδάνου κηρύσσων βάπτισμα μετανοίας εἰς ἄφεσιν ἁμαρτιῶν.

37. Fitzmyer, *The Gospel according to Luke I–IX*, 681.

38. Garland, *Luke*, 317.

of this generation refuse to join the Son of God at the table with joy. They do not accept true laughter provided by Jesus, and by default fail to understand true weeping. They say, ἰδοὺ ἄνθρωπος φάγος καὶ οἰνοπότης, φίλος τελωνῶν καὶ ἁμαρτωλῶν ("Look at him! A glutton and a drunkard, a friend of tax collectors and sinners"). They bring calamity upon themselves by not responding to God's message. Their fortune hinges on their response to the messages of Jesus and John.

There is a difficulty in interpreting v. 35. Because this proverbial saying concludes the pericope, its meaning certainly sheds light on the interpretation of the whole parable. The wisdom (σοφία) noted here does not directly point to Jesus himself, for Luke does not use wisdom to indicate Jesus in his gospel. Instead wisdom here is "a personification of God's counsel and means 'God in his wisdom.'"[39] In the OT and Second Temple literature, the personification of wisdom is a popular theme (Prov 1:20–33; 8:1–9:6; Sir 1 and 24; Bar 3 and 4; *1 Enoch* 42; 4 Ezra 5:10; Wis 7:22–11:1, etc.). Wisdom here is described as God's way of communicating with his children, i.e., his chosen people.[40]

This wisdom is said to be justified by "all her children." To whom does "all her children" refer? First, it should be noted that v. 35 is not a part of the parable of v. 32; it is the ending remark of the pericope (7:31–35). Therefore, one must not make the mistake of identifying wisdom's children here with the marketplace children mentioned in the parable. This implies that the referent is not Jesus. Instead God's wisdom is demonstrated through Jesus (and John the Baptist) and is "proven right" by those who respond positively. As Meier rightly points out, wisdom is God's wise, well-ordered plan of salvation, which is now reaching its climax through the words and works of His prophets, John and Jesus.[41] Put differently, those who respond to Jesus' message and accept him are wisdom's children. In this sense, the Jewish leaders and the Pharisees are not wisdom's children, although they consider themselves so. Luke replaces Matthew's "deeds" (τῶν ἔργων) with "all her children," but both demonstrate the same point.[42] Unresponsive people cannot share in God's wisdom, while those who accept them do so.

---

39. Ibid., *contra* Fitzmyer.

40. "She here stands for divinity in its concern with humanity, particularly with the chosen people, and she receives her due through her loyal dependents, her 'children.' In the course of salvation, and perdition, history, she has recognized, proclaimed, and to this extent been justified again and again by these few 'children'" (Bovon, *Luke*, 1:287).

41. Meier, *A Marginal Jew*, 2:152.

42. "It is hard to explain this difference, other than to suggest that wisdom's works in Matthew's Gospel are referred to in Luke's Gospel in terms of the product—the responding people. In other words, Luke's version lacks the figure" (Bock, *Luke*, 1:684).

Concerning the reversal of weeping, the pericope seems to have no explicit statement of the reversal of weeping at first sight. However, as stated above, the parable is about judgment. Jesus' charge is that this generation does not receive the true joy and forgiveness that he has brought. In the context of the reversal of weeping, this generation will weep in the near future. John the Baptist's charge is that this generation does not weep, or in other words, repent. They are satisfied with their present situation. Thus, they will weep. This parable, its application and conclusion, illustrates the woe in 6:25b in that it pronounces judgment on an unresponsive generation.

From the pericope as a whole, we can find several common factors of the reversal of weeping. First, the one who can bring about the reversal is Jesus. This is made clear through his saying in v. 35; he is the true medium of God's wisdom.[43] Second, one of the significant elements in the reversal of weeping is the recipient's response. Like the stories of the reversal of weeping that are located immediately before and after, this pericope emphasizes the importance of one's response to God's messengers and messages. Those who accept God's message possess God's wisdom; those who reject it face judgment; they are not to be vindicated. Third, unresponsiveness is deeply rooted in a present-oriented way of life, and this generation attempts to receive God's wisdom by way of this orientation. This is one of the aspects of laughter. They will eventually weep because their accusers have already charged them. Their fortunes will be reversed to weeping. On the whole, Luke 7:31–35 shows an important picture of those who laugh. They are an unresponsive generation satisfied with this present world that rejects God's wisdom.

The Weeping Savior (Luke 19:41–44)

Luke 19:41–44 is the second lament of Jesus over Jerusalem; the first is recounted in 13:31–35.[44] This lament of Jesus follows his entry into Jerusalem, where he is met with joy and the welcome of the crowds (19:28–38). Luke relates that as Jesus is on his way, he rebuffs the Pharisees' criticism (19:38–40). When he draws near Jerusalem, he weeps and predicts the

---

43. Paul says that Jesus is God's wisdom (1 Cor 1:24, 30), but Luke does not express Paul's idea here.

44. See the excellent article of Fisk, "See My Tears," 147–48, for these passages. See also Tannehill, "Israel in Luke–Acts," 69–85. Tannehill sees the text, along with three others (13:33–35; 21:20–24; 223:27–31) in the context of "speak of Jerusalem," "its rejection of Jesus," and "its coming destruction." Notice that Eklund sees Jesus' lament in 19:41–44 as a dirge. Eklund, "LORD, Teach Us How to Grieve."

doom of the city in a lament recorded only in Luke. After this lament, Jesus enters the temple and cleanses it.

In v. 41, Luke uses the word ἤγγισεν, a word used frequently throughout the travel narrative as part of the journey motif.[45] This occurrence in 19:41 is the last in the travel narrative, perhaps implying that the journey of Jesus is almost over. In addition, this occurrence of ἔκλαυσεν is the only mention of Jesus weeping in the Synoptic Gospels.[46] By adding the preposition to the verb, ἔκλαυσεν ἐπ' ("wept *over*"), Luke wants to demonstrate that the emotion of Jesus is stronger than that expressed by δακρύω ("shed tears"; [Luke 7:38, 44]).[47] Jesus is weeping not for himself, but for Jerusalem, the city of God, the city of Peace. "In contrast to Luke 13, Jesus' lament lacks entirely the self-conscious ἐγώ: he sheds no tears for himself, only for Jerusalem."[48] Wright expands the point: "He did not see himself as a prophet entrusted with a task simply for his own generation, one member of a long, continuing line. . . . The stories he told, and acted out, made it clear that he envisaged his own work as bringing Israel's history to its fateful climax. He really did believe he was inaugurating the kingdom."[49] In v. 41, the weeping of Jesus is the center of the scene. It not only calls up the reversal of weeping motif by using ἔκλαυσεν, but also provides the context for the lament that follows. There are three points that can be made concerning Jesus' weeping.

First, Jesus' weeping over the city is a prophetic gesture that echoes the actions of the OT prophets, especially Jeremiah.[50] In Jer 8:23 of the LXX, the prophet foresees the destruction of Jerusalem and weeps over it: τίς δώσει κεφαλῇ μου ὕδωρ καὶ ὀφθαλμοῖς μου πηγὴν δακρύων καὶ κλαύσομαι τὸν λαόν μου τοῦτον ἡμέρας καὶ νυκτὸς τοὺς τετραυματισμένους θυγατρὸς λαοῦ μου ("Oh that my head were waters, and my eyes a fountain of tears, so that I might weep day and night for the slain of the daughter of my people!"). Likewise, as Jesus weeps for his own city's destruction, he is portrayed as a prophet like Jeremiah.[51] This is in fact constant throughout the whole Gospel

---

45. For the travel narrative, see chapter 3. The word ἤγγισεν is Lukan. It appears eighteen times in Luke, seven times in Matthew, and only three times in Mark.

46. The other occasion that shows Jesus' weeping is John 11:35.

47. Bovon, *Luke*, 3:17.

48. Fisk, "See My Tears," 173.

49. Wright, *Jesus and the Victory of God*, 197.

50. 2 Kgs 8:11; Neh 1:4; Ps 136:1; Jer 9:1; 14:17; and Lam 1:1. Fitzmyer, *The Gospel according to Luke X–XXIV*, 298.

51. Jesus' portrayal as a Jeremiah-like prophet is well attested in the work of Zamfir. Like Jeremiah's prophecy, the prophecy of Jesus is against the Temple, and he is also a model of a persecuted prophet. Although Zamfir does not deal with 19:41–44 explicitly, as she does with 13:31–35 because the former is rather lament than indictment, the

of Luke, and all the more in the reversal of weeping stories. For example, in the story of the widow of Nain, the people who witnessed the miracle confess that Jesus is a great prophet who has arisen among them (7:16). In the story of the sinful woman, Simon the Pharisee thinks that Jesus is a prophet (7:39). In the story of the unresponsive generation, Jesus is in the same line with John the Baptist, God's messenger, a prophet (7:31-35). In the lament in 19:41-44 as well, Jesus is presented as the true prophet, the antitype of Jeremiah. Jesus' pronouncement and lament for Jerusalem are prophetical.

Second, the weeping of Jesus foreshadows the reversal of fortune that the people of Jerusalem would soon experience. His weeping is not about peace or joy but about judgment and punishment from God. The lament that follows Jesus' weeping confirms the point. In other words, Jesus' weeping is an indication of reversal for he knows what will happen to them: weeping will become reality for the people.

Third, the cause of this reversal of fortune can be found in the response of the people toward the God-sent prophets. As stated in the previous section (7:31-35), the response of "this generation" to God's messenger is determinative of this reversal. Jesus weeps for those who laugh now. Jerusalem here can be equated to "this generation" in 7:32. With these points in mind, we now turn to Jesus' lamentation. It is with these points in mind that Jesus' lamentation needs to be discussed.

The *aposiopesis*, which means "sudden-silence,"[52] in v. 42 (εἰ ἔγνως ἐν τῇ ἡμέρᾳ ταύτῃ) indicates an unfulfilled wish that is contrary to reality.[53] Thus, Jerusalem fails to recognize τὰ πρὸς εἰρήνην ("the things that make for peace in reality"), seen also in 13:31-35. The expression ἐν τῇ ἡμέρᾳ ταύτῃ καὶ σύ ("on this day also/even you") has at least three alternative readings in different manuscript families.[54] The interpretation of v. 42b depends on the

---

echoes of Jeremiah are obvious in 19:41-44. Zamfir, "Jeremian Motifs," 139-76. For the Lukan presentation of Jesus as a prophet, see Verheyden, "Calling Jesus a Prophet," 177-210. The work of Boring is worth consulting: Boring, *The Continuing Voice of Jesus*. However, for intensive discussion on this topic, Jesus as a prophet, see Wright, *Jesus and the Victory of God*, 147-97. For Jesus as an Elijah-like prophet, see chapter 3.2.

52. It refers to the "sudden breaking off of what is being said (or written), so that the mind may be the more impressed by what is too wonderful, or solemn, or awful for words: or written a thing may be, as we sometimes say, 'better imagined than described.' Its use is to call our attention to what is being said, for the purpose of impressing us with its importance" (Bullinger, *Figures of Speech Used in the Bible*, 151).

53. Marshall, *The Gospel of Luke*, 718. "The force is: 'If only you knew now . . . the future would hold something better for you, *or* it would be pleasing to me.'"

54. Bock categorizes the options according to the manuscripts. "(1) ἐν τῇ ἡμέρᾳ ταύτῃ καὶ σύ ("in this day also you"; ℵ, B, L, Origen), (2) καὶ σὺ ἐν τῇ ἡμέρᾳ ταύτῃ ("and you in this day"; D, Θ, many Itala, some Coptic), (3) καὶ σὺ καί γε ἐν τῇ ἡμέρᾳ ταύτῃ ("and you also indeed in this day"; A, Ψ, family 1), and (4) καὶ σὺ καί γε ἐν τῇ ἡμέρᾳ σου

rendering of καί, which can be translated either as "even" because it helps listeners recall the privileges of the holy city,[55] or as "also" in connection with vv. 37–38.[56] The former rendering is more persuasive because neither the multitude nor the disciples did not clearly recognize that the day of Jesus' coming to Jerusalem would be the day of vindication and visitation of God. Taking καί as "even" points out the failure of Jerusalem to recognize the way to make peace even in this late hour of judgment.[57]

Clearly, τῇ ἡμέρᾳ ταύτῃ has a theological dimension; it is used differently here from its usage in, for example, v. 43, where it is the coming of Jesus to Jerusalem, rather than the day of judgment, that is eschatological.[58]

What Jerusalem has not recognized is τὰ πρὸς εἰρήνην. Contrary to her name, Jerusalem, the city of peace, she has been blinded from peace.[59] "Jerusalem . . . stands as a cipher for Israel as a whole; hence, not only must it be the ultimate destination of the prophet proclaiming a message of reform, but it is there, where the message of reform contrasts most sharply with accepted beliefs and practices, that resistance to the prophet will reach its acme."[60] "Peace" in v. 42, is "peace with God," i.e., salvation.[61] In rejecting the

---

ταύτῃ ("and you also indeed in this your day"; W, Δ, family 13, Byz, Lect, many Syriac)." Bock, *Luke*, 2:1566. He prefers the first reading, which has superior external evidence in the major Alexandrian witnesses, but all make the point that the city has missed its day. However, Bock does not leave the option for rendering καί as "even" rather than "also." The nuance and meaning of "this day" can be different when καί is taken as "even." See the discussion above.

55. Bovon, *Luke*, 3:17. Fitzmyer, Garland, Green, Marshall, Johnson, and Stein agree with Bovon. Most English versions take καί as "even" (ESV, NIV, NRSV, and so on).

56. Nolland, *Luke*, 3:931.

57. Evans' detailed and lengthy comment on this expression is helpful: "The manuscripts vary here between 'in this day, even you', 'even in this day' and 'even you at least (even) in this day'. Behind these variations may lie two different conceptions. 'in this day' refers in the context to the coming of Jesus to Jerusalem, or his whole mission to Israel, as the crucial moment in her history, perhaps as the fulfillment of what prophets had said would happen 'in that day', i.e., in the eschatological time. The failure to recognize this, shown by the rejection of Jesus—which is here seen in advance, and before Jerusalem has been given a chance to show her mind (cf. 9:22; 18:31f., and possibly 1335)—will be the evidence that Jerusalem's eyes have been blinded. 'in your day' means the day of divine visitation (cf. Jer 50:31; Ezek 22:4); but this generally denotes the day of destruction already determined, when the time for recognition and repentance has passed. If kai in the sense of 'even' is to be taken with *today* the meaning could be 'even at this late hour.' If taken with *you* in the sense of 'also', the meaning could be 'you, like my disciples'" (Evans, *Saint Luke*, 683–84).

58. Ibid.

59. Jerusalem here indicates the Israel.

60. Green, *The Gospel of Luke*, 537.

61. Green encapsulates the concept of peace in v. 42. "'Peace' in Luke has no

God-sent Messiah, Jesus, Jerusalem has failed to be reconciled with God. Jerusalem did not understand the true meaning of God's coming in Jesus. She thought she was already at peace with God. But Jesus rejects her confidence by pronouncing judgment.

This peace with God, i.e., salvation, is now hidden from Jerusalem: νῦν δὲ ἐκρύβη ἀπὸ ὀφθαλμῶν σου. This blindness of Jerusalem is the tragic result of failure to respond to God and bears the fruit of weeping.[62] One interesting feature of this blindness is that only God can reverse it (cf. Isa 29:18; 35; 42:16), since it is a result of God's judgment. The concept of blindness and restoration from it is clearly connected to Jesus' rebuke of the Jewish leaders in the Gospels.[63] Thus, νῦν δὲ ἐκρύβη ἀπὸ ὀφθαλμῶν σου implies that God has judged Jerusalem's inability to understand the truth of God and her unresponsive attitude towards God's eschatological prophet. This blindness is intensified by the use of νῦν. She is still failing to recognize God's salvific offer even now. Jerusalem is the prime example of one who presently laughs with the false belief that laughter, which is current conditions, will continue.[64] However as Jesus proclaims, a reversal of fortunes is imminent.

The portrayal of Jesus in vv. 41–42 is, no doubt, that of a prophet. As said above, weeping over the city like that of Jeremiah provides the background for Jesus' weeping as a prophet. However, there is a critical difference between Jesus and the other prophets in the Old Testament: Jesus' prediction or prophecy is fulfilled with his coming. In other words, Jesus' coming is the fulfillment of his prophecy of judgment over Jerusalem. His coming inaugurates the kingdom of God (Luke 4:16–21).

---

connection to harmony with the Roman Empire or with the temple leadership, nor does it refers to subjective or individualistic tranquility. Peace, rather, is a soteriological term—shalom, peace and justice, the gift of God that embraces salvation for all in all of its social, material, and spiritual realities" (ibid., 690). "Peace includes the absence of war, as the rest of the oracle makes clear, but the word is shorthand for much more: justice, reconciliation, prosperity, friendship, tranquility, safety, security, and redemption (cf. 13:34; Isa 52:7–9)" (Fisk, "See My Tears," 174). For further study of peace in the Gospel of Luke, see Comblin, "La Paix Dans La Théologie de Saint Luc," 439–60. See also the more recent work of Kilgallen, "'Peace' in the Gospel of Luke and Acts of Apostles," 55–79.

62. The image of blindness that relates to the inability to recognize truth or respond to God is found in the OT (Deut 28:28–29; Isa 6:9–10; 29:9–10).

63. The most recent is Hartsock, *Sight and Blindness in Luke-Acts*, which surveys the contemporary literature and the OT as well as other portions of the NT and Luke-Acts. For a similar work, see Parsons, *Body and Character in Luke and Acts*.

64. Of course, the laughter of those who laugh here is to indicate the state of being satisfied with their present condition in metaphorical sense. This is consistent in Luke's use of "laughing" in presenting the reversal of weeping, especially in neative direction.

Prophecy (vv. 43–44) quickly follows Jesus' lament, more evidence that Jesus is being presented as a prophet. The prophetic formula ὅτι ἥξουσιν ἡμέραι ἐπὶ σὲ ("for the days will come upon you") is a phrase commonly used not only in the OT (Joel 9:7; Amos 4:2; 8:11; 9:13; Zech 14:1; Mal 4:1; Isa 39:6; Jer 19:6) but also in Luke (5:35 and 23:29). It signifies impending significant events, obviously judgment here. "Jerusalem's rejection of him (42a, 44b) is now to be matched by God's rejection of the city (43–44a)."[65] This prophetic portrayal of Jesus is intensified by use of the series of future verbs in v. 43, ἥξουσιν, παρεμβαλοῦσιν, περικυκλώσουσίν, and συνέξουσίν.

Jesus uses the image of war to pronounce judgment on Jerusalem: the city will be surrounded by enemies, who will set up barricades on every side. Scholars have debated whether the saying is a *vaticinium ex eventu* concerning the destruction of the Temple in A.D. 70.[66] Bultmann writes that it is: "The saying of Jesus in vv. 42–44 is a *vaticinium ex eventu*. Whether it was conceived together with the introductory scene in v. 41 it is impossible to say. But it is no imaginary scene."[67] Due to their revelatory nature, Bultmann thinks these verses are a Christian construction; they are not Jesus' original sayings.[68] However, recent scholars have been uncertain about identifying these verses as a *vaticinium ex eventu*, because vv. 43–44a contain apparent echoes from the OT as well as general descriptions of besiegement in ancient war.[69] Wright sees more of the latter: "It is far more plausible to regard the details of the passage as extrapolations from ancient biblical prophecy than to read them as lame and inaccurate attempts to turn history, after the event, into pseudo-prophecy."[70] Dodd, on the other hand sees a direct correlation between vv. 43–44a and the OT: "It appears, then, that not only are the two Lucan oracles composed entirely from the language of the Old Testament, but the conception of the coming disaster which the author has in mind is a generalized picture of the fall of Jerusalem as imaginatively presented by

---

65. Fisk, "See My Tears," 174–75.

66. Thus, the question of *vaticinium ex eventu* brings out the problem of dating Luke. If v. 43 refers to the actual event of A.D. 70, the date of Luke is later than A.D. 70, and Luke wrote his work after the fall of Jerusalem. For the description of Josephus, see *War* 5.11.4 §466; 5.12.2 §508. See also ibid., 6.418.

67. Bultmann, *The History of the Synoptic Tradition*, 36.

68. This weakness is typical of Bultmann's theology. He is convinced that it is almost impossible to know the original setting of the history in which the historical Jesus lived, so he thinks the Gospels are work theologically and confessionally colored by the early church.

69. This make Bultmann's argument likely implausible because the portrayal of Jesus in this passage is that of a prophet who continues in the tradition of OT prophecy and is at the same time the fulfiller of it.

70. Wright, *Jesus and the Victory of God*, 349.

the prophets."[71] Dodd rightly argues that the picture and conception of the destruction of Jerusalem comes from the prophets, though he overstates that the Lukan composition comes entirely from the OT. It is more reasonable to think that Luke uses both the OT *and* the general image of warfare and revises his sources, mostly from the LXX, according to his purposes. The five threats in vv. 43–44 demonstrate this point more fully.

There are five threats that are prophesied about Jerusalem; each threat is rooted in OT themes. Three threats appear in v. 43 and the other two in v. 44. The first threat is χάρακά, which means "palisade," or "entrenchment."[72] Jesus prophesies that enemies will set up a palisade around Jerusalem. The second threat is περικυκλώσουσίν, that is, surround or encircle: the enemies will encircle Jerusalem. The third threat is συνέξουσίν[73] σε πάντοθεν ("press on you from every side"): enemies will not only encircle Jerusalem but allow no one to flee by closing off every side. These threats are clear echoes of Isa 29:3 (LXX), which reads, καὶ κυκλώσω ὡς Δαυιδ ἐπὶ σὲ καὶ βαλῶ περὶ σὲ χάρακα καὶ θήσω περὶ σὲ πύργους ("And like David I will camp against you all around, and will besiege you with towers and I will raise siegeworks against you").[74] In the context of Isaiah, it is YHWH who encamps, besieges, and raises siegeworks against Jerusalem. If Luke borrowed this concept from Isaiah, it is reasonable to assume that the one who brings judgment over Jerusalem in vv. 43–44a is YHWH. In other words, the true enemy of Jerusalem is none other than YHWH. Luke wants to show that the judgment of YHWH is behind this formidable attack by enemies on Jerusalem. The prophecy is *now* fulfilled. The fourth and fifth threats appear in v. 44. The fourth is ἐδαφιοῦσίν σε καὶ τὰ τέκνα σου ἐν σοί, which echoes Ps 137:9 in LXX (MT Ps 136). Here the word ἐδαφιοῦσίν denotes "to destroy or tear down by causing something to be brought to ground level, dash to the ground,"[75] so it means the violence of war, especially a form of genocide.[76] It is used in the LXX to express the throwing to the ground of women and children in the context of the sacking of a city.[77] Luke adds "you" to "your children" to increase the horror of the judgment. The final threat is οὐκ ἀφήσουσιν λίθον ἐπὶ λίθον ἐν σοί, which echoes Mic 3:12. All these threats that allude to the

71. Dodd, *More New Testament Studies*, 79. See also Gaston, *No Stone on Another*, 359.

72. "χάραξ," BDAG, 1078. ESV translates it a more modern way: "barricade."

73. This denotes "to press in and around so as to leave little room for movement, press hard, crowd" ("συνέχω," BDAG, 970).

74. LXX adds ὡς Δαυιδ, which is not in the MT.

75. "ἐδαφίζω," BDAG, 275.

76. Fitzmyer, *The Gospel according to Luke X–XXIV*, 1258.

77. Nolland, *Luke*, 3:932. Thus, Isa 3:26; Ezek 31:12, Nah 3:10; Hos 10:14; 14:1.

OT show that Jerusalem's rejection of Jesus is reminiscent of the apostasy that preceded the destruction of Jerusalem in 586 B.C. Following suit, the rejection of Jesus results in the destruction of the Temple in A.D. 70.

Luke uses general war imagery to describe the judgment of Jerusalem. Similar language is found in 1QpHab 9:5–7.

> Its interpretation concerns the last priests of Jerusalem, who will accumulate riches and loot from plundering the peoples. However, in the last days their riches and their loot will fall into the hands of the army of the Kittim. . . . For they are the greatest of the peoples.[78]

This is commentary on Hab 2:8, which reads, "Because you have plundered many nations, all the remnant of the peoples shall plunder you, for the blood of man and violence to the earth, to cities and all who dwell in them." This prophecy was originally against the Chaldeans, but the Qumran community brings this charge against the last priests of Jerusalem. 1QpHab 9:5–7 clearly demonstrates how the leadership of the Jewish people, symbolized as Jerusalem, is in danger of destruction. In doing so, it makes use of war imagery. In this regard, Luke's use of war imagery is not only from the OT but also from the ancient Jewish concept of the war in his days.

The last part of 19:44 provides a more specific reason for Jerusalem's judgment. Here the word ἐπισκοπῆς is the center of interest. In the context of the pericope, the time of visitation refers to the eschatological time of YHWH's coming. Specifically, ἐπισκοπῆς can be used to denote God's intervention either for punishment and judgment (Jer 6:15; Deut 28:25; Sir 23:24; Isa 24:22) or for salvation (Gen 50:24–25; Exod 3:16; 13:19).[79] The time of God's visitation is now (v. 42), but Jerusalem has not recognized this and as a result is blind toward God's judgment. Throughout chapter 19, Luke presents the coming of Jesus as YHWH's coming. Luke demonstrates that the visitation of YHWH, bringing with it judgment, is now fulfilled by the eschatological prophet Jesus. "There is thus ample evidence that most Second-Temple Jews who gave any thought to the matter were hoping for YHWH to return, to dwell once again in the Temple in Jerusalem as he had done in the time of the old monarchy."[80] Luke portrays that YHWH's eschatological prophet is Jesus. Jesus brings a double-edged sword of salvation and judgment to his people. The time of visitation is intended to bring salvation, but the rejection of Jesus will result in horrible judgment. Those

---

78. Martínez and Tigchelaar, *The Dead Sea Scrolls*, 201. See also *War* 6.300 in ibid.

79. For the discussion of God's coming as visitation, see chapter 3.2. God's coming as visitation is also shown in 1QS3. 18; 4. 19; CD 7. 9; 8:2–3.

80. Wright, *Jesus and the Victory of God*, 623.

who are satisfied with their status are now under the judgment of God. Their fortunes will be reversed. In this regard, Jesus weeps in v. 42 for the people who laugh now—those who have not recognize the eschatological vindication of God.

From Luke 19:41–44 we can also identify several marks of the reversal to weeping. First, the reversal to weeping is related to the pronouncement of woe and judgment, as seen in 6:25b. By identifying Jesus' coming as the coming of YHWH, Luke shows an aspect of the day of the LORD, which is judgment.[81] If the stories of the widow of Nain, the sinful woman, and the daughter of Jairus show the salvific aspect of Jesus' coming as the day of the LORD, the lament concerning Jerusalem shows the opposite. Second, the reversal to weeping pertains to those who laugh. In Luke 19:41–44, those who laugh metaphorically, in this case Jerusalem, are blinded from the truth so that they cannot recognize the fulfillment of the promise of God in its eschatological form. They cannot identify the right time of God's visitation through Jesus. Rather, they overlook what God has promised. Luke tries to illustrate the portrayal of this laughter. From their perspective, reversal comes in a sudden, quick, and surprising way. Finally, Jesus is the only one to bring this reversal to weeping. As discussed earlier, Jesus' coming is that of YHWH. As YHWH is the only bringer of a reversal to weeping throughout the OT, so now Jesus is that bringer in the pericope. He brings judgment on Jerusalem and is rejected by her unto death. But God will vindicate and exalt him at last, which is the true and ultimate reversal.

The Weeping Women (Luke 23:27–31)

The story of the weeping women is located immediately before Jesus' crucifixion. After Simon of Cyrene is compelled to carry Jesus' cross, a group of women lament Jesus' fate in 23:26, after which Jesus warns those who follow. This episode of the weeping women (23:27–31) is only recorded in Luke's gospel, while v. 26 is matched most closely in Mark 15:21. Thus, most scholars believe that it comes from a source unique to Luke.[82] Whether

---

81. There are two aspects to the day of the LORD. On the one hand, it is the refinement or restoration of God's people. On the other, it comes with destructive force, so that those who oppose YHWH will be punished and ruined.

82. See, Plummer, *Gospel according to St. Luke*, 528; Fitzmyer, *The Gospel according to Luke X–XXIV*, 1494–96; and Bovon, *Luke*, 3:293–99. However, see *Gospel of Thomas* 79, which is similar to and only slightly different from Luke. It reads: "A woman in the crowd said to him, 'Blessed are the womb that bore you and the breasts that fed you.' He said to [her], 'Blessed are those who have heard the word of the Father and have truly kept it. For there will be days when you will say, 'Blessed are the womb that has not

Luke used his own source or revised other sources, the real focus should be on Luke's intent on including this story in his gospel.

Jesus was followed by πολὺ πλῆθος τοῦ λαοῦ καὶ γυναικῶν ("a great multitude of the crowd and women"). The expression πλῆθος πολὺ τοῦ λαοῦ is also used in 6:17, the difference between the two usages being the inclusion of "women" (γυναικῶν) here. In 6:17, Luke attempts to show that many people from all areas have come to Jesus and have become beneficiaries of the kingdom of God. This is not, however, the case in 23:27. Throughout the narrative, Luke presents λαός as the group that is favorable towards Jesus. According to Kodell, Luke uses λαός to distinguish the crowd from the Jewish leaders, especially in the passion narrative starting in 19:47.[83] The word λαός is used to refer to people who are favorable toward Jesus (19:47-48; 20:1-6, 19, 26,45; 22:2; 23:5; 24:19-20). But when it is used in relation to Jerusalem, it is depicted negatively. As Neyrey points out, "In Luke 21.23 'this people' is the object of God's wrath, the explanation for which is surely found in Jerusalem's rejection both of God's messengers (13.33-34) and of Jesus' own ministry (19.44)."[84] Minear insists that λαός refers "the largest, most inclusive audience. With few exceptions this term refers to Israel as God's covenant community, as represented by Jerusalem or by the crowds which come to hear Jesus, God's appointed messenger to them. This term bulks largest in the accounts of Jesus' birth and Passion."[85] Though Minear rightly understands λαός as referring to Israel as God's people,[86] he overlooks the fact that Israel is the recipient of not only God's blessing but also God's judgment and punishment. Thus Neyrey's point is more persuasive since he highlights both facts. Indeed, λαός is used in both ways in the Gospel of Luke.

The question is, then, how is Luke using λαός in 23:27? Is the crowd described positively or negatively? Further, why does Luke use λαός with γυναικῶν? Here the interpretive key lies in the word γυναικῶν, Jesus calls "daughters of Jerusalem" in the following verse. It is certain that λαός and γυναικῶν are not being used synonymously, since Luke specifies the referent

---

conceived and the breasts that have not given milk'" (Valantasis, *The Gospel of Thomas*, 158).

83. Kodell, "Luke's Use of *Laos*," 328-31. For more information on "people" or "crowd" in Luke, see chapter 3.3. See also Fitzmyer, *The Gospel according to Luke X-XXIV*, 1497.

84. Neyrey, "Jesus' Address to the Women of Jerusalem," 75.

85. Minear, "Jesus' Audience, according to Luke," 81-109. Especially see 89. He analyzes "the people" (λαός), "the crowd" (ὄχλοι), "the disciples" (μαθηταί), and "the twelve" and "the seventy-two," all of which have different meanings.

86. See also Dahl, "'A People for His Name,'" 319-27.

in v. 27 in relation to v. 28. In other words, many people follow Jesus but γυναικῶν are the specific group among the λαός that Jesus targets.[87] This passage runs parallel to 19:41–44 and 7:32, which are both reversal of weeping stories. In all three passages Luke depicts two groups: a group of people who are onlookers (both Jerusalem's inhabitants and visitors for the festival), and a group of women who are beating their breasts and lamenting as they follow Jesus. Once again, Luke's focus is on the latter. For this reason, the question of who these women in v. 27 are is important. Various suggestions have been made by scholars.

First, a number of scholars classify γυναικῶν as sympathizers.[88] The word used to describe the women's lamenting (ἐθρήνουν) denotes verbal mourning or singing of dirges, possibly echoing Zech 12:10–14.[89] However, some argue that this kind of lamenting by women was prohibited in public because they were mourning for a man who is condemned to death. Klein asserts, "Es war nicht gestattet, einen zum Tode Verurteilten zu betrauern. Aber da Pilatus selbst Jesus dem Volk überläßt, können auch die Stimmen derer zu Wort kommen, die um Jesus trauern. So wird die Menge hier zur Prozessionsgemeinde"[90] This line of thought is based on Deut 21:22–23, which says a man hanged on a tree is cursed. In this regard, the women are seen as sympathizers carrying out a religious ritual. But Klein seems to be reading too much into the text. The group of women who mourn and lament Jesus' fate is not a funeral procession or a sign of protestation of his death.

Another suggestion is to view the women as symbolic figures. They represent Jerusalem or Israel; they are a literary symbol,[91] and so it is not necessary to discuss the cultural customs of mourning, since Jesus has

---

87. "Although many of 'the people' are following Jesus, it is the Daughters of Jerusalem—as distinguished from 'the people'—who are addressed in 23.27–31. For, they are the element of Israel who continually rejected God's messengers" (Neyrey, "Jesus' Address to the Women of Jerusalem," 75).

88. They have been seen from many different angles, but it can be better said that they are "sympathizers." See Marshall, *The Gospel of Luke*, 863. See also Ellis, *The Gospel of Luke*, 266.

89. However, Moo does not think that v. 27 is from Zech 12:10–14. "While Zech 12:10 is appropriated as a *testimonium* to Christ's death, in the NT, Luke evinces no knowledge of it, and this renders very unlikely the hypothesis that he has utilized this context in Lk. 23:27" (Moo, *The Old Testament in the Gospel Passion Narratives*, 221). See also Nolland, *Luke*, 3:1136. NA28 also has a question mark for v. 27, which shows that the editors consider any allusion to the Zechariah passage unclear at best.

90. Klein, *Das Lukasevangelium*, 705.

91. Neyrey, "Jesus' Address to the Women of Jerusalem," 74. The same position is held by Käser. See Käser, "Exegetische und Theologische," 240–54.

already provided many warnings against the fate of nations.[92] Moreover, v. 27 is also one of many passages where Luke positively depicts the role of women in Jesus' ministry (1:39–56; 2:36–38; 7:11–15, 36–50; 8:1–3; 10:38–42; 11:27; 13:10–17).[93] While it is appropriate to stress the function of women in the Gospel of Luke and understand that it is unnecessary to suddenly create symbolic figures in the text, Neyrey's view cannot be totally left out of the pericope, because Jesus addresses not the whole crowd, but the group of women. The women are not symbolic figures per se, but they are synecdochic to Israel: they represent Israel.

In v. 28, Jesus is noted to have "turned" to the women. The phrase στραφεὶς πρὸς αὐτὰς is a common Lukan expression (7:9; 9:55; 10:23; 22:61). It might be the same expression used in 22:61, which is essentially a call to repentance.[94] Neyrey, however, thinks that the best analogy for this turning of Jesus can be found in Acts 7:42, where God's judgment falls upon those who reject God's messenger. Thus, "Jesus' turning in 23.28, then, is not necessarily a call to repentance, but may be an act of judgment."[95]

The point made by Neyrey is appropriate when the reversal of weeping is considered. In 22:61, Peter weeps because Jesus turns to look at him. This moves Peter to repentance. In other words, Jesus' turning is a harbinger of reversal for those who weep by making his people repent. Also, Peter's weeping is the result of what he recognized in his deed. However, Jesus' turning in v. 28 is not the same as 22:61. In the former Jesus explicitly tells the women not to weep for him but for themselves and their children. More to the point, the turning of Jesus to the weeping women is not so much a call to repentance as it is a pronouncement of judgment.

Jesus calls the women θυγατέρες Ἰερουσαλήμ, which is often used in the OT to refer to the people of Israel, the inhabitants of Jerusalem, or the holy city itself (LXX Ps 9:14; 72:28; Mic 1:8. 13, 15; 4:8, 10; Zech 3:14; Zeph 2:10; 9:9; Isa 6:23; 16:1; 62:11; Jer 6:2). Since Jerusalem is the capital city of Israel, θυγατέρες Ἰερουσαλήμ can refer the first and the second sense above. Jesus says to them μὴ κλαίετε, a command used also in 7:13 when he raised the son of the widow of Nain. The expression μὴ κλαίετε in both instances indicates a reversal. In other words, the readers are confronted with a different ending. As the young dead man was alive after Jesus' words μὴ κλαίετε, so also will something happen in the future in 23:28. However joyful news will not come this time. Rather, tragic judgment will follow, for

---

92. Bock, *Luke*, 2:1844.
93. Ibid.
94. Danker, *Jesus and the New Age*, 229. See chapter 3.5.
95. Neyrey, "Jesus' Address to the Women of Jerusalem," 76.

Jesus says, "Do not weep for *me* but weep for *yourselves and for your children* (μὴ κλαίετε ἐπ' ἐμέ· πλὴν ἐφ' ἑαυτὰς κλαίετε καὶ ἐπὶ τὰ τέκνα ὑμῶν)." Jesus is telling the women that they are weeping for the wrong person; their weeping is misdirected. Bock points out that the women should be directing their sympathy not to Jesus but to themselves.[96] Their weeping is not the result of what they recognize. Rather, it comes from their own standards. It runs parallel with 19:42: "Would that you, even you, had known on this day the things that make for peace! But now they are hidden from your eyes." Thus, Jesus points out that they should have wept for their destiny. The following verses that pronounce judgment over Jerusalem confirm this fact. In this regard, the weeping of women indicates their blindness to or ignorance of what will happen to them.

Concerning the ignorance of Jerusalem, as in 19:41–44, Schaefer asserts that judgment over her is limited and temporary.

> Die Trauer des Lukas darüber ist in Stellen wie Lk 19:41 und 23:28 noch zu erkennen. So hofft er darauf, dass es sich letztlich um eine zeitlich begrenzte Abwendung Gottes von seinem Volk handelt. In der (wohl unsprünglichen) lectio brevior ist der Text offen für die Hoffnung, dass die Zertretung der Stadt Jerusalem begrenzt sei. Diese Begrenzung liegt im Heilsplan Gottes begründet, der Zeiten und Zeitbegrenzungen festlegt.[97]

However, this pericope does not explicitly provide evidence for Schaefer's line of thought. Instead, it presents how ignorant and blind the Jerusalemites are, as seen in 19:41–44. Schaefer reads in too much from the after-resurrection vantage point by adopting God's saving plan for His people. For the Jerusalemites, there is a judgment over them, which will be literally fulfilled and clearly seen as God's judgment over them. The important point of v. 28 is not the temporary nature or limited scope of God's judgment over Jerusalem, but the judgment itself and its imminent fulfillment. Therefore, Neyrey's argument that vv. 27–31 is a judgment oracle is right.[98] From this perspective, it is not an exaggeration to say that the ignorance and blindness of the daughters of Jerusalem imply that they fall into the category of those who laugh. As in 19:41–44, or even 7:32, they are satisfied with their present situation and status, a situation and status that are going to undergo

---

96. Bock, *Luke*, 2:1845. See also Fitzmyer, *The Gospel according to Luke X–XXIV*, 1498.

97. Schaefer, *Die Zukunft Israels bei Lukas*, 182. Bovon also thinks that this ignorance of the inhabitants of Jerusalem is not fatal because there is one more chance to repent, the message of resurrection. Bovon, *Luke*, 3:303.

98. Neyrey, "Jesus' Address to the Women of Jerusalem," esp. p. 76.

reversal. They should weep for themselves and their children, not for Jesus. Accordingly, they must recognize the precise reason for weeping: impending disaster. "The present statement is a reprise of the earlier one. Now the time of reversal is near. Those who were involved in the rejection will themselves face disaster, and it will spill over onto all the city's inhabitants."[99] Jesus' word to weep not for him but for themselves and their children is a clear indication of a reversal to weeping of those who laugh. In addition, the women's weeping should be the same as Jesus' in the context of Jerusalem's impending judgment. Hence, "The Lukan Jesus has already so wept (19:41), and he invites the women to do the same."[100]

Jesus gives more reason to weep in vv. 29–30, which again contain echoes from the OT. The expression ἰδοὺ ἔρχονται ἡμέραι used in v. 29 (similar to 19:43) has apocalyptic and prophetic force, although here it is closer to the latter.[101] The expression appears throughout the narrative (5:35; 17:2; and 21:6), and it is used specifically for lamenting over Jerusalem in 13:35 and 19:43. When this expression is used of Jerusalem in the Gospel of Luke, it is always in the context of judgment. The following supports the point more specifically. Luke provides a more detailed feature of the coming day in the form of a beatitude: "μακάριαι αἱ στεῖραι καὶ αἱ κοιλίαι αἳ οὐκ ἐγέννησαν καὶ μαστοὶ οἳ οὐκ ἔθρεψαν." This beatitude may be alluding to Isa 54:1. While Isa 54:1 promises a new beginning after the disaster, v. 29 gives no hope at all. Although many commentators, such as Marshall, Nolland, and Bock, are reluctant to see v. 29 as an allusion to or echo of Isa 54:1, it is clear that Luke borrows and utilizes the image of barrenness in Isa 54:1 to emphasize the impending judgment and reversal in v. 29.[102] Thus, Russam's idea that Luke gives new meaning to Isa 54:1 is significant:

> Diese Aufforderung wird begründet: "Es kommen Tage . . ." Der Satz beginnt wie eine Prophetie und will es auch sein. Aber wie nicht das kommende Ereignis selbst, sondern dessen Wirkung auf das Volk in den Blick genommen. Man wird dann die Unfruchtbaren selig preisen, die hier dreifach genannt sind, als solche, die nicht empfangen, nicht gebären und nicht säugen können. Gemeint ist, daß über die Kinder eine solche

---

99. Johnson, *The Gospel of Luke*, 372.
100. Nolland, *Luke*, 3:1137.
101. LXX Jer 7:32; 9:24; 16:14; 19:6; 23:5; 38:27.
102. Specifically, see Nolland, *Luke*, 3:1137. Also Marshall, *The Gospel of Luke*, 864. Bock, *Luke*, 2:1846, agrees with Marshall. These scholars do not argue that v. 29 is not an allusion or echo of Isa 54:1. Rather, they cannot see any obvious parallel between Isa 54:1 and v. 29 because they have different contexts. NA28 lists Isa 54:1 as a possible allusion.

Katastrophe kommt, daß Frauen, die nie Mutterglück erlebt haben, besser dran sind als die Mütter. Lk hat den jüdischen Krieg im Blick, bei dem nach dem Bericht des Josephus in den besiegten Ortschaften immer nur ganz wenige Menschen überlebten, auch in Jerusalem. Ein Segensspruch, wie er hier begegnet, ist ohne Parallele.[103]

As Russam points out, v. 29 shows worse situation and formidable effect of the coming event compared to Isa 54:1. Indeed, the point of v. 29 is in the reversal of the present situation; "the barren and childless women are blessed." This implies that a worse and more horrible situation will occur. In contrast to v. 29, Isa 54 is a promise for a bright future that will reverse the present dark situation of barrenness. However, Luke calls the barren blessed. This is ironic because barrenness is considered a woe or a shameful state in the OT (Gen 30:23; Isa 4:1; even Luke 1:25). Having the ability to bear children is considered a blessing from God. But here in Luke it becomes a woe. Luke's intention is not to highlight barrenness as a positive and genuine blessing from God. Rather, it underlines the dreadful result of judgment and its impact on the people of Jerusalem. In other words, it is better to be barren than to experience the impending judgment.

Another reason Jesus addresses the weeping women is shown in v. 30. This verse contains an obvious echo of Hosea 10:8 (LXX) and is used also in Rev. 6:16.[104] The Hosean text speaks a judgment oracle against the northern kingdom for its idolatry and injustice. God's destruction of the high places is so formidable that "those who survive will desire to live no longer and therefore they cry out for a great earthquake. It seems better to them to be crushed and buried by falling rocks than to have to live with no refuge among the destroyed sanctuaries."[105] Luke uses the Hosean image of judgment for Jerusalem's destruction. The pronoun "they" is not the women in v. 27, but anyone involved in the judgment. As the northern kingdom, especially Samaria, is punished for her idolatry and rejection of God, so Jerusalem faces the same things for rejecting Jesus. Thus, Luke may be relating rejecting Jesus to the sin of idolatry. Indeed, "Israel's decision under Hosea

---

103. Klein, *Das Lukasevangelium*, 705. Also see Rusam, *Das Alte Testament bei Lukas*, 234 and Pao, "Luke," 394.

104. καὶ ἐξαρθήσονται βωμοὶ Ων ἁμαρτήματα τοῦ Ισραηλ ἄκανθαι καὶ τρίβολοι ἀναβήσονται ἐπὶ τὰ θυσιαστήρια αὐτῶν καὶ ἐροῦσιν τοῖς ὄρεσιν καλύψατε ἡμᾶς καὶ τοῖς βουνοῖς πέσατε ἐφ' ἡμᾶς (Hos 10:8 LXX). Rev 6:16 (καὶ λέγουσιν τοῖς ὄρεσιν καὶ ταῖς πέτραις· πέσετε ἐφ' ἡμᾶ ς καὶ κρύψατε ἡμᾶς ἀπὸ προσώπου τοῦ καθημένου ἐπὶ τοῦ θρόνου καὶ ἀπὸ τῆς ὀργῆς τοῦ ἀρνίου) is another quotation of or allusion to Hos 10:8.

105. Wolff, *Hosea*, 176.

was only a prelude to Israel's last decision before the crucified and resurrected Christ, in whom the offer of salvation to Israel came with finality."[106]

The pericope ends with an ambiguous proverbial saying by Jesus in v. 31. The image used in v. 31 is, as expected, rooted in the OT. YHWH will punish and refine his people, who are called a "green tree" (Jer 11:16), with fire (Isa 10:16–19). Verse 31 is most likely an echo of Ezek 17:24.[107] Though both passages use the word ξηρός ("dry, withered"), Luke does not entirely adopt the concept shown in Ezekiel. Rather, Luke recalls and warns the people of Jerusalem who reject Jesus of the tragic and horrible effects of God's judgment. While in Ezek 17:24 the green tree dries up and the dry tree flourishes, for Luke both trees will dry up regardless.

The difficulty in interpreting v. 31 is in identifying the referent "these things" (ταῦτα). Now what Jesus is saying in this verse is clear: things will be far worse than they are now. However, depending on how one renders ταῦτα, the verse can be construed in a number of ways. There are five suggestions concerning the referent of ταῦτα. The first option has ταῦτα refer to the Romans. In this case v. 31 can be paraphrased as, "If the Romans treat an innocent man like Jesus this way, how much more will they mistreat a nation in revolt?" However, the weakness of this option is that the Romans do not appear in the scene. The second option has ταῦτα refer to the Jews and paraphrases as "If the Jews treat Jesus this way for coming to deliver them, how will the Jews be treated after they destroy him?" The weakness is that the subject shifts in v. 31b from plural to singular (from ποιοῦσιν to γένηται). The third option has ταῦτα refer to God; thus, "If God has not spared Jesus, how much more will the nation of the unrepentant not be spared when God's judgment comes?" However, ταῦτα is a third-person plural reference to God (12:20 has a similar reference). It is easier to burn dry wood than lush, moisture-filled green wood. The fourth refers ταῦτα to humankind: "If humankind is this wicked, how much more will it be when wickedness overflows?" The weakness here is that it does not make good sense, since the concept of a green tree is never used negatively elsewhere. The fifth takes the entire passage as a general proverb for impending judgment that lacks a specific referent.[108]

Bock thinks the second and fourth options are most persuasive and finds it difficult to choose between them. But he leans toward the fourth,

---

106. Ibid., 177.

107. καὶ γνώσονται πάντα τὰ ξύλα τοῦ πεδίου διότι ἐγὼ κύριος ὁ ταπεινῶν ξύλον ὑψηλὸν καὶ ὑψῶν ξύλον ταπεινὸν καὶ ξηραίνων ξύλον χλωρὸν καὶ ἀναθάλλων ξύλον ξηρόν ἐγὼ κύριος λελάληκα καὶ ποιήσω (Ezek 17:24 LXX).

108. Bock, *Luke*, 2:1847. See also the same explanation in Bovon, *Luke*, 3:305.

as do most commentators.[109] Wright, however, agreeing with Caird, holds to the first option of interpretation: "The saying does not carry any sort of atonement-theology such as characterized the church's understanding of Jesus' death from very early on. . . . Jesus understood his death as being organically linked with the fate of the nation. He was dying as the rejected king, who had offered the way of peace which the city had rejected; as the representative king, taking Israel's suffering upon himself, though not here even with any hint that Israel would thereby escape."[110] Even Rome is the tool of God to punish God's own people. Thus, considering the whole context of the pericope and its usage in 12:20, the fourth option is likely the best interpretation. With this, the pericope can be seen as a judgment oracle rather than a call to repentance.[111] The coming days in v. 29 are considered to be "the day of the LORD." Though this "day" has two aspects—salvation and judgment—Jesus is referring to the latter here in this passage.

Gathering all the observations made above, several points on this reversal to weeping are worth mentioning. First, and interestingly, those who "laugh" are portrayed as those who weep: the women who weep for Jesus' fate. However, their weeping is misdirected. They do not know whom they really have to weep for—themselves and their children. In this sense, the women do not know their present situation. They should be weeping for themselves and their children because of the impending catastrophe. Soon the word of Jesus in 6:25b will be realized. Those who laugh now shall weep. Here those who laugh are described as those who do not recognize Jesus (cf. 19:41–44). Second, Jesus is the bringer of the reversal to weeping. Because of Jesus' death, the tragic things will come upon them. As we have seen, if God has not spared Jesus, how much more will the impenitent nation not be spared when divine judgment comes? Thus, the death of Jesus is the reason and cause of reversal brought about by God. Finally, as seen in 19:41–44, the reversal comes in a sudden, horrible, and tragic fashion. All the OT passages echoed by Luke illustrate that point. In this sense, Jesus is presented as the prophet. His word will be fulfilled shortly.

---

109. Fitzmyer, *The Gospel according to Luke X–XXIV*, 1498–99, Marshall, *The Gospel of Luke*, 865, and Danker, *Jesus and the New Age*, 372 are supporters of this option. However, Neyrey thinks that the second option, which renders the referent as the Jews, is the best. "The particular sense of the aphorism in 23.31 seems to imply that 'if *they* do this' refers to what the Jerusalemites are doing to Jesus" (Neyrey, "Jesus' Address to the Women of Jerusalem," 79). Garland, *Luke*, 919–20, thinks that these different options are not mutually exclusive.

110. Wright, *Jesus and the Victory of God*, 570. See also Caird, *Saint Luke*, 249–50.

111. Neyrey, "Jesus' Address to the Women of Jerusalem," esp. p. 79–83.

Conclusion

In this chapter, we have examined the reversal to weeping: those who laugh shall weep. The passages discussed illustrate this. Those who laugh are usually described as those who do not know their present status or situation. They are blind to the things that will happen. They are ignorant of their destiny. Their common fault is rejecting and denying the prophet and messenger of God, Jesus. Those who laugh have their own misguided ideas about the coming of the Messiah (7:32–35). This leads them to destruction (19:41–44; 23:27–31). Although they weep for Jesus' fate, the final judgment will fall upon them. They do not understand what is going on in God's history. The self-satisfied one who laughs is in danger of God's impending judgment. By emphasizing the present situation of those who laugh ("now" in 6:25b), Luke shows how their destiny will be reversed by the bringer of reversal, Jesus. The focus is on Jesus more than anything or anyone else. Thus, the reversal to weeping is centered on Christ.

CHAPTER FIVE

THE NARRATIVE INTENTION AND IMPLICATION OF THE REVERSAL OF WEEPING

The foregoing examination offers a reading of Luke's use of κλαίω in relation to reversal in the Gospel of Luke. The focus is not the overall, broad range of weeping but Luke's specific use of κλαίω with the theme of reversal. The exegesis of seven stories illustrates this Lukan reversal of weeping in particular, although some passages may be more persuasive than others. However, all the stories, which are based on the overarching statement of 6:21 and 6:25, reveal Luke's intention to use κλαίω in presenting one of his significant themes, reversal. By using weeping as a crucial element in presenting reversal, Luke wants to achieve his narrative goals as well as underline a theme of reversal.[1] The narrative purposes of Luke include separating the reversal of weeping as a distinctive theme from other aspects of reversals; highlighting the theme of reversal; focusing on people who suffer in this world, symbolized by those who weep; portraying Jesus as the Christ, the long-awaited promised prophet. Luke successfully achieves these narrative goals throughout by recounting instances when Jesus reversed the fortunes of those who were weeping of reversal of weeping.

The purpose of this chapter is to investigate Luke's narrative goals and achievements. The theological implication of reversals of weeping is also discussed in the context of the kingdom of God. The analysis will synthesize the previous discussions according to Luke's narrative purpose. Thus,

---

1. For the unity and narrative role and function of Luke (and Luke–Acts), see Tannehill, *The Narrative Unity of Luke–Acts*. See also O'Toole, *The Unity of Luke's Theology*.

the scope of the chapter will be holistic and multidimensional, examining Luke's use of weeping in the context of reversal.

Luke's Purpose in Telling of the Reversal of Weeping

Reversal of Weeping as a Distinctive Theme

Luke is unique in seeing the reversal of weeping as a distinctive theme and purposing to develop it. As seen in chapter 1, the theme of reversal has been discussed by previous commentators under the rubric of poor versus rich.[2] Specifically, those who weep, hunger, and are persecuted are subsumed under the category of the poor. For this reason, other aspects of reversal have not been much discussed or considered as significant. However, the Lukan connection of κλαίω with reversal underscores the importance of the reversal of weeping as a significant theme that is independent of the poor/rich distinction. As Alter asserts, a theme is established by the repetition of a word or word root, and the word repeated here is κλαίω, "weep."[3] The repetition of κλαίω is intentional for Luke, since there is no use of other word for weeping in the Gospel of Luke. The only exception is 6:25, which uses πενθέω, but here πενθέω is used with κλαίω. Thus, the repetition of κλαίω intensifies the theme of reversal and establishes the reversal of weeping as a independent theme.[4]

Luke successfully identifies the theme of reversal of weeping from other reversals by arranging the stories of reversal of weeping into his narrative. From the Beatitudes and Woes in 6:20–26 to Jesus' walk to his execution in 23:27–32, Luke illustrates that reversal of weeping occurs in people's lives in Jesus' day. There is no single cause for weeping, but Luke attempts to reveal that the weeping of people is not strange. Rather, it coexists in people's *Sitz im Leben*. The stories of reversal of weeping clearly show that the reversal of weeping is a great exercise of God's power.

Luke presents the reversal of weeping as going in two directions. On the one hand, those who weep shall laugh, as we saw in chapter 3: the dead are raised, the sick are healed, sinners are forgiven, and the rejected are restored. The final destiny of those who weep is that they will laugh. By contrast, those who laugh now will weep: "this generation," which rejects the God-sent messenger and the Messiah, and the people of Israel who reject their true king, Jesus. The important feature of the reversal to weeping

---

2. For the issue of the poor and rich in the Gospel of Luke, see chapter 1.
3. Alter, *The Art of Biblical Narrative*, 95.
4. See note 2 in Chapter 2 for word and its concept distinction.

is judgment: those who laugh are satisfied with their present life with no concern for the future. However, the destiny and fortune of these people are reversed by one man, Jesus. By him their fortune is made good or bad. They are under the judgment of God. Their laughter will soon disappear and weeping will appear.

Since the reversal of weeping is brought about by Jesus, the focus of Luke is christological. Luke is not only concerned for the marginalized people by describing them as those who weep; he is also focused on Jesus Christ's saving power for them. Specifically, Luke portrays Jesus as a prophet. All these points are discussed below and show more detailed features of the reversal of weeping.

Focusing on Marginalized People

The reversal of weeping in the Gospel of Luke is illustrated by Luke's use of the word κλαίω. As examined in chapters 3 and 4, Luke attempts to demonstrate the reversal of weeping through various stories in his narrative. The theme of reversal is revealed best in the Beatitudes and Woes in the Sermon on the Plain (Luke 6:20-26). Luke introduces the theme of reversal in the Sermon on the Plain, and he develops and unfolds it throughout his narrative.[5] Through many stories Luke highlights how reversal occurs in the lives of people, especially people marginalized in this world, doing so through the use of κλαίω, detailing the theme of reversal by focusing on those who either presently weep or will weep in the certain future. Those who weep are not only the poor but also women and those who suffer from sickness, loss of a child, and sin. Luke consistently shows that God is interested in them.[6] God's interest in marginalized people is specifically found in the positive reversal of weeping stories.

In the story of the widow of Nain (7:11-17), Jesus brings reversal to the weeping widowed mother by raising up her dead son. Jesus consistently keeps the disadvantaged woman, not only her dead son, at the center of the story.[7] Jesus comes to *her*, tells *her* not to weep, and gives *her* son back to

---

5. Dunn, *Jesus Remembered*, 412-14. See chapter 1.

6. Blomberg places the outcast of society in the Gospel of Luke into four categories: (1) Samaritans and Gentiles, (2) tax collectors and sinners, (3) women, and (4) the poor. Blomberg, *Jesus and the Gospels*, 163-65.

7. For studies of women in Luke, see Newsom and Ringe, *Women's Bible Commentary*, especially Schaberg, "Luke," 363-80; Seim, *The Double Message*; D'Angelo, "Women in Luke-Acts," 441-61; Sullivan, *Women in the New Testament*; Arlandson, *Women, Class, and Society in Early Christianity*; Bauckham, *Gospel Women*; France, *Women in the Church's Ministry*.

her. Her weeping is the center of Jesus' concern. The fortunes of a woman who was suffering in this world and has just experienced the death of her only son were restored, and she could live in happiness and comfort. This reversal provides the woman with a means of support as well as a source of true joy.[8] She now comes back to her normal life because of God's great consolation.

Luke keeps showing special interest in women. The sinful woman in 7:36–50 is shown as marginalized even among women. She is regarded as a sinner by her community. Being a woman means to live a marginalized and disadvantaged life, but being a sinner *and* a woman means much more than a marginalized life. Her seemingly unclean action, washing Jesus' feet with her tears and drying them with her hair, is not acceptable by the social conventions of her day. However, her fortunes are reversed by Jesus' proclamation that she is forgiven. Witherington points out that Jesus' breaking down of "the barrier of clean and unclean and of social ostracism by forgiveness opened the door for a return of such women to a more normal life and perhaps even a place in His community."[9] She was made a precious member of God's people by Jesus.

The story of the raising of Jairus' daughter (8:40–56) shows another dimension of Luke's interest in marginalized people through reversal of weeping: not only is Jairus' daughter a child and female, but also Jairus is a noble man. Moreover, another story sandwiched into Jairus' story, the story of the bleeding woman, also demonstrates Luke's interest in women. This woman was unclean and kept away from others, but Jesus heals her and brings true reversal to her. The weeping father, Jairus, finally experiences the reversal of fortune for him and his daughter. Here the faith of Jairus is highlighted in contrast to those who were scoffing at Jesus. Jairus' faith is recompensed by Jesus' raising up his daughter. As with the sinful woman, Jairus' fortunes were reversed by Jesus through his faith. Jesus includes the marginalized people into his new community through their faith.

The weeping disciple, Peter, is shown as well. He was the central figure among the disciples, but his denial of Jesus three times marginalizes him. When Peter sees Jesus turn to him, he runs out weeping. His weeping is that of repentance and it leads him to restoration. The story of Peter's denial also exemplifies the greatest/least motif through the reversal of weeping. Dunn states that "there will be a reversal of status: those who expect high recognition will be disappointed and those held in low esteem will be shown to be

---

8. Witherington, *Women in the Ministry of Jesus*, 77.
9. Ibid., 57.

highly esteemed by God."[10] Dunn's comment is relevant in that the reversal is dealt with in the context of the kingdom of God. In the kingdom of God, anyone can be marginalized or made great by reversal of fortune. Peter experienced both statuses in his life.

Finally, the story of the daughters of Jerusalem also shows Luke's concern for women. As noted, the expression "daughter of Jerusalem" is synecdochic, representing all Jerusalemites or Israelites who reject Jesus. By using this expression, Luke demonstrates that women are the equal members of society as man. Luke has Jesus show his concern for women by identifying with their plight, for they would confront suffering and judgment as Jesus had at his execution.

It is clear that Luke achieves his purpose of showing that God has compassion for weeping people who are suffering in this world by employing the technique of *Leitwort*. In this regard, Lukan weeping symbolizes the agony, grief, suffering, and hardship of people in their present lives. However, the saving power of Jesus through healing, resuscitating, and raising up his people reverses their fortunes, which shows that the kingdom of God is present now.

Jesus as the Prophet

Another feature of the reversal of weeping is Luke's portrayal of Jesus as a prophet.[11] Of the seven stories of reversal *of* weeping and reversal *to* weeping, six explicitly describe Jesus as a prophet. The story of the widow of Nain is the first example: astonished after witnessing Jesus reverse the weeping of the widow by raising her son, the people said that a great prophet had arisen among them (7:16). This amazement of the people illustrates not only their apocalyptic expectation but also their anticipation that God would fulfill what he had promised in the OT. The similarity between Jesus and Elijah and Elisha makes the latter point more persuasive:[12] Luke portrays Jesus as

---

10. Dunn, *Jesus Remembered*, 417.

11. A number of works have been published concerning the issue of Jesus as a prophet, the most significant of which is Sanders, *Jesus and Judaism*; Meier's four-volume work, *A Marginal Jew* deals with the issue intensively, although there is no section exclusively devoted to the issue. See also Allison, *Jesus of Nazareth*. Also worth mentioning is Bock, *Proclamation from Prophecy and Pattern*. For discussions of the detailed descriptions of Jesus as a prophet in each pericope, see chapter 3 and 4.

12. For the role of Jesus as the prophet, see Schneider, *Jesus, Der Prophet*. See also Minear, *To Heal and to Reveal*. Minear presents Jesus as an Elijah-like and Moses-like prophet in this work. See also Dunn and Donnelly, "From Elijah-like Prophet to Royal Davidic Messiah," 45–83; Feiler, "Jesus the Prophet."

their eschatological antitype who reverses the conventions of the time and brings the new order of God. The story of the sinful woman also makes the same point. However, it is Simon the Pharisee who thinks that Jesus is the prophet. The thought of Simon shows that the contemporaries of Jesus thought that his identity was a prophet.[13] This implies that Jesus was thought of at least as a God-sent messenger. However, in this story, Jesus reveals him not only as a prophet, but as God who can forgive people's sin. In other words, he is the eschatological prophet who brings good news to weeping people by forgiving their sin. Going even beyond what the people thought, Luke identifies Jesus with God. The third story in which Jesus is depicted as a prophet is Peter's denial of Jesus. Peter's denial is expected because Jesus has already told him that he would do so in 22:31-34. The story of Peter's weeping is a realization and fulfillment of Jesus' word. Luke purposefully uses the expression that Peter remembered the saying of the LORD in 22:61 in order to emphasize his portrayal of Jesus as a prophet.

The stories of reversal *to* weeping also show Jesus as a prophet. Although it is not explicitly stated, 7:31-35 describes Jesus as a messenger sent by God along with John the Baptist. The teaching and lesson of Jesus in this pericope is "this generation's" sin of rejecting Jesus and John the Baptist. Interestingly, John the Baptist is described and assessed as a great prophet among men by Jesus. Accordingly, it is not an overstatement to say that Jesus is greater than John. In this respect, Jesus reveals himself to people as a prophet, although he calls himself the Son of Man here.[14]

Another example is Jesus' lament over Jerusalem in 19:41-44. This picture of Jesus weeping over the city is undoubtedly that of the Prophets, especially Jeremiah. Jesus pronounces judgment over the disobedient and unresponsive people of Israel, which is typical of the prophets of Israel. Of significance is that Jesus brought this impending judgment over Jerusalem with his coming, while the other prophets in the OT expected that God

---

13. Verheyden argues, "Luke does not want Jesus to be called a prophet or to be presented like one. It is a category that is pursed by some of his opponents who challenge his authority and question his identity (and by Jesus himself in replying to them), or by some among his own disciples who do not understand what he is, or still by the first missionaries, as a stratagem of the Early Church (Acts). . . . For Luke, 'prophet' is the category used by those who do not understand; it is a useful category to *help* understand, almost as if by contrast, who Jesus really, is not to stick with it" (Verheyden, "Calling Jesus a Prophet," 204). However, Verheyden's argument is not persuasive in that Jesus regarded himself as a prophet. See Dunn's summary of the issue. Dunn, *Jesus Remembered*, 655-66.

14. Meier has an intensive discussion of John the Baptist as the greatest prophet among men. See Meier, *A Marginal Jew*, 2:100-236. See also Böhlemann, *Jesus und der Täufer*.

would come in the future whether it is near or far.[15] Luke tries to present Jesus, then, more than prophets in the OT. He is the greatest prophet of them all. Moreover, he is the God who can control the fortunes of individuals and nations' destinies. The same point is found in the road to the cross in 23:27-31 as well. Here Jesus pronounces tragic and formidable judgment on the daughters of Jerusalem, who symbolize the people of Israel. As in the lament over Jerusalem, Jesus speaks words clearly quoted from the Prophetic books of the OT. Jesus here also brings tragedy to those who have rejected him. They will understand and recognize that the saying of Jesus will be fulfilled in the near future. By pronouncing the impending judgment, Jesus identifies himself with the prophets of the OT.

Describing Jesus as a prophet is one of the most important goals that Luke wants to achieve throughout his narrative. Jesus not only brings blessings and judgment to this world, but reverses people's fortunes. In other words, he is the bringer of God's reversal. Luke tries to show how this portrayal of Jesus fits that of the eschatological prophet promised in the OT.

The Significance of the Present

One final feature and a narrative goal of Lukan reversal of weeping is his emphasis on "now." The significance of the present is emphasized by the use of νῦν in 6:21 and 6:25. The concern of Luke is for those who weep now in this world. Luke demonstrates the importance of the present world by showing that the reversal of weeping occurs *now* (at least near future). Although the people who weep suffer now, they experience the reversal in this present world: their present suffering "serves to bring out explicitly the greatness of the reversal that God will perform."[16] Luke follows this picture faithfully throughout the stories of reversal of weeping, emphasizing that the kingdom of God is present. In other words, Luke's eschatology is not exclusively future; it is also present.[17] By illustrating that reversal of weeping

---

15. The tradition of rejection of the prophet is well argued and explained by Steck, *Israel und das Gewaltsame Geschick der Propheten*. See also the death of Jesus in the tradition of the prophets: Ruzer, "Jesus' Crucifixion," 173-91.

16. Bock, *Luke*, 1:576.

17. For Luke's eschatology, see note 13 in Introduction. "Realized eschatology" here is not the same notion as that of C. H. Dodd, who states that Luke appreciates both the present and the future kingdom of God. I am aware that Luke pictures and provides both aspects of the kingdom of God. However, Luke stresses the importance of the present kingdom and its realization through Jesus in the reversal of weeping stories. For "realized eschatology," see Dodd, *The Parables of the Kingdom*. In this book, Dodd finds himself unconvinced by the "consequente Eschatologie" of Schweitzer, and

occurs in the present world to those who suffer now, "Luke still has a firm hope for an imminent eschatological event, while at the same time affirming a belief in the present as in a very real sense a realization of some of these eschatological events."[18] Thus, for Luke, the present world is as significant as the future world. The fortunes of suffering people can be reversed not only in the future but also in this world. Although complete and final restoration belongs to the future, a foretaste of the final day is given in the stories of the reversal of weeping. Luke's emphasis on the significance of the present leads to the crucial theological implication that the reversal of weeping is a kingdom phenomenon, as will be discussed in the following section.

Theological Implication: Phenomenon of the Kingdom of God

As James Dunn rightly recognizes, eschatological reversal is one of persistent themes in Jesus tradition.[19] Luke's Gospel is not an exception to the rule that the kingdom of God is marked by a reversal of fortunes.[20] Interestingly, the Gospel of Luke is full of reversal stories in relation to the kingdom of God. The Magnificat eloquently speaks of God's favor being extended to the humble, powerless, and poor. Jesus' inaugural sermon at Nazareth makes the same point: His mission is for those who are poor, those who are captive, and those who are oppressed, which is a critical sign that God's kingdom has come. In the beatitudes and woes in the Sermon on the Plain, the theme of reversal is more explicitly described than in any other passage in the Gospel of Luke. Powell points out that "these reversals and rewards are more descriptive of general blessings that God's reign brings to the world at large than of specific blessings realized within communities of faith."[21] Besides,

---

he introduces his famous concept of "realized eschatology," into the kingdom of God debate. See the most important passage of the presence of the kingdom in Luke 17:21. The exegesis of Meier is excellent. Meier, *A Marginal Jew*, 2:398–506.

18. Riches et al., "Luke," 284. Here Tuckett effectively refutes Conzelmann's thesis, the delay of the parousia. See Conzelmann, *The Theology of St. Luke*.

19. Dunn, *Jesus Remembered*, 412.

20. The phrase "kingdom of God" contains various concepts and notions according to E. P. Sanders. First, it is only by covenant that one enters. Second, it is still to be fully established. Third, it is an unexpected coming event that will separate the righteous from the wicked. Fourth, the kingdom will involve a decisive future event which will result in a recognizable social order involving Jesus' disciples and presumably Jesus himself. Fifth, it is the present experience of Jesus' words and deeds. Finally, it is a characteristic of God and his kingly rule. Most scholars see the present and future entity of God's reign among these concepts. Sanders, *Jesus and Judaism*, 141–50.

21. Powell, "Matthew's Beatitudes," 460.

many parables of Jesus and other discourses of Jesus reveal the theme of reversal of fortunes in the context of the kingdom of God.²²

Specifically, the reversal of fortune in the kingdom of God is the most common of the teachings of Jesus.²³ However, the theme of reversal is not only the topic of Jesus' teaching in the context of God's kingdom, it is also demonstrated by the deeds of Jesus. Meier notes,

> The most significant *sayings* of Jesus about the kingdom's presence contain references to significant *actions* of Jesus that communicate or symbolize this presence. As we have seen any number of times, one cannot separate the words and deeds of Jesus into two neat packets of information, they are inextricably bound together in the Gospel traditions.²⁴

Meier's argument is useful in that he points out the inseparability of Jesus' words and deeds (actions) in his portrait of the kingdom as present. More to the point, Jesus proclaims that the kingdom of God has already come through his words *and* deeds. Not only Jesus' proclamation of reign of God (Luke 4:16–21) but also many stories of Jesus' healings (Luke 9:1–6; Matt 9:35, 10:1, 9–11; Mark 6:6–12), exorcisms (Matt 12:28; Luke 11:20), and control of nature (Matt 8:27) are proofs that the kingdom has come.²⁵ Without doubt, the theme of reversal of weeping is included in all these stories of the present kingdom. In this regard, the theme of reversal of weeping is used to depict the present rule of God and the nature of his kingdom. Thus, reversal of weeping is a kingdom phenomenon in which God's power is presented and displayed through Jesus' words and deeds. In addition, Luke's

---

22. One of the popular parables of reversal is that of the Rich Man and Lazarus in Luke 16:19–31. For more discussion, see chapter 1. For Jesus' discourse to illustrate reversals (in general), see Luke 14:11 and 18:14.

23. Thus, Ridderbos affirms, "The central theme of Jesus' message, as it has come down to us in the synoptic gospels, is the coming of the kingdom of God" (Ridderbos, *The Coming of the Kingdom*, xi). Many scholars in addition to Ridderbos have made the same point, Joachim Jeremias among them: "Our starting point is the fact that the central theme of the public proclamation of Jesus was the kingly reign of God" (Jeremias, *New Testament Theology*, 96). This is explicitly expressed in the parables of Jesus, as we have seen in chapter 1. For an exclusive discussion of reversal in Luke, especially Jesus' parables in Luke 14–16, see Emmrich, *At the Heart of Luke*.

24. Meier, *A Marginal Jew*, 2:451.

25. Meier cites many sources to explain the details of the signs of the present kingdom. (ibid., 398–508). Actually, Meier's volume 2 devotes the most chapters to explain these signs of the present kingdom. See also Dunn, *Jesus Remembered*, 437–65. Also see McCartney, "ECCE HOMO," 1–21.

emphasis on "now" enables us to see that the present kingdom is inaugurated by Jesus.²⁶

Marilyn Adams discusses the theme of reversal in the context of the kingdom of God to show that reversal is an important phenomenon of the kingdom of God. First, she shows that the kingdom reverses the criteria for citizenship. The poor, women, and the physically deformed are disqualified to be citizens of this world, but "Jesus demonstrates *God's willingness to reverse the putative disqualifying conditions*" by miracles and the forgiveness of sins.²⁷ Those who suffer in this present world will have citizenship in the kingdom through reversal. In the stories of the reversal of weeping, many disqualified and marginalized people appear, such as the widowed mother, the sinful woman, the Gentile father of a sick daughter, and a betrayer. However, God reverses their disqualified condition through Jesus' words and deeds.

Second, she shows that the order of entry is reversed:

> Reversal of criteria for admission result in a reversal of populations who enter easily. Whereas external criteria were designed by and for the scrupulous and exclusive, the offer of salvation by the forgiveness of sins is open to all. This surprising news finds its most enthusiastic reception, not among the self-righteous whose capital was thereby devalued, but among the outcast.²⁸

This point is best exemplified by the story of the sinful woman in 7:36–50. Luke describes Simon the Pharisee as self-righteous, while the sinful woman is a true citizen of God's family and has salvation by the forgiveness of her sin.

Third, he shows that the roles are reversed for the elect:

> To be sure, Luke–Acts shares with the apocalyptic literature the idea that the elect will suffer in the present at the hands of those who reject God's purpose for their lives. Jesus himself, the righteous one par excellence, forecasts that his proclamation of the Kingdom of God will lead to persecution and death at the hands of the religious establishment. His disciples, who act in his name can expect the same.²⁹

---

26. Dunn seems to think that reversal is eschatological. However, he qualifies that by saying, "The poor are comforted in the present, not because their situation has already changed, but because they can be confident that God has not forgotten them and that their place in his kingdom is assured" (Dunn, *Jesus Remembered*, 413).

27. Adams, "Separation and Reversal in Luke–Acts," 97–100.

28. Ibid., 101.

29. Ibid., 102.

In this world, God's elect meet persecution and rejection as Jesus did, but the roles will be reversed. This is the destiny of the elect, and a hope for them. Adams' explains his analysis of reversal well, although he seems to limit the reversal to the context of entry into the kingdom or preconditions to entering the kingdom. Without doubt, reversal is kingdom phenomenon.

Conclusion

We have delved into the narrative intentions and achievements of Luke's presentation of reversal of weeping. Most of all, Luke's primary intention is to highlight the reversal of weeping as a significant and independent theme. His repeated use of κλαίω is intentional, and it exemplifies the modern literary term *Leitwort*. By positioning κλαίω in each of the reversal of weeping stories, Luke tries to show his readers that reversal of weeping is one of the important topics of his narrative. In addition, four features are demonstrated in Luke's presentation of the reversal of weeping: identifying the theme of reversal of weeping as distinctive theme in the narrative; his focus on marginalized people, especially women; his portrayal of Jesus as the prophet; and the significance of the present time. Luke meets these narrative goals through seven stories of reversal of weeping. All these achievements reflect Lukan theology.

Luke not only fulfills his narrative goals but also provides the basis for an important theological implication. The reversal of weeping is a kingdom phenomenon in which God's power comes through one man, Jesus. Specifically, reversal of weeping stories are significant signs for the present kingdom, which means the kingdom of God has already come. With the arrival of Jesus, God's kingdom has already entered into this world, and with the words and deeds of Jesus, the fortunes of those who weep have already changed. Those who weep now shall laugh, and those who laugh now shall weep.

CHAPTER SIX

CONCLUSION

This study hopes to make several contributions in the field of the NT studies, especially studies of the Gospel of Luke. Most of all, it highlights the theme of reversal from the angle of weeping. The study of reversal has been mostly carried out from a single perspective, the distinction between poor and rich. Accordingly, other aspects of reversal have been overlooked or subcategorized under the distinction of the poor and the rich. Although weeping, hunger, and persecution can be viewed as characteristics of the poor, it is also possible to see each feature as a unique illustration of the theme of the reversal of fortune. Using the beatitudes and woes (6:20–26) as a touchstone passage, Luke employs the technique of repetition, (*Leitwort*), specifically the repetition of κλαίω, to connect his stories of reversal of weeping. This is shown in chapter 1.

Chapter 2 deals with the reversal of weeping in the OT and other Second Temple literature. The Greek word κλαίω is regularly translate the Hebrew verb הָכָב, while another verb for mourning, לְבָא, is not used for κλαίω. Thus, the passages from the OT and other literature are selected by their use of κλαίω. The examination of the passages from the OT points out that the most important cause for weeping is Israel's exile. The fortune of Israel is finally reversed when YHWH intervenes in the lives of his people. YHWH's reversal of his weeping's people fortunes is so sudden, quick, and powerful that the people cannot expect it.

Other reversal of weeping stories are found in Second Temple literature. Specifically, *1 Enoch*, *Baruch*, and some Qumran documents explicitly feature the theme of the reversal of weeping. The most important point is that the Jews who lived in the Second Temple period had an apocalyptic worldview, believing that God would vindicate His people by defeating the enemies and foreign powers that oppressed them. Based on this worldview, they thought they were still in exile, as N. T. Wright argues. The stories of the reversal of weeping in Second Temple literature illustrate this worldview very well. Those who weep recognize that their misfortune is due to their sin and mischief against God. However, their weeping will disappear when God vindicates them. In the meantime, those who laugh are described as the wicked, powerful, and oppressors in contrast to those who weep. Punishment and judgment on the wicked as well as reward and joy for the righteous who weep will come suddenly and unexpectedly. The most significant feature of the reversal of weeping in the OT and Second Temple literature is that YHWH is the one who brings about the reversal of fortunes of both those who laugh and those who weep. This point provides an important launching pad for the trajectory of the Lukan reversal of weeping.

Chapter 3 investigates the positive direction of the reversal of weeping: those who weep now shall laugh. The touchstone statement for the reversal of weeping is Luke 6:20b. Four stories of the reversal of weeping, all of which use κλαίω, are great illustrations of this statement. The resurrection of the son of the widow of Nain, the forgiving of the sinful woman, the resurrection of Jairus' daughter, and the restoration of Peter show that Jesus, as God, is the only bringer of reversal. As seen in the OT and Second Temple literature, reversal of weeping is sudden and unexpected. It is also based on the compassion of Jesus. Interestingly, Jesus is portrayed as the prophet, which is one of Luke's narrative goals.

Chapter 4 deals with reversal *to* weeping: those who laugh shall weep. In these stories, the focus is judgment for those who laugh. Here those who laugh now are depicted as those who are satisfied with their present condition and were blinded mostly by their own standards of righteousness. "This generation" in 7:31–35, the Jerusalemites, and the "daughters of Jerusalem" in 23:27–31 are those who laugh now but would experience God's formidable judgment. As in chapter 3, Jesus is also presented as the prophet. However, the reversal-to-weeping stories more clearly illustrate Jesus as the prophet than do the reversal of weeping stories. The lament over the city of Jerusalem, the pronouncement of judgment through an oracle, and the quotation from the OT make this point obvious. Here Jesus is identified as the bringer of reversal to both those who laugh and to those who weep. Their fortunes will be dramatically reversed by the words and deeds of Jesus.

Chapter 5 is a synthesis of the previous discussion and statement of the theological implications. Luke' repetitive use of κλαίω implies his narrative intensions. By employing the technique of *Leitwort*, Luke attempt to intensify the theme of reversal in the perspective of weeping.

With the technique of *Leitwort*, Luke successfully achieves his aims other than separating and highlighting the reversal of weeping as a distinctive theme. He focuses on marginalized people, especially women, who are suffering and seemingly disqualified from their community in this present world: the reversal of their tragic fortunes is not merely promise for the future. Rather, it will happen in this world, or at least near future. He portrays Jesus as the prophet, as seen in chapters 3 and 4.

We also looked at the theological implications the reversal of weeping has for the kingdom of God. The reversal of weeping is a kingdom phenomenon, especially as it shows the kingdom as a present entity. Along with Luke's emphasis on "now," seven stories of the reversal of weeping give new hope to the suffering people of God: the kingdom of God through Jesus' words and deeds has already come, and God rules this world, although it seems that agony and hardship are still going on in the lives of the people. By showing that the reversal of weeping happens in this world, Luke shows that God's saving power for His people is not a false hope but a reality. The people who live in the tension between the already and not yet thus can live according to kingdom ethics through witnessing the reversal of fortune. By trusting and focusing on Jesus, the only bringer of reversal of weeping and the eschatological prophet, the people of God's kingdom engage in their lives with endurance and faith, being careful not to be in the seat of those who laugh.

I am aware of a few things that are necessary for further study. First, this study only examines the reversal of weeping in the Gospel of Luke. Since Luke's work is a two-volume set, the theme should be considered in the context of Acts as well. Second, the other aspects of reversal can be useful topics of study. As shown in the beatitudes and woes, hunger and persecution are not only the condition or characterization of the poor but the same kind of distinctive topics for reversal as reversal of weeping has been. Although they are not presented as reversal of weeping, they deserve to be discussed for further study.

BIBLIOGRAPHY

Aalen, Sverre. *Heilsverlangen und Heilsverwirklichung: Studien zur Erwartung des Heils in der Apokalyptischen Literatur des Antiken Judentums und im Ältesten Christentum*. Arbeiten zur Literatur und Geschichte des hellenistischen Judentums 21. Leiden: Brill, 1990.

———. "St. Luke's Gospel and the Last Chapters of I Enoch." *NTS* 13/1 (1966) 1–13.

Abrams, M. H. *A Glossary of Literary Terms*. 4th ed. New York: Holt, Rinehart and Winston, 1981.

Adams, Marilyn McCord. "Separation and Reversal in Luke–Acts." In *Philosophy and the Christian Faith*, edited by Thomas V. Morris, 92–117. Notre Dame: University of Notre Dame Press, 1988.

Adams, Sean A. *Baruch and the Epistle of Jeremiah: A Commentary Based on the Texts in Codex Vaticanus*. Septuagint Commentary. Leiden: Brill, 2014.

Allen, Leslie C. *Psalms 101–150*. WBC 21. Waco, TX: Word, 1983.

Allison, Dale. C. "Elijah Must Come First." *JBL* 103 (1984) 256–58.

———. *Jesus of Nazareth: Millenarian Prophet*. Minneapolis: Fortress, 1998.

Alomia, Merling. "The Psalm of the 'Blessed Hope': Comments on Psalm 126." In *To Understand the Scriptures: Essays in Honor of William H. Shea*, edited by David Merling, 45–56. Berrien Springs, MI: Institute of Archaeology, Siefgried H. Horn Archaeological Museum, Andrews University, 1997.

Alter, Robert. *The Art of Biblical Narrative*. New York: Basic, 2011.

Anderson, Janice Capel. *Matthew's Narrative Web: Over, and Over, and Over Again*. JSNTSup 91. Sheffield: Sheffield Academic Press, 1994.

Anderson, Kevin L. *"But God Raised Him from the Dead": The Theology of Jesus' Resurrection in Luke–Acts*. Paternoster Biblical Monographs. Milton Keynes, UK: Paternoster, 2006.

Applegate, Judith K. "'And She Wet His Feet with Her Tears': A Feminist Interpretation of Luke 7:36–50." In *Escaping Eden New Feminist Perspectives on the Bible*, edited by Harold C. Washington, Susan Lochrie Graham, and Pamela Lee Thimmes, 69–90. Biblical Seminar 65. New York: New York University Press, 1999.

Aristotle. *Aristotle's Poetics*. Edited by John Baxter and Patrick Atherton. Translated by George Whalley. Montreal: McGill–Queen's, 1997.

Arlandson, James Malcolm. *Women, Class, and Society in Early Christianity: Models from Luke–Acts*. Peabody, MA: Hendrickson, 1997.

Arnold, Clinton E. "The Kingdom, Miracles, Satan, and Demons." In *The Kingdom of God*, edited by Christopher W. Morgan and Robert A. Peterson, 153–78. Wheaton, IL: Crossway, 2012.

Ascough, Richard S. "Narrative Technique and Generic Designation: Crowd Scenes in Luke-Acts and in Chariton." *CBQ* 58/1 (1996) 69–81.

Bailey, James L. "Sermon on the Mount: Model for Community." *Concordia Theological Monthly* 20 (1993) 85–94.

Bailey, Kenneth. E. *Jesus through Middle Eastern Eyes: Cultural Studies in the Gospels.* Downers Grove, IL: InterVarsity, 2008.

———. *Poet and Peasant.* Grand Rapids: Eerdmans, 1976.

———. "The Song of Mary: Vision of a New Exodus (Luke 1:46–55)." *TR (Near East School of Theology)* 2 (1979) 29–35.

Barker, Margaret. *The Lost Prophet: The Book of Enoch and Its Influence on Christianity.* Nashville: Abingdon, 1988.

Barton, Ernest DeWitt. *Syntax of Mood and Tenses in N.T. Greek.* 3rd ed. Edinburgh: T. & T. Clark, 1987.

Batey, Richard A. *Jesus and the Poor.* New York: Harper & Row, 1972.

Bauckham, Richard. *Gospel Women: Studies of the Named Women in the Gospels.* Grand Rapids: Eerdmans, 2002.

———. "The Rich Man and Lazarus: The Parable and the Parallels." *NTS* 37/2. (April 1991) 225–46.

Beale, G. K. *A New Testament Biblical Theology: The Unfolding of the Old Testament in the New.* Grand Rapids: Baker Academic, 2011.

———. *The Temple and the Church's Mission: A Biblical Theology of the Dwelling Place of God.* New Studies in Biblical Theology 17. Leicester: InterVarsity, 2004.

———. *The Use of Daniel in Jewish Apocalyptic Literature and in the Revelation of St. John.* Eugene, OR.: Wipf & Stock, 2010.

Beale, G. K., and D. A. Carson, eds. *Use of the Old Testament.* Grand Rapids: Baker Academic, 2007.

Beavis, Mary Ann. "'Expecting Nothing in Return': Luke's Picture of the Marginalized." *Interpretation* 48/4 (1994) 357–68.

Bellinger, W. H. *Psalmody and Prophecy.* Journal for the Study of the Old Testament Supplement Series 27. Sheffield: Sheffield Academic Press, 1984.

Bemile, Paul. *The Magnificat within the Context and Framework of Lukan Theology: An Exegetical Theological Study of Luke 1:46–55.* Regensburger Studien zur Theologie Bd. 34. Frankfurt: P. Lang, 1986.

Berlin, Adele. "Qumran Laments and the Study of Lament Literature." In *Liturgical Perspectives: Prayer and Poetry in Light of the Dead Sea Scrolls, Proceeding of the Fifth International Symposium of the Oriental Center 19–23 January 2000,* edited by Esther G. Cazon et al., 1–17. Studies on the Texts of the Desert of Judah. Leiden: Brill, 2003.

Berlin, Walter. *Wirs sind wie Träumende: Studien zum 126. Psalm.* Stuttgarter Bibel Studien 89. Stuttgart: Katholisches Bibelwerk Stuttgart, 1978.

Betz, H. D., and A. Yarbro. *The Sermon on the Mount: A Commentary on the Sermon on the Mount, Including the Sermon on the Plain (Matthew 5:3—7:27 and Luke 6:20–49).* Hermeneia. Minneapolis: Fortress, 1995.

Beuken, Willem A. M. *Isaiah II.* Historical Commentary on the Old Testament. Leuven: Peeters, 2000.

Bishop, E. F. "A Yawning Chasm." *EVQ* 45/1 (1973) 3–5.
Blenkinsopp, Joseph. *Isaiah: A New Translation with Introduction and Commentary.* 3 vols. AB 19–19B; New York: Doubleday, 2000–2003.
Bloch, R. "Midrash." In *Approaches to Judaism: Theory and Practice*, edited by W. S. Green Brown, 272–93. Judaic Studies 1. Missoula, MT: Scholars, 1978.
Blomberg, Craig. *Jesus and the Gospels: An Introduction and Survey.* 2nd ed. Nashville: B & H Academic, 2009.
———. "The Wright Stuff: A Critical Overview of *Jesus and the Victory of God.*" In *Jesus, Paul and the People of God: A Theological Dialogue with N. T. Wright*, edited by Carey C. Newman, 19–39. Downers Grove, IL: InterVarsity, 2011.
Bock, Darrell L. *Luke 1:1—9:50.* BECNT. Grand Rapids: Baker Academic, 1994.
———. *Luke 9:51—24:53.* BECNT. Grand Rapids: Baker Academic, 1996.
———. *Proclamation from Prophecy and Pattern: Lucan Old Testament Christology.* JSNTSup 12. Sheffield: Sheffield Academic, 1987.
Böhlemann, Peter. *Jesus und der Täufer: Schlüssel zur Theologie und Ethik des Lukas.* Society for New Testament Studies 99. New York: Cambridge University Press, 1997.
Boomershine, Thomas. "Epistemology at the Turn of the Ages in Paul, Jesus, and Mark: Rhetoric and Dialectic in Apocalyptic and the New Testament." In *Apocalyptic and the New Testament: Essays in Honor of J. Louis Martyn*, edited by Joel Marcus and Marion L. Soards, 147–68. JSNTSup 24. Sheffield: Sheffield Academic Press, 1989.
Boring, M. Eugene. *The Continuing Voice of Jesus: Christian Prophecy and the Gospel Tradition.* Louisville: Westminster/John Knox, 1991.
Bosworth, David A. "Weeping in the Psalms." *VT* 63/1 (2013) 36–46.
Bovon, Francois. *Luke 1:1— 9:50.* Hermeneia. Minneapolis: Augsburg Fortress, 2002.
———. *Luke 19:28—24:53.* Hermeneia. Minneapolis: Augsburg Fortress, 2012.
———. *Luke 9:51—19:27.* Hermeneia. Minneapolis: Augsburg Fortress, 2013.
Boyd, W. P. "Apocalyptic and Life after Death." *SE* 5 [= *TU* 103] (1968) 39–56.
Brodie, Thomas L. *The Crucial Bridge: The Elijah-Elisha Narrative as an Interpretive Synthesis of Genesis-Kings and a Literary Model for the Gospels.* Collegeville, MN: Liturgical, 2000.
———. "Towards Unravelling Luke's Use of the Old Testament: Luke 7:11–17 as an Imitation of 1 Kings 17.17–24." *NTS* 32 (1986) 247–67.
Brown, Francis, S. R. Driver, and Charles A. Briggs, eds. *A Hebrew and English Lexicon of the Old Testament.* Oxford: Clarendon, 1906.
Brown, Raymond Edward. "The Annunciation to Mary, the Visitation, and the Magnificat (Luke 1:26–56)." *Worship* 62/3 (1988) 249–59.
———. *The Birth of the Messiah: A Commentary on the Infancy Narratives in Matthew and Luke.* The Anchor Yale Bible Reference Library. Garden City, NY: Doubleday, 1977.
Bruce, F. F. *Biblical Exegesis in the Qumran Texts.* Grand Rapids: Eerdmans, 1960.
Brueggemann, Walter. *Isaiah 1–39.* Westminster Bible Companion. Louisville: Westminster John Knox, 1998.
Buber, Martin. "Leitwort Style in Pentateuch Narrative." In *Scripture and Translation*, 211–38. Indiana Studies in Biblical Literature. Bloomington: Indiana University Press, 1994.
———. "Leitwortstil in der Erzählung des Pentateuchs." In *Werke: Zweiter Band: Schriften zur Bible*, 1131–49. Munich: Kösel, 1964.

Bullinger, E. W. *Figures of Speech Used in the Bible: Explained and Illustrated.* Grand Rapids: Baker, 1968.
Bultmann, Rudolf. *The History of the Synoptic Tradition.* New York: Harper & Row, 1968.
Burke, David G. *The Poetry of Baruch: A Reconstruction and Analysis of the Original Hebrew Text of Baruch 3:9–5:9.* Chico, CA: Scholars, 1982.
Burke, Kenneth. *Language as Symbolic Action.* Berkeley: University of California Press, 1966.
Cadbury, Henry J. "The Name of Dives." *JBL* 84/1 (March 1965) 73.
Caird, G. B. *Saint Luke.* Westminster Pelican Commentaries. Philadelphia: Westminster, 1978.
Card, Michael. *Luke: The Gospel of Amazement.* Downers Grove, IL: InterVarsity, 2011.
Carson, D. A. *Exegetical Fallacies.* 2nd ed. Grand Rapids: Baker, 1996.
———. "Redaction Criticism: On the Legitimacy and Illegitimacy of a Literary Tool." In *Scripture and Truth*, edited by John D. Woodbridge and D. A. Carson, 119–42. Grand Rapids: Baker, 1992.
Casey, Maurice. "Where Wright Is Wrong: A Critical Review of N. T. Wright's *Jesus and the Victory of God*." *JSNT* 69 (1998) 95–103.
Charlesworth, James H., ed. *The Old Testament Pseudepigrapha.* 2 vols. Anchor Bible Reference Library. New York: Doubleday, 1983–1985.
Chazon, Esther Glickler. "Pesher." In *The Oxford Dictionary of the Jewish Religion*, edited by R. J. Zwi Werblowsky and Geoffrey Wigoder, 560. Oxford: Oxford University Press, 1997.
Clements, R. E. *Jeremiah.* Interpretation. Atlanta: John Knox, 1988.
Coggins, Richard J. *Sirach.* Sheffield: Sheffield Academic Press, 1998.
Collins, John J. *The Apocalyptic Imagination: An Introduction to Jewish Apocalyptic Literature.* The Biblical Resource Series. Grand Rapids: Eerdmans, 1998.
Comblin, José. "La Paix Dans La Théologie de Saint Luc." *Ephemerides Theologicae Lovanienses* 32/3–4 (1956) 439–60.
Conzelmann, Hans. *The Theology of St. Luke.* Translated by Geoffrey Buswell. New York: Harper, 1960.
Cosgrove, Charles H. "A Woman's Unbound Hair in the Greco-Roman World, with Special Reference to the Story of the 'Sinful Woman' in Luke 7:36–50." *JBL* 124/4 (2005) 675–92.
Cotter, Wendy J. "The Parable of the Children in the Market-Place, Q(Lk) 7:31–35: An Examination of the Parable's Image and Significance." *NT* 29/4 (1987) 289–304.
Cousland, J. R. C. *The Crowds in the Gospel of Matthew.* Novum Testamentum. New York: Brill, 2002.
Craddock, Fred B. *Luke.* Interpretation. Louisville: John Knox, 1990.
Creed, John Martin. *The Gospel according to St. Luke: The Greek Text with Introduction, Notes, and Indices.* London: Macmillan, 1930.
Crossan, John Dominic. *In Parables: The Challenge of the Historical Jesus.* New York: Harper & Row, 1973.
Crow, Loren D. *The Songs of Ascents (Psalms 120–134): Their Place in Israelite History and Religion.* Society of Biblical Literature Dissertation Series 148. Atlanta: Scholars, 1996.
Cullmann, Oscar. *The Christology of the New Testament.* Translated by Shirley C. Guthrie and Charles A. M. Hall. Philadelphia: Westminster, 1963.

Culpepper, R. Alan. *The New Interpreter's Bible: Luke—John*. New Interpreter's Bible 9. Nashville: Abingdon, 1996.

Dahl, Nils Alstrup. "'A People for His Name' (Acts 15:14)." *NTS* 4/4 (1958) 319–27.

———. "The Purpose of Luke-Acts." In *Jesus in the Memory of the Early Church: Essays*, edited by Nils Alstrup Dahl, 87–98. Minneapolis: Augsburg, 1976.

Dahood, Mitchell J. *Psalms 3*. AB 17A. Garden City, NY: Doubleday, 1966.

Daly, Robert J., ed. *Apocalyptic Thought in Early Christianity*. Holy Cross Studies in Patristic Theology and History. Grand Rapids: Baker Academic, 2009.

Dancy, J. C. *The Shorter Books of the Apocrypha: Tobit, Judith, Rest of Esther, Baruch, Letter of Jeremiah, Additions to Daniel, and Payer of Manasseh*. London: Cambridge University Press, 1972.

D'Angelo, Mary Rose. "Women in Luke-Acts: A Redactional View." *JBL* 109/3 (1990) 441–61.

Danker, Frederick W., ed. *A Greek-English Lexicon of the New Testament and Other Early Christian Literature*. 3rd ed. Chicago: University of Chicago Press, 2000.

———. *Jesus and the New Age: A Commentary on St. Luke's Gospel*. Philadelphia: Fortress, 1988.

Davies, Philip R. "Biblical Interpretation in the Dead Sea Scrolls." In *A History of Biblical Interpretation*, edited by Alan J. Hauser and Duane F. Watson, 1:144–66. Grand Rapids: Eerdmans, 2003.

Davies, W. D., and Dale C. Allison. *A Critical and Exegetical Commentary on the Gospel according to Saint Matthew*. 3 vols. ICC. Edinburgh: T. & T. Clark, 1988–2000.

De Long, Kindalee Pfremmer. *Surprised by God: Praise Responses in the Narrative of Luke-Acts*. Beihefte zur Zeitschrift für die Neutestamentliche Wissenschaft 166. Berlin: Walter de Gruyter, 2009.

Di Lella, Alexander A., and Patrick W. Skehan. *The Wisdom of Ben Sira: A New Translation with Notes*. AB 39. New York: Doubleday, 1987.

Dodd, C. H. *More New Testament Studies*. Grand Rapids: Eerdmans, 1968.

———. *The Parables of the Kingdom*. New York: Scribner's, 1961.

Drake, Larry Keith. "The Reversal Theme in Luke's Gospel." PhD diss., Saint Louis University, 1985.

Drury, John. *Tradition and Design in Luke's Gospel: A Study in Early Christian Historiography*. London: Darton Longman and Todd, 1976.

Dunn, James D. G., and Doris Donnelly, eds. "From Elijah-like Prophet to Royal Davidic Messiah." In *Jesus: A Colloquium in the Holy Land*, 45–83, New York: Continuum, 2001.

———. *Jesus, Paul, and the Gospels*. Grand Rapids: Eerdmans, 2011.

———. *Jesus Remembered*. Grand Rapids: Eerdmans, 2003.

Edwards, James R. *The Gospel according to Mark*. Pillar New Testament Commentary. Grand Rapids: Eerdmans, 2002.

Eklund, Rebekah Ann. "Lord, Teach Us How to Grieve: Jesus' Lament and Christian Hope." PhD diss., Duke University, 2011.

Ellis, E. Earle. *The Gospel of Luke*. New Century Bible. London: Nelson, 1966.

Emmrich, Martin *At the Heart of Luke: Wisdom and Reversal of Fortune*. Eugene, OR: Wipf & Stock, 2013.

Esler, Philip Francis. *Community and Gospel in Luke-Acts: The Social and Political Motivations of Lucan Theology*. Cambridge: Cambridge University Press, 1989.

Evans, C. F. *Saint Luke*. Trinity Press International New Testament Commentaries. Philadelphia: SCM, 1990.
Evans, Craig A. "Aspects of Exile and Restoration in the Proclamation of Jesus and the Gospels." In *Exile: Old Testament, Jewish, and Christian Conceptions*, edited by James M. Scott, 299–328. Leiden: Brill, 1997.
Feiler, Paul Frederick. "Jesus the Prophet: The Lucan Portrayal of Jesus as the Prophet like Moses." PhD diss., Princeton Theological Seminary, 1986.
Finger, Reta Halteman. *Of Widows and Meals: Communal Meals in the Book of Acts*. Grand Rapids: Eerdmans, 2007.
Fishbane, Michael. "Use, Authority, and Interpretation of Mikra at Qumran." In *Mikra: Text, Translation, Reading, and Interpretation of the Hebrew Bible in Ancient Judaism and Early Christianity*, edited by Martin J. Mulder and Harry Sysling, 339–77. Grand Rapids: Baker Academic, 2004.
Fisk, Bruce N. "See My Tears: A Lament for Jerusalem (Luke 13:31–35; 19:41–44)." In *Word Leaps the Gap*, edited by J. Ross Wagner, C. Kavin Rowe, and A. Katherine Grieb, 147–78. Grand Rapids: Eerdmans, 2008.
Fitzmyer, J. A. *The Gospel according to Luke I–IX: Introduction, Translation, and Notes*. Anchor Bible 28. Garden City, NY: Doubleday, 1981.
———. *The Gospel according to Luke X–XXIV*. AB 29. Garden City, NY: Doubleday, 1985.
France, R. T. *The Gospel of Matthew*. New International Commentary of the New Testament. Grand Rapids: Eerdmans, 2007.
———. *Women in the Church's Ministry: A Test-Case for Biblical Interpretation*. Grand Rapids: Eerdmans, 1997.
Friberg, Timothy, Barbara Friberg, and Neva F. Miller. *Analytical Lexicon of the Greek New Testament*. Victoria, BC: Trafford, 2006.
Garland, David E. *Luke*. Zondervan Exegetical Commentary on the New Testament 3. Grand Rapids: Zondervan, 2011.
Gaston, Lloyd. *No Stone on Another: Studies in the Significance of the Fall of Jerusalem in the Synoptic Gospels*. Supplements to Novum Testamentum 23. Leiden: Brill, 1970.
Getty-Sullivan, Mary Ann. *Women in the New Testament*. Collegeville, MN: Liturgical, 2001.
Glueck, Nelson. *Rivers in the Desert: A History of the Negev*. New York: Farrar, Straus and Cudahy, 1959.
Goldingay, John. *Psalms*. Baker Commentary on the Old Testament Wisdom and Psalms. Grand Rapids: Baker Academic, 2006.
Goulder, M. D. *Luke: A Paradigm*. Journal for Study of the New Testament 20. Sheffield: Sheffield Academic Press, 1999.
Green, Joel B. *The Gospel of Luke*. NICNT. Grand Rapids: Eerdmans, 1997.
Gundry, Robert H. *Matthew: A Commentary on His Handbook for a Mixed Church under Persecution*. Grand Rapids: Eerdmans, 1994.
Hagner, Donald A. *Matthew 1–13*. WBC 33A. Dallas: Word, 1993.
Haenchen, Ernst. *Der Weg Jesu: Eine Erklärung des Markus-Evangeliums und der kanonischen Parallelen*. Berlin: Walter de Gruyter, 1968.
Hanson, Paul D. *The Dawn of Apocalyptic*. Philadelphia: Fortress, 1975.
Harmon, Allen M. "The Setting and Interpretation of Psalm 126." *RTR* 44/3 (1985) 74–80.
Harrington, Daniel J. *Invitation to the Apocrypha*. Grand Rapids: Eerdmans, 1999.

Harris, R. Laird, Gleason L. Archer, and Bruce K. Waltke, eds. *Theological Wordbook of the Old Testament*. Chicago: Moody, 1981.

Hartsock, Chad. *Sight and Blindness in Luke-Acts: The Use of Physical Features in Characterization*. Biblical Interpretation Series 94. Leiden: Brill, 2008.

Hays, Christopher M. *Luke's Wealth Ethics: A Study in Their Coherence and Character*. WUNT2. Reihe 275. Tübingen: Mohr Siebeck, 2010.

Hays, Richard B., ed. *Jesus, Paul and the People of God: A Theological Dialogue with N. T. Wright*. Downers Grove, IL: InterVarsity, 2011.

———. *The Moral Vision of the New Testament: Community, Cross, New Creation: A Contemporary Introduction to New Testament Ethics*. San Francisco: Harper, 1996.

———. "Reading the Bible with Eyes of Faith: The Practice of Theological Exegesis." JTI 1/1 (Spring 2007) 5–21.

———. "Reading the Bible with Eyes of Faith: Theological Exegesis from the Perspective of Biblical Studies." In *Sharper than a Two-Edged Sword: Preaching, Teaching, and Living the Bible*, edited by Michael Root and James Joseph Luckely, 82–102. Grand Rapids: Eerdmans, 2008.

Hendriksen, William. *Exposition of the Gospel according to Luke*. New Testament Commentary 3. Grand Rapids: Baker, 1978.

Himmelfarb, Martha. *Tours of Hell: An Apocalyptic Form in Jewish and Christian Literature*. Philadelphia: Fortress, 1983.

Hintzen, Johannes. *Verkündigung und Wahrnehmung: Über das Verhältnis von Evangelium und Leser am Beispiel Lk 16, 19–31 im Rahmen des lukanischen Doppelwerks*. Bonner Biblische Beiträge 81. Frankfurt: Hain, 1991.

Hoffmann, Paul. *Studien zur Frühgeschichte der Jesus-Bewegung*. Stuttgarter Biblische Aufsatzbände, Neues Testament 17. Stuttgart: Katholisches Bibelwerk, 1994.

Holladay, William Lee. *Jeremiah 2: A Commentary on the Book of the Prophet Jeremiah, Chapters 26–52*. Hermeneia. Minneapolis: Fortress, 1989.

Holmås, Geir Otto. *Prayer and Vindication in Luke-Acts: The Theme of Prayer within the Context of the Legitimating and Edifying Objective of the Lukan Narrative*. Library of New Testament Studies 433. London: T. & T. Clark, 2011.

Horgan, Maurya P. "A Lament over Jerusalem (4Q179)." *JSS* 18/2 (1973) 222–34.

Hossfeld, Frank-Lothar. *Psalms 3: A Commentary on Psalms*. Hermeneia. Minneapolis: Fortress, 2005.

Hotze, Gerhard *Jesus Als Gast: Studien Zu Einem Christologischen Leitmotiv Im Lukasevangelium*. Biblical Research 111. Würzburg: Echter, 2007.

Hoyt, Thomas, Jr. "The Poor/Rich Theme in the Beatitudes." *Journal of Religious Thought* 37/1(1980) 31–41.

Hunter, Archibald Macbride. *A Pattern for Life: An Exposition of the Sermon on the Mount*. Philadelphia: Westminster, 1965.

Hur, Ju. *A Dynamic Reading of the Holy Spirit in Luke-Acts*. JSNTSup 211. Sheffield: Sheffield Academic Press, 2001.

Inselmann, Anke. *Die Freude im Lukasevangelium: Ein Beitrag zur Psychologischen Exegese*. Scientific Studies of the New Testament Series 2:322. Tübingen: Mohr Siebeck, 2012.

Jeremias, Joachim. *New Testament Theology: The Proclamation of Jesus*. New York: Scribner's, 1971.

———. *The Parable of Jesus*. New Testament Library. London: SCM, 1963.

Johnson, Luke Timothy. *The Literary Function of Possessions in Luke–Acts*. SBLDS 39. Missoula, MT: Scholars, 1977.

———. *The Gospel of Luke*. Sacra Pagina 3. Collegeville, MN: Liturgical, 1991.

Karris, Robert J. "The Literary Function of Possessions in Luke–Acts." *CBQ* 41/4 (1979) 653–54.

———. *Luke: Artist and Theologian: Luke's Passion Account as Literature*. Theological Inquires. New York: Paulist, 1985.

Käser, Walter. "Exegetische und Theologische Erwägungen zur Seligpreisung der Kinderlosen, Lc, 23:29b." *ZNW* 54/3–4 (1963) 240–54.

Kawin, Bruce F. *Telling It Again and Again: Repetition in Literature and Film*. Ithaca, NY: Cornell University Press, 1972.

Keesmaat, Sylvia C., and Brian J. Walsh, "Outside of a Small Circle of Friends: Jesus and the Justice of God." In *Jesus, Paul and the People of God: A Theological Dialogue with N. T. Wright*, edited by Nicholas Perrin and Richard B. Hays, 66–89. Downers Grove, IL: InterVarsity, 2011.

Kilgallen, John J. "Forgiveness of Sins (Luke 7:36–50)." *NT* 40/2 (1998) 105–16.

———. "John the Baptist, the Sinful Woman and the Pharisee." *JBL* 104/4 (1985) 675–79.

———. "'Peace' in the Gospel of Luke and Acts of Apostles." *Studia Missionalia* 38 (1989) 55–79.

Kingsbury, Jack. "Jesus as the 'Prophetic Messiah' in Luke's Gospel." In *Future Christology: Essays Honor Leander E. Keck*, edited by Abraham J. Malherbe and Wayne A. Meeks, 35–41. Minneapolis: Fortress, 1993.

Kissinger, Warren S. *The Parables of Jesus: A History of Interpretation and Bibliography*. American Theological Library Association, BS 4. Metuchen, NJ: Scarecrow, 1979.

Klein, Hans. *Das Lukasevangelium*. Kritisch-exegetischer Kommentar über das Neue Testament / begründet von Heinrich August Wilhelm Meyer Bd. I/3 -10. Göttingen: Vandenhoeck & Ruprecht, 2006.

Knibb, Michael A. *Essays on the Book of Enoch and Other Early Jewish Texts and Traditions*. Leiden: Brill, 2009.

———. *The Qumran Community*. Cambridge: Cambridge University Press, 1987.

Kodell, Jerome. "Luke's Use of *Laos*, 'People,' especially in the Jerusalem Narrative: Lk 19:28–24:53." *CBQ* 31/3 (1969) 327–43.

Kraus, Hans-Joachim. *Psalms: A Continental Commentary*. Minneapolis: Fortress, 1993.

Kuckhoff, Antonius. *Psalm 6 und die Betten im Psalter: Ein Paradigmatisches Betten und Klagegebet im Horizont des Gesamtpsalters*. BBB 160. Göttingen: Bonn University Press, 2011.

Kurz, William S. *Reading Luke–Acts: Dynamics of Biblical Narrative*. Louisville: Westminster John Knox, 1993.

Lange, Armin, and Matthias Weigold. *Biblical Quotations and Allusions in Second Temple Jewish Literature*. Göttingen: Vandenhoeck & Ruprecht, 2011.

Longenecker, Richard N. *Biblical Exegesis in the Apostolic Period*. 2nd ed. Grand Rapids: Eerdmans, 1999.

Longman, Tremper. *Jeremiah, Lamentations*. New International Biblical Commentary 14. Peabody, MA: Hendrickson, 2008.

Loretz, Oswald. "Psalm 6: Klagelied eines Einzeln: Totenklage im Keret-Epost und Weinen in Ps 6, 7b-8 und 55, 4." In *Psalmstudien: Kolometrie, Strophik und Theologie Ausgewählter Psalmen*, 75-102. Berlin: Walter de Gruyter, 2002.

Luccio, Pino Di. "La Megillá de Ester Y El Magníficat de María de Nazaret." *Estudios Eclesiásticos* 86/336 (2011) 39-55.

Lundbom, Jack R. *Jeremiah: A New Translation with Introduction and Commentary*. Anchor Bible 21B. New York: Doubleday, 1999.

Luz, Ulrich. *Matthew 1-7: A Commentary*. Translated by James E. Crouch. Hermeneia. Minneapolis: Augsburg Fortress, 2007.

Malbon, Elizabeth Struthers, and Adele Berlin. "Characterization in Biblical Literature." *Semeia* 63 (1993) 3-227.

Malina, Bruce J. *The New Testament World: Insights from Cultural Anthropology*. 3rd ed. Louisville: Westminster John Knox, 2001.

———. *Social Science Commentary on the Synoptic Gospels*. Minneapolis: Fortress, 1992.

Marsh, Clive. "Theological History? N. T. Wright's *Jesus and the Victory of God*." *JSNT* 69 (1998) 77-94.

Marshall, Christopher D. *Faith as a Theme in Mark's Narrative*. Society for New Testament Studies 64. Cambridge: Cambridge University Press, 1989.

Marshall, I. Howard. *The Gospel of Luke: A Commentary on the Greek Text*. New International Greek Testament Commentary. Exeter: Paternoster, 1978.

———. *Luke, Historian and Theologian*. Exeter: Paternoster, 1970.

Martínez, Florentino García, and Eibert J. C Tigchelaar, eds. *The Dead Sea Scrolls Study Edition*. Leiden: Brill, 1997.

Mayes, James Luther. *Psalms*. Interpretation. Louisville: John Knox, 1994.

McAlpine, Thomas H. *Sleep, Divine and Human in the Old Testament*. JSOT 38. Sheffield: Sheffield Academic Press, 1987.

McCane, Byron R. *Roll Back the Stone: Death and Burial in the World of Jesus*. Harrisburg, PA: Trinity, 2003.

McCartney, Dan G. "ECCE HOMO: The Coming of the Kingdom of God as the Restoration of Human Vicegerency." *WTJ* 56/1 (Spring 1994) 1-21.

McKane, William. *A Critical and Exegetical Commentary on Jeremiah*. ICC. Edinburgh: T. & T. Clark, 1986.

McNamara, Martin. *Palestinian Judaism and the New Testament*. Good News Studies 4. Wilmington, DE: Michael Glazier, 1983.

Meadors, Gary T. "The 'Poor' in the Beatitudes of Matthew [5:3] and Luke." *Grace Theological Journal* 6/2 (1985) 305-14.

Meier, John P. *A Marginal Jew: Rethinking the Historical Jesus*. 4 vols. ABRL. Garden City, NY: Doubleday, 1991.

Menken, Martinus J J. "The Position of ΣΠΛΑΓΧΝΙΖΕΣΘΑΙ and ΣΠΛΑΓΧΝΑ in the Gospel of Luke." *NT* 30/2 (1988) 107-14.

Mercer, Calvin R. *Norman Perrin's Interpretation of the New Testament: From "Exegetical Method" to "Hermeneutical Process."* Studies in American Biblical Hermeneutics 2. Macon, GA: Mercer, 1986.

Midgley, Mary. *Science and Poetry*. 1st ed. London: Rutledge, 2001.

Miller, Amanda C. "Bridge Work and Seating Charts: A Study of Luke's Ethics of Wealth, Poverty, and Reversal." *Interpretation* 68/4 (October 2014) 416-27.

Minear, Paul Sevier. "Jesus' Audiences, according to Luke." *NT* 16/2 (1974) 81-109.

———. "Luke's Use of the Birth Stories." In *Studies in Luke-Acts; Essays Presented in Honor of Paul Schubert*, edited by Leander E. Keck et al., 111–30. Nashville: Abingdon, 1966.

———. *To Heal and to Reveal: The Prophetic Vocation according to Luke*. New York: Seabury, 1976.

Moessner, David P. *Lord of the Banquet: The Literary and Theological Significance of the Lucan Travel Narrative*. Minneapolis: Augsburg Fortress, 1989.

Molin, G. "Elijahu der Prophet und sein Weiterleben in den Hoffnungen des Judentums und der Christenheit." *Judaica* 8 (1952) 65–94.

Moo, Douglas J. *The Old Testament in the Gospel Passion Narratives*. Eugene, OR.: Wipf & Stock, 2007.

Moore, Carey A. *Daniel, Esther and Jeremiah: The Additions*. AB 44. Garden City, NY: Doubleday, 1977.

Morris, Leon. *Luke*. Tyndale New Testament Commentaries. Downers Grove, IL: InterVarsity, 1988.

Motyer, J. A. *The Prophecy of Isaiah: An Introduction and Commentary*. Downers Grove, IL: InterVarsity, 1993.

Murphy, Frederick James. *Apocalypticism in the Bible and Its World: A Comprehensive Introduction*. Grand Rapids: Baker Academic, 2012.

Neale, David A. *None but the Sinners: Religious Categories in the Gospel of Luke*. JSNTSup 58. Sheffield: Sheffield Academic Press, 1991.

Neusner, Jacob. *Invitation to Midrash: The Workings of Rabbinic Bible Interpretation: A Teaching Book*. San Francisco: Harper & Row, 1989.

Neusner, Jacob, and Alan J. Avery-Peck, eds. *George W. E. Nickelsburg in Perspective: An Ongoing Dialogue of Learning*. 2 vols. Journal for the Study of Judaism 80. Leiden: Brill, 2003.

Newsom, Carol A., and Sharon H. Ringe, eds. *Women's Bible Commentary*. Louisville: Westminster John Knox, 1998.

Neyrey, Jerome H. "Jesus' Address to the Women of Jerusalem (Lk 23:27–31)—A Prophetic Oracle." *New Testament Studies* 29/1 (1983) 74–86.

———. *The Passion according to Luke: A Redaction Study of Luke's Soteriology*. Theological Inquires. New York: Paulist, 1985.

Nickelsburg, George W. E. *1 Enoch 1: A Commentary on the Book of 1 Enoch, Chapters 1–36; 81–108*. Hermeneia. Minneapolis: Fortress, 2001.

———. *1 Enoch: A New Translation, Based on the Hermeneia Commentary*. Minneapolis: Fortress, 2004.

Nolland, John. *Luke 1:1—9:20*. WBC 35a. Dallas: Word, 1989.

———. *Luke 9:21—18:34*. WBC 35b. Dallas: Word, 1993.

———. *Luke 18:35—24:53*. WBC 35c. Waco, TX: Word, 1993.

Omanson, Roger. "Lazarus and Simon." *BT* 40/4 (1989) 416–19.

Osborne, Grant. "Redaction Criticism." In *Dictionary of Jesus and the Gospels*, edited by Joel Green, 662–69. Downers Grove, IL: InterVarsity, 1992.

Pao, David. "Luke." In *Commentary on the New Testament*, edited by G. K. Beale and D. A. Carson, 251–414. Grand Rapids: Baker Academic, 2007.

Parsons, Mikeal Carl. *Body and Character in Luke and Acts: The Subversion of Physiognomy in Early Christianity*. Grand Rapids: Baker Academic, 2006.

Perrin, Norman. *What Is Redaction Criticism?* Guides to Biblical Scholarship, New Testament Series. Philadelphia: Fortress, 1969.

Pilgrim, Walter E. *Good News to the Poor: Wealth and Poverty in Luke–Acts.* Minneapolis: Augsburg, 1981.
Plummer, Alfred. *A Critical and Exegetical Commentary on the Gospel according to St. Luke.* ICC. New York: Scribner, 1896.
Powell, Mark Allan. "Matthew's Beatitudes: Reversals and Rewards of the Kingdom." *CBQ* 58/3 (1996) 460–79.
———. "Narrative Criticism." In *Methods of Biblical Interpretation*, edited by John H. Hays, 169–72. Nashville: Abingdon, 2004.
———. "Toward a Narrative-Critical Understanding of Luke." *Interpretation* 48/4 (1994) 341–46.
Poythress, Vern S. "Kinds of Biblical Theology." *WTJ* 70/1 (2008) 129–42.
Rahlfs, Alfred. *Septuaginta.* Stuttgart: German Bible Society, 1935.
Ransom, John Crowe. *The New Criticism.* Westport, CT: Praeger, 1979.
Resseguie, James L. *Narrative Criticism of the New Testament: An Introduction.* Grand Rapids: Baker Academic, 2005.
Rice, Peter. "The Rhetoric of Luke's Passion: Luke's Use of Common-Place to Amplify the Guilt of Jerusalem's Leaders in Jesus' Death." *Biblical Interpretation* 21/3 (2013) 355–76.
Richards, I. A. *Principles of Literary Criticism.* 2nd ed. London: Routledge, 2001.
Riches, John Kenneth, et al. "Luke." In *The Synoptic Gospels*, 251–342. New Testament Guides. Sheffield: Sheffield Academic Press, 2001.
Ridderbos, Herman N. *The Coming of the Kingdom.* Philadelphia: Presbyterian and Reformed, 1962.
Robertson, A. T. *A Grammar of the Greek New Testament in the Light of Historical Research.* 4th ed. Nashville: Broadman, 1934.
Rosner, Brian S. *Paul, Scripture and Ethics: A Study of 1 Corinthians 5–7.* Arbeiten zur Geschichte des antiken Judentums und des Urchristentums Bd. 22. Leiden: Brill, 1994.
Rowe, C. Kavin. *Early Narrative Christology: The Lord in the Gospel of Luke.* Grand Rapids: Baker, 2009.
Rusam, Dietrich. *Das Alte Testament Bei Lukas.* BZNW 112. Berlin: Gruyter, 2003.
Ruzer, Serge. "Jesus' Crucifixion in Luke and Acts: The Search for a Meaning Vis-À-Vis the Biblical Pattern of Persecuted Prophet." In *Judaistik und Neutestamentliche Wissenschaft*, 173–91. Göttingen: Vandenhoeck & Ruprecht, 2008.
Sacchi, Paolo. *Jewish Apocalyptic and Its History.* Journal for the Study of the Pseudepigrapha Supplement Series 20. Sheffield: Sheffield Academic Press, 1996.
Sakenfeld, Katharine Doob, ed. *New Interpreter's Dictionary of the Bible.* 5 vols. Nashville: Abingdon, 2006.
Sanders, E. P. *Jesus and Judaism.* Philadelphia: Fortress, 1985.
Schaberg, Jane. "Luke." In *Women's Bible Commentary*, edited by Carol A. Newsom and Sharon H. Ringe, 363–80. Louisville: Westminster John Knox, 1998.
Schaefer, Christoph. *Die Zukunft Israels bei Lukas: Biblisch-Frühjüdishe Zukunftsvorstellungen im Lukanischen Doppelwerk in Vergleich zu Röm 9–11.* BZNW 190. New York: De Gruyter, 2012.
Schiffman, Lawrence H. *Qumran and Jerusalem: Studies in the Dead Sea Scrolls and the History of Judaism.* Studies in the Dead Sea Scrolls and Related Literature. Grand Rapids: Eerdmans, 2010.

Schneider, Franz. *Jesus, Der Prophet*. Orbis biblicus et orientalis 2. Universitätsverlag Freiburg. Göttingen: Vandenhoeck & Ruprecht, 1973.

Schneider, Gerhard. *Verleugnung, Verspottung und Verhör Jesu nach Lukas 22, 54–71: Studien zur Lukanischen Darstellung der Passion*. SANT 22. Munich: Kösel, 1969.

Schramm, Tim. *Der Markus-Stoff Bei Lukas: Eine Literakritische und Redaktionsgeschichtliche Untersuchung*. Cambridge: Cambridge University Press, 1971.

Seccombe, David Peter. *Possessions and the Poor in Luke–Acts*. Studien zum Neuen Testament und seiner Umwelt. Linz: Harrachstraße, 1982.

Seim, Turid Karlsen. *The Double Message: Patterns of Gender in Luke–Acts*. Nashville: Abingdon, 1994.

Shaver, Brenda Jean. "The Prophet Elijah in the Literature of the Second Temple Period: The Growth of a Tradition." PhD diss., University of Chicago, 2001.

Silva, Moisés. *Biblical Words and Their Meaning: An Introduction to Lexical Semantics*. Grand Rapids: Zondervan, 1994.

Simons, R. "The Magnificat: Cento, Psalm or Imitatio?" *TynBul* 60/1 (2009) 25–46.

Smalley, Stephen S. "Redaction Criticism." In *New Testament Interpretation: Essays on Principles and Methods*, edited by Howard I. Marshall, 181–98. Grand Rapids: Eerdmans, 1977.

Snaith, John G. *Ecclesiasticus or The Wisdom of Jesus Son of Sirach*. Cambridge Bible Commentaries on the Apocrypha. Cambridge: Cambridge University Press, 1974.

Snodgrass, Klyne R. *Stories with Intent: A Comprehensive Guide to the Parables of Jesus*. Grand Rapids: Eerdmans, 2008.

Soards, Marion L. *The Passion according to Luke: The Special Material of Luke 22*. JSNTSup 14. Sheffield: Sheffield Academic Press, 1987.

Soulen, Richard N. *Handbook of Biblical Criticism*. 3rd ed. Louisville: Westminster John Knox, 2001.

Spencer, F. Scott. "Neglected Widows in Acts 6:1–7." *CBQ* 56 (1994) 714–33.

———. *Salty Wives, Spirited Mothers, and Savvy Widows: Capable Women of Purpose and Persistence in Luke's Gospel*. Grand Rapids: Eerdmans, 2012.

Stanford, Thomas J. F. *Luke's People: The Men and Women Who Met Jesus and the Apostles*. Eugene, OR: Wipf & Stock, 2014.

Steck, Odil Hannes. *Israel und Das Gewaltsame Geschick Der Propheten. Untersuchungen zur Überlieferung des deuteronomistischen Geschichtsbildes im Alten Testament, Spätjudentum und Urchristentum*. WMANT 23. Neukirchen-Vluyn: Neukirchener, 1967.

Stein, Robert H. *Luke*. NAC 24. Nashville: Broadman, 1992.

Sternberg, Meir. *The Poetics of Biblical Narrative: Ideological Literature and the Drama of Reading*. Indiana Studies in Biblical Literature. Bloomington: Indiana University Press, 1985.

Stone, Michael E., ed., *Jewish Writings of the Second Temple Period: Apocrypha, Pseudepigrapha, Qumran, Sectarian Writings, Philo, Josephus*. Compendia Rerum Iudaicarum ad Novum Testamentum 2/2. Assen: Van Gorcum, 1984.

Strack, H., and Paul Billerbeck. *Kommentar zum Neuen Testament aus Talmud und Midrasch*. 6 vols. Munich: Beck, 1922–61.

Strauss, Mark L. *The Davidic Messiah in Luke–Acts: The Promise and its Fulfillment in Lukan Christology*. JSNTSup 110. Sheffield: Sheffield Academic Press, 1995.

Stuckenbruck, Loren T. *1 Enoch 91–108*. Berlin: Walter de Gruyter, 2007.

Talbert, Charles H. *Literary Patterns, Theological Themes and the Genre of Luke-Acts*. Society of Biblical Literature Monograph Series 20. Missoula, MT: Scholars, 1974.

Tan, Randall K. J. "Recent Developments in Redaction Criticism: From Investigation of Textual Prehistory Back to Historical-Grammatical Exegesis?" *JETS* 44/4 (2001) 599-614.

Tannehill, Robert C. "Israel in Luke-Acts: A Tragic Story." *JBL* 104/1 (1985) 69-85.

———. "Magnificat as Poem." *JBL* 93/2 (January 1974) 263-75.

———. *The Narrative Unity of Luke-Acts: A Literary Interpretation*. Vol. 1, *The Gospel according to Luke*. Philadelphia: Fortress, 1991.

———. *The Narrative Unity of Luke-Acts: A Literary Interpretation*. Vol. 2, *The Acts of the Apostles (Foundations and Facets)*. Philadelphia: Fortress, 1989.

———. *The Sword of His Mouth*. Missoula, MT: Scholars, 1975.

Telford, William. "Pre-Markan Tradition in Recent Research (1980-1990)." In *The Four Gospels: Festschrift Frans Neirynck*, edited by Frans van Segbroeck et al., 693-723. Leuven: Leuven University Press, 1992.

Thaidigsmann, Edgar. "Gottes Schöpferisches Sehen: Elemente einer Theologischen Sehschule im Anschluss an Luthers Auslegung des Magnificat." *Neue Zeitschrift für Systematische Theologie und Religionsphilosophie* 29/1 (1987) 19-38.

Theissen, Gerd. *The Miracle Stories of the Early Christian Tradition*. Philadelphia: Fortress, 1983.

Theissen, Gerd, and Annette Mertz. *The Historical Jesus: A Comprehensive Guide*. Translated by John Bowden. Minneapolis: Fortress, 1996.

Tiede, David L. "The Literary Function of Possessions in Luke-Acts." *JBL* 98/3 (1979) 445-46.

Tov, Emanuel. *The Book of Baruch, also Called 1 Baruch (Greek and Hebrew)*. Missoula, MT: Scholars, 1975.

Turner, David L. *Matthew*. Baker Exegetical Commentary on the New Testament. Grand Rapids: Baker Academic, 2008.

Tyson, Joseph B. "The Jewish Public in Luke-Acts." *NTS* 30/4 (1984) 574-83.

Valantasis, Richard. *The Gospel of Thomas*. New Testament Readings. London: Routledge, 1997.

Vander Hart, Mark D. "The Transition of the Old Testament Day of the Lord into the New Testament Day of the Lord Jesus Christ." *AJT* 9/1 (1993) 3-25.

VanderKam, J. C. *Enoch: A Man for All Generations*. Studies on Personalities of the Old Testament. Columbia, SC: University of South Carolina Press, 1995.

———. "Righteous One, Messiah, Chosen One, and Son of Man in 1 Enoch 37-71." In *Messiah: Developments in Earliest Judaism and Christianity; The First Princeton Symposium on Judaism and Christian Origins*, edited by R. H. Charlesworth, 145-68. Minneapolis: Fortress, 1992.

VanderKam, J. C., and William Adler, eds. *The Jewish Apocalyptic Heritage in Early Christianity*. Minneapolis: Fortress, 1996.

Van Til, Kent. "Three Anointings and One Offering: The Sinful Woman in Luke 7.36-50." *Journal of Pentecostal Theology* 15/1 (October 2006) 73-82.

Verhey, Allen. *The Great Reversal: Ethics and the New Testament*. Grand Rapids: Eerdmans, 1984.

Verheyden, Joseph. "Calling Jesus a Prophet, as Seen by Luke." In *Prophets and Prophecy in Jewish and Early Christian Literature*, 177-210. Tübingen: Mohr Siebeck, 2010.

Vermès, Géza. *Jesus the Jew: A Historian's Reading of the Gospels*. Philadelphia: Fortress, 1981.

Verseput, D. J. "The Davidic Messiah and Matthew's Jewish Christianity." In *SBL 1995 Seminar Papers*, 102–16. Atlanta: Scholar's, 1995

Vogels, Walter. "Having or Longing: A Semiotic Analysis of Luke 16:19–31," *Église et Théologie* 20/1 (January 1989) 27–46.

———. "A Semiotic Study of Luke 7:11–17." *Église et Théologie* 14/3 (1983) 282–83.

Voorwinde, Stephen. *Jesus' Emotions in the Gospels*. London: T. & T. Clark, 2011.

Wallace, Daniel B. *Greek Grammar Beyond the Basic: An Exegetical Syntax of the New Testament*. Grand Rapids: Zondervan, 1996.

Watts, John D. W. *Isaiah 1–33*. WBC 24. Waco, TX: Word, 1985.

Weiser, Artur. *Das Buch Des Propheten Jeremia*. Das Alte Testament Deutsch 20–21. Göttingen: Vandenhoeck & Ruprecht, 1952.

Wenkel, David. "The Emotion of Joy and the Rhetoric of Reversal in Luke–Acts." PhD diss., University of Aberdeen, 2011.

Wiarda, Timothy. *Peter in the Gospels: Pattern, Personality, and Relationship*. WUNT 127. Tübingen: Mohr Siebeck, 2000.

Wiefel, Woflgang. *Das Evangelium nach Lukas*. Theologischer Handkommentar zum Neuen Testament 3. Berlin: Evangelische Verlagsanstalt, 1988.

Wildberger, Hans. *Isaiah: A Commentary*. Continental Commentaries. Minneapolis: Fortress, 1991.

Witherington, Ben. *Women in the Ministry of Jesus: A Study of Jesus' Attitudes to Women and Their Roles as Reflected in His Earthly Life*. Society for New Testament Studies 51. Cambridge: Cambridge University Press, 1985.

Witte, Markus. "Theologien im Buch Jesus Sirach." In *Die Theologische Bedeutung der Alttestamentlichen Weisheitsliteratur*, edited by Markus Saur, 91–128. Düsseldorf: Neukirchener Theologie, 2012.

Wolff, Hans Walter. *Hosea: A Commentary on the Book of the Prophet Hosea*. Hermeneia. Philadelphia: Fortress, 1974.

Wolter, Michael. *Das Lukasevangelium*. Handbuch zum Neuen Testament 5. Tübingen: Mohr Siebeck, 2008.

———. "Eschatology in the Gospel according to Luke." In *Eschatology of the New Testament and Some Related Document*, edited by Jan G. Van Der Watt, 91–108. Wissenschaftliche Untersuchungen zum Neuen Testament 2. Reihe 315. Tübingen: Mohr Siebeck, 2011.

Wright, N. T. *Jesus and the Victory of God*. Minneapolis: Augsburg Fortress, 1997.

———. *The New Testament and the People of God*. Minneapolis: Augsburg Fortress, 1992.

———. *The Resurrection of the Son of God*. Minneapolis: Augsburg Fortress, 2003.

York, John O. *The Last Shall Be First: The Rhetoric of Reversal in Luke*. JSNTSup 46. Sheffield: Sheffield Academic Press, 1991.

Zamfir, Korinna. "Jeremian Motifs in the Synoptics' Understanding of Jesus." In *Prophets and Prophecy in Jewish and Early Christian Literature*, edited by Joseph Verheyden, Korinna Zamfir and Tobias Nicklas, 139–76. Tübingen: Mohr Siebeck, 2010.

Zeller, Dieter. "Die Bildlogik Des Gleichnisses Mt 11:16f/Lk 7:31f." *Zeitschrift für Neutestamentliche Wissenschaft. Kunde Älteren Kirche* 68/3–4 (1977) 252–57.

www.ingramcontent.com/pod-product-compliance
Lightning Source LLC
Chambersburg PA
CBHW071457150426
43191CB00008B/1371